便携版

GRE
核心词汇
考法精析

第2版

陈琦 周书林 / 主编

颜余真、戈弋、肖雪 编著

浙江教育出版社·杭州

图书在版编目(CIP)数据

GRE核心词汇考法精析：便携版／陈琦主编. —2
版. -- 杭州：浙江教育出版社，2017.3（2019.7重印）
ISBN 978-7-5536-5139-2

Ⅰ．①G… Ⅱ．①陈… Ⅲ．①GRE—词汇—自学参考资
料 Ⅳ．①H313.1

中国版本图书馆CIP数据核字（2016）第291985号

GRE核心词汇考法精析：便携版（第2版）
GRE HEXIN CIHUI KAOFA JINGXI: BIANXIEBAN (DI 2 BAN)
陈 琦 主编

责任编辑	罗　曼
美术编辑	韩　波
封面设计	大愚设计
责任校对	刘文芳
责任印务	时小娟
出版发行	浙江教育出版社
	地址：杭州市天目山路40号
	邮编：310013
	电话：（0571）85170300－80928
	邮箱：dywh@xdf.cn
	网址：www.zjeph.com
印　　刷	三河市良远印务有限公司
开　　本	787mm×1092mm　1/32
成品尺寸	120mm×185mm
印　　张	8.75
字　　数	186 000
版　　次	2017年3月第2版
印　　次	2019年7月第16次印刷
标准书号	ISBN 978-7-5536-5139-2
定　　价	19.80元

前　言

　　本书是《GRE核心词汇考法精析：第2版》的浓缩精华版，开本小巧，方便考生随身携带。

　　本书保留了大本书中最核心的部分——单词及其中英文释义，删除了例、派、同反义词。书中共收录3041个单词，涵盖上一版中的核心高频词汇，删除了部分低频词，加入2014年以来新GRE考试中出现的新词。

　　本书特色具体如下：

　　结构科学：本书共有31个List，每个List 100个单词（除最后一个List以外）。考生可以循序渐进地进行学习，更加牢固地掌握每个单词。

　　释义准确：所有单词的解释均结合GRE考试的常考含义进行筛选。英文释义出自《美国传统词典》（*American Heritage Dictionary*）及GRE官方指定的《韦氏大学词典》（*Merriam-Webster's Collegiate Dictionary*）。

　　结合实战：每条英文解释中均以下划线标记出单词考点所在，便于考生迅速把握单词的考法特征，在平时背诵的过程中逐步由中式思维转换为英式思维。

　　逆序编排：对所有单词进行逆序编排，避免只是记住单词的位置而不是单词意思的情况出现。同时，逆序的排列也将一些形近词排列在了一起，方便考生区分（更多形近词的区分可以参考微臣培训学校的"形近词卡片"）。

考生可将本书作为备考 GRE 第一阶段的词汇书。在 GRE 备考起步时，将本书刷三遍（每遍约 20 个小时）。重点关注单词的中英文释义，最大程度地避免考生对单词理解的偏差，攻克 GRE 考试中最核心的词汇，确保背诵单词的命中率。三遍之后，可以认真学习《GRE 核心词汇考法精析：第 2 版》，确保核心单词识记的深度。对于要参加 GRE 培训班的学员，建议在培训之前至少将本书翻看一遍。

编　者

目　录

音 频

coda	[ˈkoʊdə] *n.* 终曲：the <u>concluding passage</u> of a movement or composition
panacea	[ˌpænəˈsiːə] *n.* 万能药，万灵药：a <u>remedy for all ills</u> or difficulties
nostalgia	[nəˈstældʒə] *n.* 怀旧，怀念：a wistful or excessively <u>sentimental yearning for return</u> to or of some past period or irrecoverable condition
mania	[ˈmeɪniə] *n.* 热衷，狂热：an excessively <u>intense enthusiasm</u>, interest, or desire; a craze
cornucopia	[ˌkɔːrnjuˈkoʊpiə] *n.* 大量：an <u>overflowing</u> store; an abundance
euphoria	[juːˈfɔːriə] *n.* 感觉极其愉快：a state of <u>overwhelming usually pleasurable</u> emotion
sequela	[siˈkwiːlə] *n.* 结果：a <u>secondary</u> consequence or <u>result</u>
anathema	[əˈnæθəmə] *n.* 令人讨厌的事物：a ban or <u>curse</u> solemnly pronounced by ecclesiastical authority and accompanied by excommunication
enigma	[ɪˈnɪgmə] *n.* 难以理解或解释的事物，谜：something <u>hard to understand</u> or explain
stigma	[ˈstɪgmə] *n.* 耻辱，污名：a <u>mark of shame</u> or discredit
coma	[ˈkoʊmə] *n.* 昏迷，深度无知觉：a state of <u>profound unconsciousness</u> caused by disease, injury, or poison

1

charisma [kəˈrɪzmə] *n.* 魅力，吸引力：a special magnetic charm or appeal

nirvana [nɪrˈvɑːnə] *n.* 天堂，极乐世界：an often imaginary place or state of utter perfection and happiness

stamina [ˈstæmɪnə] *n.* 耐力：physical or moral strength to resist or withstand illness, fatigue, or hardship

patina [pəˈtiːnə] *n.* 外表：a superficial covering or exterior
n. (由内而外散发的)氛围，气场：an appearance or aura that is derived from association, habit, or established character

chimera [kaɪˈmɪrə] *n.* 虚构的事物，幻觉：an illusion or fabrication of the mind, especially an unrealizable dream

plethora [ˈpleθərə] *n.* 过量，过剩：excess, superfluity

bravura [brəˈvʊərə] *adj./n.* 优秀演技(的)：brilliant technique or style in performance

quota [ˈkwoʊtə] *n.* 配额，限额：a proportional part or share

drab [dræb] *adj.* 单调的，无聊的：characterized by dullness and monotony

ad-lib [ˌædˈlɪb] *adj.* 即兴的：made or done without previous thought or preparation

glib [glɪb] *adj.* 流利圆滑的(常含有不真诚或欺诈的成分)，油腔滑调的：marked by ease and fluency in speaking or writing often to the point of being insincere or deceitful
adj. 缺乏深度的，肤浅的：lacking depth and substance

succumb [səˈkʌm] *vi.* 屈服：to yield to superior strength or force or overpowering appeal or desire *vi.* 死亡：to be brought to an end （as <u>death</u>） by the effect of destructive or disruptive forces

plumb [plʌm] *adj.* 完全的，绝对的：having <u>no exceptions</u> or restrictions
vt. 仔细深入地检查；探索，探究：to <u>examine</u> closely or <u>deeply</u>

numb [nʌm] *adj.* 麻木的，无感情的：<u>devoid of emotion</u>

barb [bɑːrb] *n.* 尖锐而严厉的批评：a biting or pointedly <u>critical</u> remark or comment

snub [snʌb] *vt.* 轻视，不理睬：to treat with <u>contempt</u> or neglect

archaic [ɑːrˈkeɪɪk] *adj.* 过时的，久远的：<u>no</u> longer <u>current</u> or applicable; <u>antiquated</u>

mosaic [mouˈzeɪɪk] *n.* 综合物，马赛克般的东西：an unorganized <u>collection</u> or mixture of various things

prosaic [prəˈzeɪɪk] *adj.* 单调的，常见的：being of the type that is encountered in the <u>normal course of events</u>

acerbic [əˈsɜːrbɪk] *adj.* （心情、心境或者语调）尖酸的：marked by the use of <u>wit</u> that is intended to <u>cause hurt feelings</u>

cherubic [tʃəˈruːbik] *adj.* 天使般可爱的：innocent looking usually chubby and <u>rosy</u>

sporadic [spəˈrædɪk] *adj.* 断断续续的：<u>not often occurring</u> or repeated

encyclopedic [ɪnˌsaɪkləˈpiːdɪk] *adj.* 全面的，百科全书式的：covering everything or all important points

episodic [ˌepɪˈsɑːdɪk] *adj.* 片段的，断断续续的：<u>lacking in steadiness</u> or regularity of occurrence

3

soporific [ˌsɑːpəˈrɪfɪk] *n.* 催眠的药剂，安眠药：a drug or other substance that <u>induces sleep</u>
adj. 催眠的：causing or tending to <u>cause sleep</u>

lethargic [ləˈθɑːrdʒɪk] *adj.* 没精打采的，行动迟缓的：of, relating to, or characterized by lethargy, <u>sluggish</u>

synergic [sɪˈnərdʒɪk] *adj.* 合作的，1 + 1 > 2：working together: <u>cooperating</u>

chic [tʃiːk] *adj.* 时髦的，潮的：being in the latest or current fashion

hagiographic [ˌhægiˈɑːgrəfik] *adj.* 捧为圣人一般的，过分谄媚的：of, relating to, or being hagiography; <u>overly or insincerely flattering</u>

monolithic [ˌmɑːnəˈlɪθɪk] *adj.* 大一统的：constituting or acting as a <u>single</u>, often rigid, <u>uniform</u> whole

diabolic [ˌdaɪəˈbɑːlɪk] *adj.* 恶魔一般的：of, relating to, or characteristic of the <u>devil</u>

catholic [ˈkæθlɪk] *adj.* 普遍，包容的：<u>not limited or specialized</u> in application or purpose

vitriolic [ˌvɪtriˈɑːlɪk] *adj.* （言辞）刻薄的：bitterly <u>scathing</u>

panoramic [ˌpænəˈræmɪk] *adj.* 全景的：of an unobstructed or <u>complete view</u> of an area in every direction

pandemic [pænˈdemɪk] *adj.* 大范围流行的：<u>widespread</u>; general

endemic [enˈdemɪk] *adj.* 地方性的：prevalent in or peculiar <u>to a particular</u> locality, <u>region</u>, or people

polemic [pəˈlemɪk] *n.* 争执：a controversial <u>argument</u>

anemic [əˈniːmɪk] *adj.* 缺乏力量、活力、精神的：<u>lacking force</u>, vitality, or spirit

arrhythmic [əˈrɪðmɪk] *adj.* 不规律的：<u>lacking</u> rhythm or <u>regularity</u>

4

mimic [ˈmɪmɪk] *adj.* 仿真的，仿造的：being such in <u>appearance</u> only and made with or manufactured from usually cheaper material
vt. 模仿：to use (someone or something) as the <u>model</u> for one's speech, mannerisms, or behavior

anthropogenic [ˌænθrəpəˈdʒenɪk] *adj.* 人为的：resulting from the <u>influence of human beings</u> on nature

laconic [ləˈkɑːnɪk] *adj.* 简洁的(以至于显得粗鲁或难以理解)：using or involving the use of a <u>minimum of words</u>: <u>concise</u> to the point of seeming rude or mysterious

histrionic [ˌhɪstriˈɑːnɪk] *adj.* 夸张做作的：dramatic, exaggerated, and insincere

chronic [ˈkrɑːnɪk] *adj.* 经常发生的，复发的：marked by long duration or <u>frequent recurrence</u>

tonic [ˈtɑːnɪk] *adj.* 滋补的，有益健康的：producing or <u>stimulating</u> physical, mental, or emotional <u>vigor</u>; <u>beneficial</u> to the health of body or mind

embryonic [ˌembriˈɑːnɪk] *adj.* 初期的，萌芽阶段的：being in an <u>early stage</u> of development

runic [ˈruːnɪk] *adj.* 神秘的：having some secret or <u>mysterious</u> meaning

cynic [ˈsɪnɪk] *n.* 反人类的喷子：a person who believes all people are motivated by <u>selfishness</u>

stoic [ˈstoʊɪk] *adj.* 隐忍的，冷静的：seemingly indifferent to or <u>unaffected by pleasure or pain</u>

epic [ˈepɪk] *adj.* 宏大的，超凡脱俗的：<u>surpassing the usual</u> or ordinary, particularly in scope or size

philanthropic [ˌfɪlənˈθrɑːpɪk] *adj.* 博爱的，为他人着想的：having or showing a concern for the <u>welfare of others</u>

| misanthropic | [ˌmɪsən'θrɑːpɪk] *adj.* 反人类的：having or showing a <u>deep distrust of human</u> beings and their motives |

| myopic | [maɪ'ɑːpɪk] *adj.* 缺乏远见的，缺乏辨别能力的：a <u>lack of foresight</u> or discernment |

| choleric | ['kɑːlərɪk] *adj.* 易怒的，暴躁的：easily <u>angered</u>; bad-tempered |

| mesmeric | [mez'merɪk] *adj.* 令人着迷的，难以抗拒的：<u>attracting</u> and holding interest as if by a spell |

| generic | [dʒə'nerɪk] *adj.* 无差别的，普遍的：having <u>no particularly distinctive quality</u> or application |

| esoteric | [ˌesə'terɪk] *adj.* 深奥难懂的：<u>difficult</u> for one of ordinary knowledge or intelligence <u>to understand</u> |

| meteoric | [ˌmiːti'ɔːrɪk] *adj.* 流星般迅速而短暂的：similar to a meteor in speed, brilliance, or <u>brevity</u> |

| eccentric | [ɪk'sentrɪk] *adj.* 行为出格的，不循规蹈矩的：<u>deviating</u> from <u>conventional</u> or accepted usage or conduct |

| panegyric | [ˌpænə'dʒɪrɪk] *n.* 赞颂之词，颂文：an <u>eulogistic</u> oration or writing |

| lyric | ['lɪrɪk] *adj.* 如诗歌般流畅甜美的：having a pleasantly flowing quality <u>suggestive of poetry or music</u> |

| intrinsic | [ɪn'trɪnsɪk] *adj.* 固有的，内在的：of or relating to the <u>essential</u> nature of a thing |

| dramatic | [drə'mætɪk] *adj.* 显著的，惹人注意的：<u>striking</u> in appearance or effect |

| melodramatic | [ˌmelədrə'mætɪk] *adj.* 感情夸张的，伤感的：<u>exaggeratedly emotional</u> or sentimental; histrionic |

| pragmatic | [præg'mætɪk] *adj.* 实用主义的，务实的：a <u>practical approach</u> to problems and affairs |

6

phlegmatic [fleg'mætɪk] *adj.* 冷静的，无感情的，淡漠的：having or suggesting a <u>calm, sluggish temperament</u>; unemotional

dogmatic [dɔːg'mætɪk] *adj.* 武断的，自以为是的：given to or marked by the forceful expression of <u>strongly held opinions</u>

axiomatic [ˌæksiə'mætɪk] *adj.* 不言自明的：taken for granted, <u>self-evident</u>

diplomatic [ˌdɪplə'mætɪk] *adj.* 使用策略的，机智的：employing <u>tact</u> and conciliation especially in situations of stress

chromatic [krə'mætɪk] *adj.* 彩色的：relating to <u>colors</u> or color

monochromatic [ˌmɑːnəkroʊ'mætɪk] *adj.* 单调无聊的：<u>lacking variety</u>, creativity, or excitement

somatic [sə'mætɪk] *adj.* 肉体的：<u>of the body</u>, especially as distinguished from a body part, the mind, or the environment

automatic [ˌɔːtə'mætɪk] *adj.* 自发的，情不自禁的：acting or done <u>spontaneously or unconsciously</u>

traumatic [traʊ'mætɪk] *adj.* 造成创伤的，痛苦的：something shocking and upsetting, and may <u>cause psychological damage</u>

fanatic [fə'nætɪk] *n.* 狂热者：a person marked or motivated by an extreme, <u>unreasoning enthusiasm</u>, as for a cause
adj. 狂热的；盲信的：marked by excessive enthusiasm and often <u>intense uncritical devotion</u>

bureaucratic [ˌbjʊrə'krætɪk] *adj.* 官僚主义的：involving <u>complicated rules</u> and procedures which can cause <u>long delays</u>

erratic [ɪ'rætɪk] *adj.* 善变的：<u>not</u> staying <u>constant</u>

7

static	[ˈstætɪk] *adj.* 静态的；停滞的：characterized by a <u>lack of movement</u>, animation, or progression
didactic	[daɪˈdæktɪk] *adj.* 喜欢说教的，思修的：designed or intended to <u>teach</u>
eclectic	[ɪˈklektɪk] *adj.* 混合的，多元化的：composed of elements drawn <u>from various sources</u>
apoplectic	[ˌæpəˈplektɪk] *adj.* 极度愤怒的：<u>extremely angry</u>; <u>furious</u>
ascetic	[əˈsetɪk] *n./adj.* 自制的（人）：practicing strict <u>self-denial</u> as a measure of personal and especially spiritual discipline
prophetic	[prəˈfetɪk] *adj.* 预言的，预示的：<u>foretelling</u> events: predictive
bathetic	[bəˈθetɪk] *adj.* 平凡的，陈腐的：characterized by exceptional <u>commonplaceness</u>
anesthetic	[ˌænəsˈθetɪk] *adj.* 无感觉的，麻木的：<u>lacking awareness or sensitivity</u>
hermetic	[hɜːrˈmetɪk] *adj.* 深奥的：relating to or characterized by occultism or <u>abstruseness</u>
peripatetic	[ˌperipəˈtetɪk] *adj.* 巡游的，四处游历：walking about or from <u>place to place</u>
politic	[ˈpɑːlətɪk] *adj.* 合时宜的，明智的，高情商的：<u>suitable</u> for bringing about a desired result under the circumstances
antic	[ˈæntɪk] *adj.* 滑稽可笑的：characterized by <u>clownish</u> extravagance or absurdity

音 频

gigantic	[dʒaɪˈgæntɪk] *adj.* 巨大的：unusually <u>large</u>
authentic	[ɔːˈθentɪk] *adj.* 真实的，非仿造的：being <u>exactly</u> as appears or as claimed
demotic	[dɪˈmɑːtɪk] *adj.* 通俗的，大众化的：popular, <u>common</u>
hypnotic	[hɪpˈnɑːtɪk] *adj.* 催眠的：tending to <u>cause sleep</u>
despotic	[dɪˈspɑːtɪk] *adj.* 专制的，暴虐的：arbitrary , autocratic, monocratic, <u>tyrannical</u>
exotic	[ɪgˈzɑːtɪk] *adj.* 外来的，不同寻常的：excitingly or mysteriously <u>unusual</u>
quixotic	[kwɪkˈsɑːtɪk] *adj.* 不切实际的，空想的：having or marked by a tendency to be guided <u>more by ideals than by reality</u>
dyspeptic	[dɪsˈpeptɪk] *adj.* 脾气坏的：<u>bad-tempered</u>
septic	[ˈseptɪk] *adj.* 腐败的，感染的：of, relating to, or causing <u>putrefaction</u>
aseptic	[ˌeɪˈseptɪk] *adj.* 消毒的，无菌的：<u>preventing infection</u>
apocalyptic	[əˌpɑːkəˈlɪptɪk] *adj.* 预言的，启示的：of a reve-latory or <u>prophetic</u> nature *adj.* 重要的，转折点的：of, relating to, or being a <u>major turning</u> point
cryptic	[ˈkrɪptɪk] *adj.* 秘密的：<u>secret</u> or occult *adj.* 难以理解的：being <u>beyond one's powers to know</u>, understand, or explain
elastic	[ɪˈlæstɪk] *adj.* 有弹性的：easily <u>resuming</u> origi-

9

nal <u>shape</u> after being stretched or expanded
adj. 能(迅速从伤痛中)恢复的：capable of <u>recov-</u>
<u>ering</u> quickly especially <u>from depression</u> or
disappointment

plastic [ˈplæstɪk] *adj.* 可塑的：susceptible of being <u>modified</u> in form or nature

majestic [məˈdʒestɪk] *adj.* 宏伟壮丽的：large and <u>impressively beautiful</u>

pessimistic [ˌpesɪˈmɪstɪk] *adj.* 悲观的：tending to stress the negative or unfavorable or to <u>take the</u> <u>gloomiest possible view</u>

chauvinistic [ˌʃəʊvɪˈnɪstɪk] *adj.* 盲目爱国的：having or show- ing <u>excessive favoritism</u> towards one's own country

egoistic [ˌegoʊˈɪstɪk] *adj.* 利己的，以自我为中心的： being <u>centered in</u> or preoccupied with <u>oneself</u> and the gratification of one's own desires

narcissistic [ˌnɑːrsɪˈsɪstɪk] *adj.* 自恋的：having an <u>undue</u> <u>fascination with oneself</u>

caustic [ˈkɔːstɪk] *adj.* 挖苦讽刺，刻薄的：marked by <u>incisive sarcasms</u>

rustic [ˈrʌstɪk] *n.* 乡下人，头脑简单的人：an <u>awkward</u> <u>or simple person</u> especially from a small town or the country
adj. 乡村的：of, relating to, associated with, or typical of <u>open areas with few buildings</u> or people
adj. 粗俗的：<u>lacking</u> in social graces or <u>polish</u>

therapeutic [ˌθerəˈpjuːtɪk] *adj.* 治疗的，有疗效的：of or relating to the <u>treatment</u> of <u>disease</u> or disorders by remedial agents or methods

ad hoc [ˌædˈhɑːk] *adj.* 专门的：concerned with a <u>particular end</u> or purpose

10

havoc [ˈhævək] *n.* 大混乱：a state in which everything is out of order

dread [dred] *n.* 恐惧：great fear especially in the face of impending evil

proofread [ˈpruːfriːd] *vt.* 校对：to read （copy or proof）in order to find errors and mark corrections

fad [fæd] *n.* （短暂的）流行，时尚：a practice or interest that is very popular for a short time

myriad [ˈmɪriəd] *adj.* 无限的，大量的：constituting a very large, indefinite number

ironclad [ˈaɪərnklæd] *adj.* 非常坚固的，坚不可摧的：so firm or secure as to be unbreakable

nomad [ˈnoʊmæd] *adj./n.* 游牧的；居无定所的人：a member of a people who have no fixed residence but move from place to place usually seasonally and within a well-defined territory

goad [goʊd] *vt.* 刺激，驱使，激发：to incite or rouse as if with a goad

embed [ɪmˈbed] *vt.* 嵌入：to enclose closely in or as if in a matrix

self-absorbed [ˌselfəbˈsɔːrbd] *adj.* 自恋的，自私的：absorbed in one's own thoughts, activities, or interests

barefaced [ˈberfeɪst] *adj.* 公然的，厚颜无耻的：undisguisedly bold; brazen

wrongheaded [ˌrɔːŋˈhedɪd] *adj.* 固执己见的，坚持(错误观点)的：stubborn in adherence to wrong opinion or principles

levelheaded [ˌlevlˈhedɪd] *adj.* 明智的：characteristically self-composed and sensible

jaded [ˈdʒeɪdɪd] *adj.* 厌倦的，没兴趣没热情的：having one's patience, interest, or pleasure exhausted

lopsided [ˌlɑːpˈsaɪdɪd] *adj.* 不平衡的，不协调的：lacking in balance, symmetry, or proportion

backhanded [ˌbæk'hændɪd] *adj.* 间接的：<u>indirect</u>, devious, especially sarcastic

ham-handed ['hæmhændɪd] *adj.* 笨手笨脚的：<u>lacking dexterity</u> or grace

outmoded [ˌaʊt'moʊdɪd] *adj.* 过时的，废弃的：<u>no longer</u> acceptable, current, or <u>usable</u>

secluded [sɪ'kluːdɪd] *adj.* 僻静的，隐蔽的：screened or <u>hidden</u> from view

ragged ['rægɪd] *adj.* 凹凸不平的，不光滑的：<u>not</u> having a level or <u>smooth</u> surface

dogged ['dɔːgɪd] *adj.* 固执的，任性的：<u>sticking to</u> an opinion, purpose, or course of action in spite of reason, arguments, or persuasion

far-fetched ['fɑːr fetʃt] *adj.* 牵强的，不可信的：<u>not likely to be true</u> or to occur

wretched ['retʃɪd] *adj.* 极差的：very <u>poor in quality</u> or ability
adj. 沮丧的：deeply afflicted, <u>dejected</u>, or distressed in body or mind

polished ['pɑːlɪʃt] *adj.* 有教养的：showing a <u>high degree of refinement</u> and the assurance that comes from wide social experience

cherished ['tʃerɪʃt] *adj.* 受喜爱的，珍爱的：<u>granted special treatment</u> or attention

watershed ['wɔːtərʃed] *n.* 重要关头，分水岭：a crucial dividing point: <u>turning point</u>

full-bodied [fʊl'bɑːdid] *adj.* 重要的：having <u>importance</u>, significance, or meaningfulness

dignified ['dɪgnɪfaɪd] *adj.* 高贵庄严的：<u>serious</u> and somewhat <u>formal</u>

serried ['serid] *adj.* 密集的：having <u>little space</u> between items or parts

12

half-baked [ˌhæf ˈbeɪkt] *adj.* 不明智的：showing or marked by a lack of good sense or judgment

wicked [ˈwɪkɪd] *adj.* 邪恶的：morally very bad

dappled [ˈdæpld] *adj.* 有斑点的，带花的：marked with small spots or contrasting with the background; mottled, spotted

ingrained [ɪnˈɡreɪnd] *adj.* 本质的，根深蒂固的：forming a part of the essence or inmost being; firmly established

thick-skinned [ˌθɪk ˈskɪnd] *adj.* 冷漠无情的，不顾及他人感受的：largely unaffected by the needs and feelings of other people

cramped [kræmpt] *n.* 狭小的，狭窄的：uncomfortably small or restricted

ill-bred [ˈɪl ˈbred] *adj.* 没有教养的，没有礼貌的：badly brought up or showing bad upbringing: impolite

kindred [ˈkɪndrəd] *adj.* 类似的；具有相似或相近的起源、本性或性质的：having a similar or related origin, nature, or character

mannered [ˈmænərd] *adj.* 不自然的，做作的：having an artificial or stilted character

unlettered [ˌʌnˈletərd] *adj.* 未受教育的，文盲的：not adept at reading and writing; deficient in the knowledge that can be acquired from books; illiterate

shred [ʃred] *n.* 少量：a small amount; a particle

enamored [ɪˈnæmərd] *adj.* 迷恋的，热爱的：filled with an intense or excessive love for

measured [ˈmeʒərd] *adj.* 深思熟虑的，审慎的：deliberated, calculated

versed [vɜːrst] *adj.* 熟知的：having information especially as a result of study or experience

13

depressed ［dɪˈprest］*adj.* 不开心的，情绪不高的，消沉的：feeling <u>unhappiness</u>

sophisticated ［səˈfɪstɪkeɪtɪd］*adj.* 精明的，老于世故的：having acquired <u>worldly knowledge or refinement</u>; lacking natural simplicity or naiveté
adj. 复杂的：very <u>complex</u> or complicated

dated ［ˈdeɪtɪd］*adj.* 过时的：having <u>passed its time of use</u> or usefulness; out-of-date

variegated ［ˈverɪgeɪtɪd］*adj.* 杂色的，斑驳的：having discrete markings of <u>different colors</u>

corrugated ［ˈkɔːrəgeɪtɪd］*adj.* 褶皱的：shaped into a series of regular <u>folds</u> that look like waves

calculated ［ˈkælkjuleɪtɪd］*adj.* 经过计算（成败得失）的，经过深思熟虑的：engaged in, undertaken, or displayed after <u>reckoning or estimating</u> the statistical probability of success or failure

antiquated ［ˈæntɪkweɪtɪd］*adj.* 古老的，过时的：outmoded or discredited by reason of age: being <u>out of style</u> or fashion

disaffected ［ˌdɪsəˈfektɪd］*adj.* 不满的，叛逆的：<u>discontented</u> and resentful especially against authority; <u>rebellious</u>

merited ［ˈmerɪtɪd］*adj.* 应得的，理所当然的：being <u>what is called for</u> by accepted standards of right and wrong

acquainted ［əˈkweɪntɪd］*adj.* 熟悉的：<u>having information</u> especially as a result of study or experience

disjointed ［dɪsˈdʒɔɪntɪd］*adj.* 不连贯的：<u>not</u> clearly or logically <u>connected</u>

unwonted ［ʌnˈwoʊntɪd］*adj.* 不习惯的，不寻常的：<u>not habitual</u> or <u>ordinary</u>; <u>unusual</u>

devoted ［dɪˈvoʊtɪd］*adj.* 投入的；忠诚的：characterized by <u>loyalty</u> and <u>devotion</u>

14

halfhearted [ˌhɑːf ˈhɑːrtɪd] *adj.* 不感兴趣的，不热情的：lacking heart, spirit, or interest

stouthearted [ˌstaʊt ˈhɑːrtɪd] *adj.* 勇敢的：having a stout heart or spirit

concerted [kən ˈsɜːrtɪd] *adj.* 共同完成的：planned or accomplished together

disinterested [dɪs ˈɪntrəstɪd] *adj.* 公正的，无偏见的：free from selfish motive or interest: unbiased

tightfisted [ˈtaɪtˌfɪstɪd] *adj.* 吝啬的：close-fisted; stingy

committed [kə ˈmɪtɪd] *adj.* 忠诚的，忠实的：loyal to a belief, organization, or group, and willing to work hard for it

convoluted [ˈkɑːnvəluːtɪd] *adj.* 复杂的，费解的：complicated; intricate

contrived [kən ˈtraɪvd] *adj.* 不自然的，刻意的：lacking in natural or spontaneous quality

reserved [rɪ ˈzɜːrvd] *adj.* 内向的，缄默的：restrained in words and actions

hackneyed [ˈhæknɪd] *adj.* 陈腐的，缺乏创新的：lacking in freshness or originality

upbraid [ʌp ˈbreɪd] *vt.* (严厉地)谴责，责骂：to reproach severely

rabid [ˈreɪbɪd] *adj.* 狂热的，不冷静的：extremely zealous or enthusiastic; fanatical

morbid [ˈmɔːrbɪd] *adj.* 疾病的，疾病所致的：affected with or induced by disease
adj. (思想性格)变态的：characterized by preoccupation with unwholesome thoughts or feelings

turbid [ˈtɜːrbɪd] *adj.* 混浊的：deficient in clarity or purity

placid	[ˈplæsɪd] *adj.* 冷静的，淡定的：free from emotional or mental agitation
flaccid	[ˈflæsɪd] *adj.* 不结实的，松弛的：not firm or stiff; lacking normal or youthful firmness
viscid	[ˈvɪsɪd] *adj.* 有粘性的：having a glutinous consistency
lucid	[ˈluːsɪd] *adj.* 表达清晰的，简单易懂的：easily understood
pellucid	[pəˈluːsɪd] *adj.* 清晰明确的，易懂的：transparently clear in style or meaning
sordid	[ˈsɔːrdɪd] *adj.* 肮脏的，不干净的：not clean *adj.* 卑鄙的：marked by baseness or grossness
frigid	[ˈfrɪdʒɪd] *adj.* 严寒的：extremely cold *adj.* 冷漠的：lacking warmth or ardor

音 频

turgid	[ˈtɜːrdʒɪd] *adj.* 浮夸的，过分装饰的：excessively <u>embellished</u> in style or language
squalid	[ˈskwɑːlɪd] *adj.* 污秽的，肮脏的：<u>dirty</u> and wretched
pallid	[ˈpælɪd] *adj.* 无生气的，缺乏活力的：<u>lacking</u> in <u>radiance</u> or <u>vitality</u>; dull *adj.* 苍白无血色的：having an abnormally <u>pale</u> or wan complexion
solid	[ˈsɑːlɪd] *adj.* 有理有据的：based on <u>sound reasoning</u> or information
stolid	[ˈstɑːlɪd] *adj.* 无动于衷的，感情麻木的：having or revealing <u>little emotion</u> or sensibility
timid	[ˈtɪmɪd] *adj.* 胆小的，不自信的：<u>lacking</u> in <u>courage</u> or <u>self-confidence</u>
paranoid	[ˈpærənɔɪd] *adj.* 多疑的，对他人极端恐惧和怀疑的：exhibiting or characterized by <u>extreme</u> and irrational <u>fear or distrust</u> of others
vapid	[ˈvæpɪd] *adj.* 无趣的，乏味的：<u>lacking</u> liveliness, animation, or <u>interest</u>
intrepid	[ɪnˈtrepɪd] *adj.* 大胆的：characterized by <u>resolute fearlessness</u>, fortitude, and endurance
tepid	[ˈtepɪd] *adj.* 不太热心的：showing <u>little or no interest</u> or enthusiasm
insipid	[ɪnˈsɪpɪd] *adj.* 平淡的，无聊的：<u>lacking</u> in qualities that <u>interest</u>, stimulate, or challenge

limpid ［'lɪmpɪd］ *adj.* 清澈透明的：characterized by transparent clearness

torpid ［'tɔːrpɪd］ *adj.* 麻木的，没有知觉的：lacking in sensation or feeling

arid ［'ærɪd］ *adj.* 干燥的：marked by little or no precipitation or humidity
adj. 无趣的，无聊的：causing weariness, restlessness, or lack of interest

hybrid ［'haɪbrɪd］ *n.* 杂交品种，混合品种：something of mixed origin or composition
adj. 杂交的：being offspring produced by parents of different races, breeds, species, or genera

acrid ［'ækrɪd］ *adj.* 刻薄的：marked by the use of wit that is intended to cause hurt feelings

florid ［'flɔːrɪd］ *adj.* 辞藻华丽的，花哨的：full of fine words and fancy expressions

torrid ［'tɔːrɪd］ *adj.* 酷热的：intensely hot
adj. 热情的，情感深厚的：having or expressing great depth of feeling

lurid ［'lʊrɪd］ *adj.* 恐怖的，令人反感的：causing horror or revulsion

fetid ［'fetɪd］ *adj.* 恶臭的：having a heavy offensive smell

languid ［'læŋgwɪd］ *adj.* 没精打采，虚弱的：lacking energy or vitality; weak

avid ［'ævɪd］ *adj.* 急切渴望的：marked by keen interest and enthusiasm

fervid ［'fɜːrvɪd］ *adj.* 酷热的：having a notably high temperature
adj. 热情的：marked by great passion or zeal

piebald ［'paɪbɔːld］ *adj.* 混合的，杂糅而成的：consisting of many things of different sorts

ribald ['raɪbɔːld] *adj.* （举止、言语）下流粗俗的：char-acterized by or indulging in vulgar, lewd humor

herald ['herəld] *vt.* 预示，预兆：to give a slight indication of beforehand

gild [gɪld] *vt.* （带欺骗性地）修改，润色：to give an often deceptively attractive or improved appearance to

chokehold ['tʃoʊkhoʊld] *n.* 压制：a force or influence that stops something from growing or developing

withhold [wɪð'hoʊld] *vt.* 抑制；扣压，不给予：to hold back from action; to refrain from granting, giving, or allowing

uphold [ʌp'hoʊld] *vt.* 支持，赞成：to give support to

untold [ʌn'toʊld] *adj.* 数不清的，无数的：too great or numerous to count

husband ['hʌzbənd] *vt.* 节俭，勤俭持家：to use sparingly or economically

offhand [ˌɔːf'hænd] *adj.* 即兴的，没有准备的：without premeditation or preparation

bland [blænd] *adj.* 无趣的：dull, insipid

countermand ['kaʊntərmænd] *vt.* 取消，撤销：to revoke（a command）by a contrary order

strand [strænd] *vt.* 遗弃，使置于困境：to leave in a strange or an unfavorable place especially without funds or means to depart

grandstand ['grænstænd] *vi.* 为了给人留下印象而表演，哗众取宠：to play or act so as to impress onlookers

descend [dɪ'send] *v.* 下降：to lead or extend downward *v.* 世代相传：to originate or come from an ancestral stock or source, to pass by inheritance

transcend	[træn'send] *vt.* 超越，超过极限：to rise above or go beyond the limits of
reprehend	[reprɪ'hend] *vt.* 谴责，责难，批评：to express one's unfavorable opinion of the worth or quality of
comprehend	[ˌkɑːmprɪ'hend] *vt.* 理解，了解：to grasp the nature, significance, or meaning of *vt.* 包括，包含：to contain or hold within a total scope, significance, or amount
commend	[kə'mend] *vt.* 赞扬：to mention with approbation: praise
suspend	[sə'spend] *vi.* 暂停，中止：to bring to a formal close for a period of time
rend	[rend] *vt.* 撕裂，猛拉：to tear or split apart or into pieces violently
contend	[kən'tend] *vi.* 竞争，争夺：to strive or vie in contest or rivalry or against difficulties *vt.* 声明，声称：to state as a fact usually forcefully
distend	[dɪ'stend] *v.* (使)膨胀：to (cause to) swell out or expand from or as if from internal pressure
rescind	[rɪ'sɪnd] *vt.* 废除，取消：to make void
abscond	[əb'skɑːnd] *v.* 偷偷离开：to depart secretly and hide oneself
moribund	['mɔːrɪbʌnd] *adj.* 即将过时的：on the verge of becoming obsolete
fecund	['fiːkənd] *adj.* 多产的，肥沃的：fruitful in offspring or vegetation
rubicund	['ruːbɪkənd] *adj.* 红润的，健康的：inclined to a healthy rosiness
jocund	['dʒɑːkənd] *adj.* 欢快的，高兴的：sprightly and lighthearted in disposition, character, or quality
bound	[baʊnd] *n.* 界限：a real or imaginary point beyond which a person or thing cannot go

adj. 投入的，坚定的：fully committed to achieving a goal

hidebound [ˈhaɪdbaʊnd] *adj.* 死板的，极度保守的：tending to favor established ideas, conditions, or institutions

confound [kənˈfaʊnd] *vt.* 使困惑：to throw into a state of mental uncertainty
vt. 证明为假，证伪：to prove to be false

compound [ˈkɑːmpaʊnd] *n.* 混合物：something composed of or resulting from union of separate elements, ingredients, or parts
adj. 混合的：consisting of two or more substances, ingredients, elements, or parts
[kəmˈpaʊnd] *vt.* 混合：to put or bring together so as to form a new and longer whole
vt. 使恶化，加重：to make worse, more serious, or more severe

foreground [ˈfɔːrɡraʊnd] *vt.* 强调，重视：to indicate the importance of by centering attention on

sound [saʊnd] *adj.* 牢固的，不可动摇的：marked by the ability to withstand stress without structural damage or distortion
adj. 健康的，强壮的：free from injury or disease; exhibiting normal health
adj. (逻辑上) 严谨的：based on valid reasoning

slipshod [ˈslɪpʃɑːd] *adj.* 粗心的，随意的：marked by carelessness or indifference to exactness, precision, and accuracy

falsehood [ˈfɔːlshʊd] *n.* 谎言：a statement known by its maker to be untrue and made in order to deceive

prod [prɑːd] *vt.* 促使…行动：to try to persuade (someone) through earnest appeals to follow a course of action

disregard [ˌdɪsrɪ'ɡɑːrd] *vt.* 漠视，不关注：to pay <u>no atten-</u><u>tion</u> to

n. 缺乏兴趣，缺乏关心：lack of <u>interest</u> or <u>concern</u>

sluggard ['slʌɡərd] *n.* 懒人：an habitually <u>lazy person</u>

diehard ['daɪhɑːrd] *adj.* 顽固的，保守的 *n.* 顽固的人，保守的人：strongly or fanatically <u>determined</u> or <u>devoted</u> / someone who <u>opposes change</u> and <u>refuses</u> to accept <u>new ideas</u>

dullard ['dʌlɑːrd] *n.* 笨蛋：a <u>stupid</u> or unimaginative person

canard [kə'nɑːrd] *n.* 谣传，误传：an unfounded or false, deliberately <u>misleading</u> story

aboveboard [ə'bʌvbɔːrd] *adj.* 无欺诈的，光明正大的：<u>free</u> <u>from</u> all traces of <u>deceit or duplicity</u>

hoard [hɔːrd] *v.* 贮藏，秘藏：to <u>keep hidden</u> or private

retard [rɪ'tɑːrd] *vt.* 减速，延迟：to <u>cause</u> to move or proceed <u>slowly</u>; delay or impede

safeguard ['seɪfɡɑːrd] *n.* 保护措施：a technical contrivance to <u>prevent accident</u>

vt. 保护：to <u>make safe</u>; protect

awkward ['ɔːkwərd] *adj.* 缺乏灵活性和技巧的：<u>lacking</u> <u>dexterity</u> or skill

adj. (处理问题)缺乏手段和智谋的：showing or marked by <u>a lack of skill and tact</u> (as in dealing with a situation)

untoward [ʌn'tɔːrd] *adj.* 倒霉的，不吉利的：<u>not favorable</u>, <u>unpropitious</u>

adj. 难以驯服的，难以驾驭的：given to <u>resisting</u> <u>control or discipline</u> by others

wayward ['weɪwərd] *adj.* 刚愎自用的，不服管束的：<u>fol-</u><u>lowing one's own</u> capricious, wanton, or depraved <u>inclinations</u>

haphazard [hæpˈhæzərd] *adj.* 无秩序的，无目标的：marked by lack of plan, order, or direction

undergird [ˌʌndərˈɡɜːrd] *vt.* 加强，巩固…的底部：to support or strengthen from beneath

accord [əˈkɔːrd] *n.* 一致：a state of consistency
vi. 相符合，相一致：to be consistent or in harmony
vt. 授予，给予：to grant or give especially as appropriate, due, or earned

concord [ˈkɑːŋkɔːrd] *n.* 一致，和睦：harmony or agreement of interests or feelings; accord

discord [ˈdɪskɔːrd] *n.* 意见不一致，不和谐：lack of agreement or harmony（as between persons, things, or ideas）

chord [kɔːrd] *vi.* 与…和谐一致；符合：to be in accord; agree

foreword [ˈfɔːrwɜːrd] *n.* 前言：a preface or an introductory note, as for a book, especially by a person other than the author

absurd [əbˈsɜːrd] *adj.* 不合理的：ridiculously unreasonable, unsound, or incongruous

shroud [ʃraʊd] *vt.* 将…从视线中隔离，遮蔽：to shut off from sight; screen

shrewd [ʃruːd] *adj.* 精明的，机敏的：having or showing a practical cleverness or judgment

minutiae [mɪˈnuːʃiiː] *n.* 次要的细节，小事：a minute or minor detail

imbibe [ɪmˈbaɪb] *v.* 喝水，摄取水分：to take in（something liquid）through small openings

gibe [dʒaɪb] *v.* 嘲弄：to deride or tease with taunting words

jibe [dʒaɪb] *vi.* 意见一致：to be in accord: agree

23

bribe	[braɪb] *v.* 贿赂，收买：to give something, such as money or a favor, to a person in a position of trust to influence that person's views or conduct
circumscribe	[ˈsɜːrkəmskraɪb] *vt.* 限制：to limit narrowly；restrict
proscribe	[proʊˈskraɪb] *vt.* 禁止，排斥：to prohibit; forbid
diatribe	[ˈdaɪətraɪb] *n.* 长篇抨击性演讲：a long angry speech or scolding
xenophobe	[ˈzenəfəʊb] *n.* 仇视(或畏惧)外国人(或外国事物)者：one unduly fearful of what is foreign and especially of people of foreign origin
probe	[proʊb] *v./n.* 深入调查：a penetrating or critical investigation
preface	[ˈprefəs] *n.* 序言：a preliminary statement or essay introducing a book that explains its scope, intention, or background and is usually written by the author
efface	[ɪˈfeɪs] *vt.* 擦掉，抹去；使不明显：to eliminate or make indistinct by or as if by wearing away a surface
solace	[ˈsɑːləs] *n.* 安慰：comfort in sorrow, misfortune, or distress *vt.* 安慰，安抚：to comfort, cheer, or console, as in trouble or sorrow
commonplace	[ˈkɑːmənpleɪs] *adj./n.* 司空见惯的(事物)，陈旧的(事物)：used or heard so often as to be dull
menace	[ˈmenəs] *vt.* 威胁，使处于危险：to make a show of intention to harm; to place in danger
embrace	[ɪmˈbreɪs] *vt.* 乐于接受：to take up willingly or eagerly
jaundice	[ˈdʒɔːndɪs] *n.* （因嫉妒或厌世而产生的）偏见：to affect with the negativity or bitterness of jaundice; bias

24

音 频

cowardice [ˈkaʊərdɪs] *n.* 懦弱，不坚定：lack of courage or resolution

edifice [ˈedɪfɪs] *n.* 大厦；大建筑物：a large or massive structure
n. 基础，基本构架：the arrangement of parts that gives something its basic form

splice [splaɪs] *vt.* 接合，叠接：to unite（as two ropes）by interweaving the strands, or to join（as two pieces of film）at the ends

rejoice [rɪˈdʒɔɪs] *vi.* 欣喜，喜悦：to feel joy or great delight

avarice [ˈævərɪs] *n.* 贪财，贪婪：excessive or insatiable desire for wealth or gain

caprice [kəˈpriːs] *n.* 反复无常，善变：an inclination to change one's mind impulsively

entice [ɪnˈtaɪs] *vt.* 诱使：to attract artfully or adroitly or by arousing hope or desire: tempt; lure

novice [ˈnɑːvɪs] *n.* 新手，初学者：a person new to a field or activity

arrogance [ˈærəgəns] *n.* 傲慢，自大：overbearing pride

allegiance [əˈliːdʒəns] *n.* 忠诚：devotion or loyalty to a person, group, or cause

variance [ˈveriəns] *n.* 不一致，不和谐：a lack of agreement or harmony

lance [læns] *vt.* 刺穿，刺破：to penetrate or hold（something）with a pointed object

25

surveillance	[sɜːrˈveɪləns] *n.* 监视，监控：close observation of a person or group, especially one under suspicion
penance	[ˈpenəns] *n.* 忏悔：something that you do in order to show that you are sorry about doing something wrong
countenance	[ˈkaʊntənəns] *vt.* 容忍：to put up with (something painful or difficult) *vt.* 赞成，推崇：to have a favorable opinion of
appurtenance	[əˈpɜːrtɪnəns] *n.* 附属物：a subordinate part or adjunct
provenance	[ˈprɑːvənəns] *n.* 来源，起源：origin, source
dissonance	[ˈdɪsənəns] *n.* (音调)不和谐；不一致，分歧：a harsh, disagreeable combination of sounds; discord; lack of agreement, consistency, or harmony; conflict
forbearance	[fɔːrˈberəns] *n.* 克制；忍耐：tolerance and restraint in the face of provocation; patience
entrance	[ˈentrəns] *n.* 进入权，进入许可：the means or right of entering or participating in [ɪnˈtræns] *vt.* 使入迷：to fill with delight, wonder, or enchantment
remonstrance	[rɪˈmɑːnstrəns] *n.* 抗议，抱怨：an expression of protest, complaint, or reproof, especially a formal statement of grievances
malfeasance	[mælˈfiːzns] *n.* 非法行为：improper or illegal behavior
complaisance	[kəmˈpleɪzəns] *n.* 愿意顺从，讨好，彬彬有礼：disposition to please or comply: affability
obeisance	[oʊˈbiːsns] *n.* 敬礼；尊重：a movement of the body made in token of respect or submission

renaissance	[ˈrenəsɑːns] *n.* 复兴：becomes popular again after a time when people were not interested in it
puissance	[ˈpwɪsəns] *n.* 权力：power; might
impuissance	[ɪmˈpjuːɪsns] *n.* 无权，虚弱：lack of power or effectiveness
pittance	[ˈpɪtns] *n.* 少量津贴：a small portion, amount, or allowance
nuance	[ˈnuːɑːns] *n.* 细微的差异：a subtle distinction or variation
abeyance	[əˈbeɪəns] *n.* 中止，搁置：temporary inactivity
decadence	[ˈdekədəns] *n.* 衰落，颓废：a process, condition, or period of deterioration or decline; a change to a lower state or level
credence	[ˈkriːdns] *n.* 坚信：firm belief in the integrity, ability, effectiveness, or genuineness of someone or something
resurgence	[rɪˈsɜːrdʒəns] *n.* 复兴：a restoration to use, acceptance, activity, or vigor
prescience	[ˈpreʃəns] *n.* 预知，先见：knowledge of actions or events before they occur
resilience	[rɪˈzɪliəns] *n.* 恢复能力：the ability to recover quickly from illness, change, or misfortune
consilience	[kənˈsɪliəns] *n.* 融合：the linking together of principles from different disciplines especially when forming a comprehensive theory
somnolence	[ˈsɑːmnələns] *n.* 瞌睡，嗜睡：the quality or state of desiring or needing sleep
persistence	[pərˈsɪstəns] *n.* 坚持，持续：uninterrupted or lasting existence
confluence	[ˈkɑːnfluəns] *n.* 汇合，混合：the coming together of two or more things to the same point

consequence ['kɑ:nsəkwens] *n.* 结果：something produced by a cause or necessarily following from a set of conditions

n. 重要性，价值：significance; importance

evince [ɪ'vɪns] *vt.* 表明：to make known (something abstract) through outward signs

province ['prɑ:vɪns] *n.* 职能范围：sphere or field of activity or authority, as of a person

wince [wɪns] *vi.* 畏缩：to shrink back involuntarily as from pain

ensconce [ɪn'skɑ:ns] *vt.* 安置：to settle (oneself) securely or comfortably

vt. 隐藏：to put in a hiding place

denounce [dɪ'naʊns] *vt.* 公开指责：to express public or formal disapproval of

renounce [rɪ'naʊns] *vt.* (正式地)放弃：to give up, refuse, or resign usually by formal declaration

farce [fɑ:rs] *n.* 闹剧：ridiculous or empty show

coerce [koʊ'ɜ:rs] *vt.* (以武力)强制：to achieve by force or threat

acquiesce [ˌækwi'es] *v.* 勉强同意；默许：to accept, comply, or submit tacitly or passively

coalesce [ˌkoʊə'les] *v.* 合并，融合：to unite into a whole: fuse

convalesce [ˌkɑ:nvə'les] *vi.* 渐渐康复，渐愈：to recover health and strength gradually after sickness or weakness

effervesce [ˌefər'ves] *vi.* 兴奋，热情洋溢：to show high spirits oranimation

seduce [sɪ'du:s] *vt.* 劝说(使不忠，使不服从)，诱…误入歧途：to attract or persuade to disobedience or disloyalty

induce [ɪn'dju:s] *v.* 引发，导致：to be the cause of (a situation, action, or state of mind)

28

truce [truːs] *n.* 休战，休战协定：a <u>suspension</u> of <u>fighting</u> especially of considerable duration by agreement of opposing forces

barricade [ˌbæriˈkeid] *n.* 障碍物：an <u>obstruction</u> or <u>rampart</u> thrown up across a way or passage
vt. 用障碍物阻止通过：to <u>prevent access</u> to by means of a barricade

cascade [kæˈskeid] *n.* 一连串，大量：something falling or <u>rushing forth in quantity</u>

renegade [ˈrenigeid] *n.* 背教者，叛徒：one who <u>rejects</u> a religion, cause, <u>allegiance</u>, or group for another; a deserter

accolade [ˈækəleid] *n.* 同意，赞赏：an expression of <u>approval</u>
v. 赞扬：to <u>praise</u> or honor

abrade [əˈbreid] *v.* 磨损，精神上折磨：to rub or <u>wear away</u> especially <u>by friction</u>; wear down spiritually

masquerade [ˌmæskəˈreid] *n.* 面具，伪装：a <u>display</u> of emotion or behavior that is <u>insincere</u> or intended to deceive
vi. 伪装，掩饰：to <u>disguise</u> oneself

retrograde [ˈretrəgreid] *adj.* 倒退的：<u>moving</u> or tending <u>backward</u>
vi. 退步，退化：to decline to a worse condition

tirade [ˈtaireid] *n.* 长篇抨击性演讲：a long <u>angry</u> or violent speech, usually of a <u>censorious</u> or <u>denunciatory</u> nature; a diatribe

dissuade [diˈsweid] *vt.* 劝阻，反对：to <u>deter</u> (a person) from a course of action or a purpose by <u>persuasion</u> or exhortation

pervade [pərˈveid] *vt.* 弥漫，充满：to be present <u>throughout</u>; permeate

cede [siːd] *vt.* (根据条约)放弃，割让：to surrender possession of, especially by treaty

accede [əkˈsiːd] *v.* 赞成：to express approval or give consent

secede [sɪˈsiːd] *vi.* 脱离，退出(组织、团体、联盟等)：to withdraw from an organization (as a religious communion or political party or federation)

concede [kənˈsiːd] *vt.* 承认：to grant as a right or privilege

impede [ɪmˈpiːd] *vt.* 妨碍，阻碍：to interfere with or slow the progress of

supersede [ˌsuːpərˈsiːd] *vt.* 取代，替代：to displace in favor of another

chide [tʃaɪd] *v.* 责备：to scold mildly so as to correct or improve

glide [glaɪd] *v.* 轻松地行动，轻松地通过：to move or proceed smoothly, continuously, and effortlessly

backslide [ˈbækslaɪd] *vi.* (情况等)倒退，变坏：to revert to a worse condition

bromide [ˈbroʊmaɪd] *n.* 陈词滥调：a commonplace or hackneyed statement or notion

deride [dɪˈraɪd] *vt.* 嘲弄，嘲笑：to speak of or treat with contemptuous mirth

override [ˌoʊvərˈraɪd] *vt.* 推翻：to set aside

subside [səbˈsaɪd] *vi.* 下陷，下沉，减弱：to tend downward

forebode [fɔːrˈboʊd] *v.* 预示，预兆：to show signs of coming ill or misfortune

decode [ˌdiːˈkoʊd] *vt.* 解码：to change (as a secret message) from code into ordinary language
vt. 对…有清晰想法，理解，解读：to have a clear idea of

30

implode	[ɪmˈploʊd] v. (使)剧烈收缩，(使)坍缩，(使)内爆：to (cause to) <u>collapse inward</u> violently
discommode	[dɪskəˈmoʊd] vt. 打扰，使不便：to cause inconvenience to: <u>trouble</u>
avant-garde	[ˌævɑːˈɡɑːrd] n. (尤指艺术上的)先锋派：an intelligentsia that <u>develops new or experimental concepts</u> especially in the arts
preclude	[prɪˈkluːd] vt. 预先阻止：to <u>make impossible</u>, as by action taken <u>in advance</u>
elude	[iˈluːd] vt. 躲闪，躲避：to <u>avoid adroitly</u> vt. 使无法理解，使困惑：to <u>escape the perception</u>, understanding, or grasp of
allude	[əˈluːd] vi. 间接提到：to convey an idea <u>indirectly</u>
collude	[kəˈljuːd] v. 串通，共谋(做坏事)：to <u>act together secretly</u> to achieve a <u>fraudulent</u>, illegal, or deceitful purpose; <u>conspire</u>
denude	[dɪˈnuːd] vt. 脱去，使赤裸：to divest of covering; make <u>bare</u>
prude	[pruːd] n. 过分正经的人：一个过分关心自己是否得体、谦逊或正确的人：a person who is <u>greatly concerned</u> with <u>seemly behavior and morality</u> especially regarding sexual matters
protrude	[proʊˈtruːd] vi. 突出：to jut out; <u>project</u>; bulge
solitude	[ˈsɑːlətuːd] n. 孤独，避世：the quality or state of <u>being alone</u> or remote from society
magnitude	[ˈmæɡnɪtuːd] n. 重要，重大：<u>greatness in significance</u> or influence
turpitude	[ˈtɜːrpətuːd] n. 卑鄙：inherent <u>baseness</u>: depravity
pulchritude	[ˈpʌlkrɪtjuːd] n. 美丽：great physical <u>beauty</u> and appeal

lassitude ['læsɪtuːd] *n.* 乏力，没精打采：a state or feeling of weariness, <u>diminished energy</u>, or listlessness

vicissitude [vɪ'sɪsɪtuːd] *n.* 自然变化，变迁兴衰：<u>natural change</u> or mutation visible in nature or in human affairs

latitude ['lætɪtuːd] *n.* (行动或言论)自由：<u>freedom</u> from normal restraints, limitations, or regulations

platitude ['plætɪtuːd] *n.* 陈词滥调：a trite or <u>banal</u> remark or <u>statement</u>, especially one expressed as if it were original or significant

rectitude ['rektɪtuːd] *n.* 正直：the quality or state of being straight; <u>moral integrity</u>

certitude ['sɜːrtɪtuːd] *n.* 确信无疑：the state of being or feeling <u>certain</u>

音 频

exude	[ɪɡˈzuːd] *v.* 分泌，流出：to <u>flow forth</u> slowly through small openings
referee	[ˌrefəˈriː] *n.* 仲裁者；裁判员：a person who <u>impartially</u> decides or <u>resolves a dispute</u> or controversy *vt.* (就纠纷或争议)给出意见：to <u>give an opinion</u> about (something at issue or in dispute)
carefree	[ˈkerfriː] *adj.* 无忧无虑的：free from care as having <u>no worries or troubles</u>
repartee	[ˌrepɑːrˈtiː] *n.* 打趣，善意的玩笑：<u>good-natured</u> <u>teasing</u> or exchanging of clever remarks
vouchsafe	[ˌvaʊtʃˈseɪf] *vt.* 允诺，给予：to <u>grant</u> or furnish often <u>in a gracious or condescending manner</u>
fail-safe	[ˈfeɪlseɪf] *n.* 保险措施：a measure taken <u>to</u> <u>preclude loss or injury</u> *adj.* 万无一失的：having <u>no chance of failure</u>
gaffe	[ɡæf] *n.* (社交上)失礼，失态：a <u>social</u> or diplomatic <u>blunder</u>
rife	[raɪf] *adj.* 丰富的，普遍的：possessing or covered with <u>great numbers</u> or amounts of something specified
disengage	[ˌdɪsɪnˈɡeɪdʒ] *vt.* 分开，使脱离：to <u>set free</u> from <u>entanglement</u> or difficulty
persiflage	[ˈpɜːrsɪflɑːʒ] *n.* 打趣：good-natured <u>teasing</u> or exchanging of clever remarks

camouflage [ˈkæməflɑːʒ] *v./n.* 伪装；伪装手段：behavior or artifice designed to <u>deceive</u> or <u>hide</u>

homage [ˈhɑːmɪdʒ] *n.* 尊敬，敬意：expression of high regard: <u>respect</u>

badinage [ˌbædənˈɑːʒ] *n.* 打趣，善意的玩笑：playful rep-artee, <u>banter</u>

rage [reɪdʒ] *n./v.* 暴怒：<u>violent</u> and uncontrolled <u>anger</u>

disparage [dɪˈspærɪdʒ] *vt.* 贬低；轻蔑地说：to <u>lower</u> in rank or reputation; to speak of in a slighting or <u>disrespectful</u> way; belittle

umbrage [ˈʌmbrɪdʒ] *n.* 不悦，生气：the <u>feeling of being offended or resentful</u> after a slight or indignity

mirage [məˈrɑːʒ] *n.* 海市蜃楼，幻想：something <u>illu-sory</u> and unattainable like a mirage

forage [ˈfɔːrɪdʒ] *vi.* 寻找：to make a <u>search</u>

barrage [bəˈrɑːʒ] *n.* 有压倒之势的、集中的倾泻（如言语）：an over-whelming, concentrated outpouring, as of words

sage [seɪdʒ] *n.* 智者：one (as a profound philoso-pher) distinguished for <u>wisdom</u>

presage [ˈpresɪdʒ] *n.* 征兆：something believed to be a <u>sign or warning</u> of a future event
vt. 预示，预言：to foretell or <u>predict</u>

montage [ˈmɒntɑːʒ] *n.* 大杂烩：an unorganized <u>collec-tion</u> or mixture of various things

sabotage [ˈsæbətɑːʒ] *n.* 妨害，破坏：treacherous action to defeat or <u>hinder a cause</u> or an endeavor; deliberate subversion
vt. 从事破坏活动，阻止：to <u>practice sabotage</u> on

assuage [əˈsweɪdʒ] *vt.* 缓和，减轻：to <u>lessen</u> the <u>inten-sity</u> of

34

salvage ['sælvɪdʒ] *vt.* (从灾难中)抢救: to save from loss or destruction

hedge [hedʒ] *v.* 闪烁其词: to avoid giving a definite answer or position

abridge [ə'brɪdʒ] *v.* 缩短，缩小: to shorten in duration or extent

dodge [dɑːdʒ] *v.* 躲避: to avoid (a blow, for example) by moving or shifting quickly aside

hodgepodge ['hɑːdʒpɑːdʒ] *n.* 大杂烩: a mixture of dissimilar ingredients; a jumble

budge [bʌdʒ] *v.* 停止抵抗，屈服: to cease resistance (as to another's arguments, demands, or control)

nudge [nʌdʒ] *vt.* 说服某人做某事: to try to persuade (someone) through earnest appeals to follow a course of action

grudge [grʌdʒ] *n.* 怨恨，仇恨: a feeling of deep-seated resentment or ill will

trudge [trʌdʒ] *vi.* 吃力而笨拙地走: to move heavily or clumsily

sacrilege ['sækrəlɪdʒ] *n.* 亵渎圣物: desecration, profanation, misuse, or theft of something sacred

renege [rɪ'niːg] *vt.* 放弃，摒弃: to solemnly or formally reject or go back on (as something formerly adhered to)

beige [beɪʒ] *adj.* 缺乏特征的: lacking distinction

prestige [pre'stiːʒ] *n.* 声望，威望: the level of respect at which one is regarded by others

vestige ['vestɪdʒ] *n.* 微小的遗迹，小痕迹: the smallest quantity or trace

bulge [bʌldʒ] *n.* 凸起: a protuberant or swollen part or place

divulge [daɪ'vʌldʒ] *vt.* 泄漏(秘密): to make known (as a confidence or secret)

estrange [ɪ'streɪndʒ] *vt.* 使疏远，离间，使感情失和：to arouse especially mutual enmity or indifference in where there had formerly been love, affection, or friendliness

revenge [rɪ'vendʒ] *n.* 报复，复仇：an act or instance of retaliating in order to get even
vt. 为…复仇：to avenge (as oneself) usually by retaliating in kind or degree

fringe [frɪndʒ] *n.* 边缘：something that resembles such a border or edging

constringe [kən'strɪndʒ] *vt.* 使紧缩：to make narrow or draw together

singe [sɪndʒ] *vt.* 轻微烧焦：to burn superficially or lightly

tinge [tɪndʒ] *vt.* 给…着上少量的色彩：to color with a slight shade or stain: tint

plunge [plʌndʒ] *vi.* 突然下降：to descend or dip suddenly

surcharge ['sɜːrtʃɑːrdʒ] *v./n.* 过高收费：to charge (someone) too much for goods or services

discharge [dɪs'tʃɑːrdʒ] *vt.* 解雇：to dismiss from employment
vt. 释放：to set free (as from slavery or confinement)

submerge [səb'mɜːrdʒ] *vt.* 使淹没：to put under water

diverge [daɪ'vɜːrdʒ] *vt.* 改变方向：to change one's course or direction
vt. (使)分叉，散开：to (cause to) go or move in different directions from a central point
vi. 分歧：to become or be different in character or form: differ in opinion
vi. 离题：to depart from a set course or norm; deviate

converge [kən'vɜːrdʒ] *v.* 汇集，交汇于一点：tending to move toward one point or one another

forge [fɔːrdʒ] *v.* 伪造：to make or imitate falsely especially with intent to defraud
v. 锻造，铸就：to form (as metal) by or as if by heating and hammering

gorge [gɔːrdʒ] *n.* 峡谷：a narrow steep-walled canyon or part of a canyon
v. 狼吞虎咽：to eat greedily or to repletion

disgorge [dɪs'gɔːrdʒ] *v.* 呕吐出：to discharge by the throat and mouth; vomit

scourge [skɜːrdʒ] *n.* 祸害：a source of harm or misfortune

gauge [geɪdʒ] *n.* 测量标准：a measurement (as of linear dimension) according to some standard or system
vt. 判定：to determine the capacity or contents of

subterfuge ['sʌbtərfjuːdʒ] *n.* 诡计：deception by artifice or stratagem in order to conceal, escape, or evade

deluge ['deljuːdʒ] *n.* 大暴雨：a drenching rain
n. 大量：a great flow of water or of something that overwhelms

cache [kæʃ] *n.* 囤货，藏货：a supply stored up and often hidden away
v. 隐藏：to put into a hiding place

panache [pə'næʃ] *n.* 炫耀：dash or flamboyance in style and action

cliché [kliː'ʃeɪ] *n./adj.* 陈词滥调（的）：a hackneyed theme, characterization, or situation

pastiche [pæ'stiːʃ] *n.* （带嘲讽的）模仿：a literary, artistic, musical, or architectural work that imitates the style of previous work, often with satirical intent

n. 大杂烩：a pasticcio of incongruous parts; a hodgepodge

gauche [gouʃ] *adj.* 笨拙的，缺乏社交经验的：lacking social experience or grace

catastrophe [kə'tæstrəfi] *n.* 大灾难：the final event of the dramatic action especially of a tragedy
n. 彻底的失败：utter failure: fiasco

loathe [louð] *vt.* 厌恶：to dislike someone or something greatly; abhor

lithe [laɪð] *adj.* 敏捷的，轻盈的：characterized by easy flexibility and grace
adj. 柔软的：easily bent or flexed

blithe [blaɪð] *adj.* 愉快高兴的：of a happy lighthearted character or disposition
adj. 无忧无虑的；漫不经心的：having or showing freedom from worries or troubles

soothe [su:ð] *vt.* 带来慰藉，安慰：to bring comfort, solace, or reassurance to

hie [haɪ] *vi.* 匆匆忙忙：to go quickly, hasten

rookie ['rʊki] *n.* 新兵；新手；菜鸟：recruit; novice

belie [bɪ'laɪ] *vt.* 掩饰：to keep secret or shut off from view
vt. 与⋯相对立；与⋯相矛盾：to be counter to; contradict

bonhomie [,bɑ:nə'mi:] *n.* 温和，和蔼：a pleasant and affable disposition; geniality

stymie ['staɪmi] *vt.* 阻碍：to present an obstacle to

camaraderie [,kɑ:mə'rɑːdəri] *n.* 友情：a spirit of friendly good-fellowship

slake [sleɪk] *vt.* 使满足：to satisfy (a craving); quench

brake [breɪk] *v.* 刹车：to cause to move or proceed at a less rapid pace

forsake	[fər'seɪk] *vt.* 彻底放弃，抛弃：to renounce or turn away from entirely
spike	['spaɪk] *v.* 激励：to give life, vigor, or spirit to
strike	[straɪk] *n.* 攻击：the act or action of setting upon with force or violence *vt.* 击打：to aim and usually deliver a blow, stroke, or thrust (as with the hand, a weapon, or a tool) *vt.* 袭击，攻击：to take sudden, violent action against *vt.* 撞击：to come into usually forceful contact with something
stoke	[stoʊk] *vt.* 增大，促进：to make greater in size, amount, or number
evoke	[ɪ'voʊk] *vt.* 唤起，引发：to call forth or up
revoke	[rɪ'voʊk] *vt.* 撤回，宣告无效：to annul by recalling or taking back
invoke	[ɪn'voʊk] *vt.* 实施：to put into effect or operation *vt.* 产生，造成：to be the cause of（a situation, action, or state of mind）
convoke	[kən'voʊk] *v.* 召集开会：to bring together by or as if by summons
provoke	[prə'voʊk] *vt.* 激怒：to incite to anger or resentment *vt.* 驱使，激起：to stir to action or feeling
yoke	[joʊk] *v.* 连接：to become joined or linked
bale	[beɪl] *n.* 痛苦，悲哀：woe, sorrow
hale	[heɪl] *adj.* 强壮的，健壮的：free from infirmity or illness; sound
finale	[fɪ'næli] *n.* 终场，结局：the closing part, scene, or number in a public performance

rationale [ˌræʃə'næl] *n.* 基本原理，解释：a statement given to <u>explain</u> a belief or act

chorale [kə'rɑːl] *n.* 赞美诗：a <u>hymn or psalm</u> sung to a traditional or composed melody <u>in church</u>

n. 合唱班，合唱团：an organized <u>group of singers</u>

stale [steɪl] *adj.* 陈旧乏味的：used or heard <u>so often as to be dull</u>

imperturbable [ˌɪmpər'tɜːrbəbl] *adj.* 沉着冷静的，淡定的：marked by <u>extreme calm</u>, impassivity, and steadiness

implacable [ɪm'plækəbl] *adj.* 固执的：<u>sticking to an opinion</u>, purpose, or course of action in spite of reason, arguments, or persuasion

adj. 无法平息的：<u>not capable of being appeased</u>, significantly changed, or mitigated

impeccable [ɪm'pekəbl] *adj.* 无瑕的，无可挑剔的：<u>free from fault</u> or blame

irradicable [ɪ'rædɪkəbl] *adj.* 不能根除的：<u>impossible</u> to uproot or <u>destroy</u>

applicable ['æplɪkəbl] *adj.* 可用的，可行的：capable of being <u>put to use</u> or account

adj. 相关的，有关的：<u>having to do with</u> the matter at hand

amicable ['æmɪkəbl] *adj.* 友善的：characterized by <u>friendly</u> goodwill; <u>amiable</u>

despicable [dɪ'spɪkəbl] *adj.* 令人鄙视的：arousing or deserving of one's <u>loathing and disgust</u>

音频

formidable	[ˈfɔːrmɪdəbl] *adj.* 艰难的：requiring considerable physical or mental effort
dependable	[dɪˈpendəbl] *adj.* 可靠的，值得信赖的：capable of being depended on
agreeable	[əˈgriːəbl] *adj.* 令人愉悦的：pleasing to the mind or senses especially as according well with one's tastes or needs *adj.* 相一致的：being in harmony
malleable	[ˈmæliəbl] *adj.* 可塑的：capable of being extended or shaped by beating with a hammer or by the pressure of rollers *adj.* 易控制的：capable of being altered or controlled by outside forces or influences
permeable	[ˈpɜːrmiəbl] *adj.* 可渗透的：capable of being permeated or penetrated, especially by liquids or gases
fable	[ˈfeɪbl] *n.* 神话，传说：a legendary story of supernatural happenings *n.* 谎言，虚构：a statement known by its maker to be untrue and made in order to deceive
affable	[ˈæfəbl] *adj.* 和蔼的，温和的：characterized by ease and friendliness
ineffable	[ɪnˈefəbl] *adj.* 难以表达的：incapable of being expressed
unimpeachable	[ˌʌnɪmˈpiːtʃəbl] *adj.* 无可置疑的：beyond doubt; unquestionable

imperishable [ɪmˈperɪʃəbl] *adj.* 不朽的，永恒的：enduring or occurring forever

appreciable [əˈpriːʃəbl] *adj.* 可感知的，明显的：capable of being perceived or measured; perceptible

pliable [ˈplaɪəbl] *adj.* 易弯曲的，柔软的：supple enough to bend freely or repeatedly without breaking
adj. 易受影响的，温顺的：easily influenced, persuaded, or swayed

amiable [ˈeɪmiəbl] *adj.* 好脾气的，友好易相处的：being friendly, sociable, and congenial

friable [ˈfraɪəbl] *adj.* 易碎的：easily crumbled or pulverized

viable [ˈvaɪəbl] *adj.* 可行的：capable of being done or carried out

unassailable [ˌʌnəˈseɪləbl] *adj.* 无可争辩的，无法否认的，不可亵渎的：not to be violated, criticized, or tampered with

estimable [ˈestɪməbl] *adj.* 值得尊敬的：deserving of esteem; admirable

inalienable [ɪnˈeɪliənəbl] *adj.* 不可剥夺的，不能让与的：cannot be transferred to another or others

amenable [əˈmiːnəbl] *adj.* 顺从的，服从的：readily brought to yield, submit, or cooperate

tenable [ˈtenəbl] *adj.* 有据可依的，无懈可击的：capable of being held or defended; reasonable

untenable [ʌnˈtenəbl] *adj.* 防守不住的，站不住脚的：not able to be defended

interminable [ɪnˈtɜːrmɪnəbl] *adj.* 无尽头的：having or seeming to have no end

unexceptionable [ˌʌnɪkˈsepʃənəbl] *adj.* 无懈可击的：not open to objection or criticism, beyond reproach

personable [ˈpɜːrsənəbl] *adj.* 风度翩翩的，吸引人的：pleasing in personality or appearance; attractive

42

palpable [ˈpælpəbl] *adj.* 明显的，易觉察的：easily perceived; obvious

culpable [ˈkʌlpəbl] *adj.* 该受谴责的，有罪的：deserving of blame or censure as being wrong, evil, improper, or injurious

unflappable [ˌʌnˈflæpəbl] *adj.* 镇定的，从容不迫的：not easily upset or excited

arable [ˈærəbl] *adj.* 适合耕种的：fit for or used for the growing of crops

considerable [kənˈsɪdərəbl] *adj.* (数量上)可观(而值得注意)的：sufficiently large in size, amount, or number to merit attention
adj. 值得考虑的，重要的：worth consideration; significant

ponderable [ˈpɑːndərəbl] *adj.* 有价值的，值得考虑的：considerable enough to be weighed or assessed

vulnerable [ˈvʌlnərəbl] *adj.* 易受攻击的，脆弱的：open to attack or damage

deplorable [dɪˈplɔːrəbl] *adj.* 可鄙的，可耻的：worthy of severe condemnation or reproach

favorable [ˈfeɪvərəbl] *adj.* 有利的：tending to promote or facilitate

inexorable [ɪnˈeksərəbl] *adj.* 无法劝阻的，不为所动的：not to be persuaded, moved, or stopped

impenetrable [ɪmˈpenɪtrəbl] *adj.* 不可渗透的，不可穿透的：impossible to get through or into
adj. 难以理解的：incapable of being comprehended

indispensable [ˌɪndɪˈspensəbl] *adj.* 必不可少的，不可或缺的：impossible to do without

palatable [ˈpælətəbl] *adj.* 感到愉悦满足的：giving pleasure or contentment to the mind or senses

redoubtable [rɪ'daʊtəbl] *adj.* 杰出的，值得尊敬的：worthy of respect or honor

adj. 可怕的：arousing fear or awe

tractable ['træktəbl] *adj.* 易驾驭的，温顺的：readily giving in to the command or authority of another

ineluctable [ˌɪnɪ'lʌktəbl] *adj.* 无法逃避的，必然的：not to be avoided, changed, or resisted

inimitable [ɪ'nɪmɪtəbl] *adj.* 无法仿效的，独特的：not capable of being imitated

inevitable [ɪn'evɪtəbl] *adj.* 不可避免的，必然的：incapable of being avoided or evaded

potable ['poʊtəbl] *n.* 饮品，尤指有酒精饮料：a beverage, especially an alcoholic beverage

adj. 适于饮用的：suitable for drinking

immutable [ɪ'mjuːtəbl] *adj.* 不可变的：not capable of changing or being changed

scrutable ['skruːtəbl] *adj.* 可以理解的：capable of being understood through study and observation; comprehensible

equable ['ekwəbl] *adj.* (脾气、性情)温和的：not easily disturbed; serene

babble ['bæbl] *v.* 发出含糊无意义的嘟囔声，胡乱说：to utter a meaningless confusion of words or sounds

v. 闲聊：to engage in casual or rambling conversation

dabble ['dæbl] *vi.* 涉猎，对…浅尝辄止：to work or involve oneself superficially or intermittently especially in a secondary interest

rabble ['ræbl] *n.* 混乱的人群；暴民；下层民众：a disorganized or disorderly crowd of people; the lowest class of people

nibble ['nɪbl] *vt.* 小口咬：to eat with small, quick bites or in small morsels

44

scribble	[ˈskrɪbl] v. 潦草地书写，乱写：to cover with scribbles, doodles, or meaningless marks
quibble	[ˈkwɪbl] vi. 吹毛求疵：to find fault or criticize for petty reasons; cavil
gobble	[ˈgɑːbl] vt. 狼吞虎咽：to swallow or eat greedily
hobble	[ˈhɑːbl] vt. 阻碍，妨碍：to hamper the action or progress of
wobble	[ˈwɑːbl] vi. 摇晃，颤抖：to move or proceed with an irregular rocking or staggering motion or unsteadily and clumsily from side to side vi. 犹豫不决：to show uncertainty about the right course of action
feeble	[ˈfiːbl] adj. 衰弱的：markedly lacking in strength
invincible	[ɪnˈvɪnsəbl] adj. 不可战胜的，不可超越的：incapable of being conquered, overcome, or subdued
irascible	[ɪˈræsəbl] adj. 易怒的：marked by hot temper and easily provoked anger
edible	[ˈedəbl] adj. 可食用的：fit to be eaten
intelligible	[ɪnˈtelɪdʒəbl] adj. 可理解的：capable of being understood
incorrigible	[ɪnˈkɔːrɪdʒəbl] adj. 不可救药的，积习难改的：incapable of being corrected or amended adj. 无法管制的：difficult or impossible to control or manage
tangible	[ˈtændʒəbl] adj. 可感知的：capable of being perceived
intangible	[ɪnˈtændʒəbl] adj. 无法感知的，无形的：incapable of being perceived by the senses
fungible	[ˈfʌndʒəbl] adj. 可互换的：capable of being substituted in place of one another
indelible	[ɪnˈdeləbl] adj. 无法忘怀的：not easily forgotten

fallible	[ˈfæləbl] *adj.* 可能出错的：tending or likely to be <u>erroneous</u> or capable of making an error
foible	[ˈfɔɪbl] *n.* 小缺点：a <u>minor flaw</u> or shortcoming in character or behavior
insensible	[ɪnˈsensəbl] *adj.* 无知觉的：having <u>lost con-</u><u>sciousness</u>, especially temporarily
ostensible	[ɑːˈstensəbl] *adj.* 表面上的，佯装的：<u>appearing</u> <u>to be true</u> on the basis of evidence that may or may not be confirmed
accessible	[əkˈsesəbl] *adj.* 可以到达的：situated <u>within</u> <u>easy reach</u> *adj.* 可理解的：capable of being <u>understood</u> or appreciated
plausible	[ˈplɔːzəbl] *adj.* 可信的：<u>superficially</u> fair, <u>reasonable</u>, or valuable but often specious
compatible	[kəmˈpætəbl] *adj.* 一致的，能共存的：capable of existing together <u>in harmony</u>
perceptible	[pərˈseptəbl] *adj.* 可察觉的：capable of <u>being</u> <u>perceived</u> especially by the senses
susceptible	[səˈseptəbl] *adj.* 容易受伤害的：being in a situation where one is <u>likely to meet with harm</u>
incontrovertible	[ˌɪnkɑːntrəˈvɜːrtəbl] *adj.* 无可争议的：<u>not open</u> <u>to question</u>
combustible	[kəmˈbʌstəbl] *adj.* 可燃的：capable of <u>igniting</u> and burning *adj.* 容易激动的：<u>easily excited</u>
flexible	[ˈfleksəbl] *adj.* 灵活的，可变的：capable of be-ing <u>readily changed</u> *adj.* 易受影响的：<u>susceptible to influence</u> or persuasion
amble	[ˈæmbl] *vi./n.* 漫步，闲逛：to <u>walk slowly</u> or <u>lei-</u><u>surely</u>; <u>stroll</u>

gamble	['gæmbl] *v.* 赌博，孤注一掷：to <u>bet</u> on an uncertain outcome, as of a contest
ramble	['ræmbl] *vi.* 漫谈；长篇大论(并经常离题)地说或写：to talk at length <u>without</u> sticking to <u>a</u> <u>topic</u> or getting to a point
dissemble	[dɪ'sembl] *v.* 用假象隐藏真相，掩饰：to put on a <u>false</u> appearance
bumble	['bʌmbl] *vi.* 含糊不清地说，杂乱无章地说：to speak <u>rapidly</u>, <u>inarticulately</u>, and usually unintelligibly
fumble	['fʌmbl] *v.* 笨拙地做：to make <u>awkward</u> <u>attempts</u> to do or find something
humble	['hʌmbl] *adj.* 谦逊的：marked by <u>meekness</u> or <u>modesty</u> in behavior, attitude, or spirit; not arrogant or prideful *adj.* 顺从的，谦卑的：showing, expressing, or offered in a spirit of <u>humility</u> or unseemly <u>submissiveness</u>
mumble	['mʌmbl] *v.* 说话含糊：to <u>utter</u> words in a low <u>confused</u> indistinct manner
grumble	['grʌmbl] *vi.* (尤指低声地)抱怨，埋怨：to <u>complain</u> in a surly manner; mutter discontentedly
ennoble	[ɪ'noʊbl] *vt.* 使尊贵：to make <u>noble</u>
garble	['gɑːrbl] *vt.* 曲解，篡改，混淆(以至使无法理解)：to mix up or <u>distort</u> to such an extent as to make <u>misleading</u> or incomprehensible
warble	['wɔːrbl] *v.* 柔和地唱歌：to <u>sing with</u> trills, runs, or other <u>melodic embellishments</u>
voluble	['vɑːljəbl] *adj.* 健谈的，话多的：characterized by <u>ready</u> or rapid <u>speech</u>
debacle	[deɪ'bɑːkl] *n.* 溃败：a <u>complete failure</u>; fiasco

47

manacle ['mænəkl] *vt.* 限制，给…制造困难：to confine or restrain with or as if with chains; to create difficulty for the work or activity of

pinnacle ['pɪnəkl] *n.* 顶峰：the highest point of development or achievement

saddle ['sædl] *vt.* 使某人负担：to load or burden

waddle ['wɑːdl] *vi.* 摇摇摆摆地走：to walk with short steps that tilt the body from side to side

meddle ['medl] *vi.* 干涉，管闲事：to intrude into other people's affairs or business; interfere

peddle ['pedl] *v.* 叫卖，兜售：to sell from place to place usually in small quantities

mollycoddle ['mɑːlikɑːdl] *vt.* 宠爱，溺爱：to treat with an excessive or absurd degree of indulgence and attention

befuddle [bɪ'fʌdl] *v.* 使困惑：to throw into a state of mental uncertainty

wheedle ['wiːdl] *v.* （用花言巧语）诱惑，哄骗：to persuade or attempt to persuade by flattery or guile

音 频

idle	[ˈaɪdl] *adj.* 闲置的，未使用的：not turned to normal or appropriate use *adj.* 懒散的：shiftless, lazy *v.* 懒散度日，无所事事：to pass (time) without working or while avoiding work
bridle	[ˈbraɪdl] *v.* 限制：to keep from exceeding a desirable degree or level (as of expression)
kindle	[ˈkɪndl] *vt.* 点燃：to build or fuel(a fire); to set fire to; ignite
dwindle	[ˈdwɪndl] *vi.* 逐渐减少：to become gradually less until little remains
swindle	[ˈswɪndl] *vt.* 欺骗，骗取：to cheat or defraud of money or property
doodle	[ˈduːdl] *vi.* （无目的地）乱涂乱画：to scribble aimlessly, especially when preoccupied *vi.* 漫无目的地打发时光：to spend time in aimless activity
dawdle	[ˈdɔːdl] *v.* 拖拖拉拉：to move or act slowly
baffle	[ˈbæfl] *vt.* 使疑惑：to throw into a state of mental uncertainty
waffle	[ˈwɑːfl] *vi.* 胡扯：to talk or write foolishly
muffle	[ˈmʌfl] *vt.* 使消声：to wrap or pad in order to deaden the sound
ruffle	[ˈrʌfl] *vt.* 使粗糙：to destroy the smoothness or evenness of

49

vt. 扰乱，打扰：to <u>disturb</u> the peace of mind of (someone) especially by repeated disagreeable acts

stifle [ˈstaɪfl] *vt.* 抑制(声音、呼吸等)；阻止，扼杀：to cut off (as the voice or breath); to keep in or <u>hold back</u>

boggle [ˈbɑːgl] *v.* (因为怀疑、恐惧)犹豫：to <u>hesitate</u> because of doubt, fear, or scruples

goggle [ˈgɑːgl] *vi.* 凝视：to <u>look</u> long and hard in wonder or surprise

inveigle [ɪnˈveɪgl] *vt.* 诱骗：to <u>win over by coaxing</u>, flattery, or artful talk

mangle [ˈmæŋgl] *vt.* 弄砸：to <u>ruin</u> or spoil through ineptitude or ignorance

wrangle [ˈræŋgl] *n.* 纷争，争端：an often noisy or angry expression of <u>differing opinions</u>
vi. 争吵：to <u>quarrel</u> noisily or angrily

tangle [ˈtæŋgl] *vt.* 纠缠，使…纠结：to seize and hold in or as if <u>in a snare</u>

entangle [ɪnˈtæŋgl] *vt.* 使卷入，使纠缠：to <u>twist</u> together into a usually <u>confused mass</u>
vt. 使变复杂或困难：to make <u>complex or difficult</u>

mingle [ˈmɪŋgl] *vt.* 混合，结合：to <u>mix</u> so that the components become united

commingle [kəˈmɪŋgl] *v.* 充分混合：to <u>blend</u> thoroughly into a harmonious whole

bungle [ˈbʌŋgl] *vt.* 办糟，失败：to act or <u>work clumsily</u> and awkwardly

labile [ˈleɪbaɪl] *adj.* 易变的，不稳定的：continually undergoing chemical, physical, or biological change; <u>unstable</u>

facile [ˈfæsl] *adj.* 表面的，浅尝辄止的：having or showing a <u>lack of depth</u> of understanding or character

domicile	['dɑːmɪsaɪl] *vt.* 为…提供住处：to establish in or provide with a domicile
reconcile	['rekənsaɪl] *vt.* 使和解，协调：to restore to friendship or harmony
fragile	['frædʒl] *adj.* 易碎的：easily broken or destroyed
simile	['sɪməli] *n.* 明喻：a figure of speech comparing two unlike things that is often introduced by like or as
rile	[raɪl] *vt.* 刺激，惹怒：to make agitated and angry
sterile	['sterəl] *adj.* 贫瘠的：not productive or effective *adj.* 无菌的：free from live bacteria or other microorganisms
puerile	['pjʊrəl] *adj.* 幼稚的，不成熟的：immature; lacking in adult experience or maturity
volatile	['vɑːlətl] *adj.* 多变的：characterized by or subject to rapid or unexpected change
versatile	['vɜːrsətl] *adj.* 多才多艺的，全能的：able to do many different kinds of things
tactile	['tæktl] *adj.* 有触觉的，能触知的：perceptible by touch: tangible
ductile	['dʌktaɪl] *adj.* 易受影响的：easily led or influenced
motile	['moʊtɪl] *adj.* 能动的：exhibiting or capable of movement
futile	['fjuːtl] *adj.* 无效的，无用的：serving no useful purpose; completely ineffective
guile	[gaɪl] *n.* 狡猾，狡诈：the inclination or practice of misleading others through lies or trickery
beguile	[bɪ 'gaɪl] *v.* 欺骗：to cause to believe what is untrue
vile	[vaɪl] *adj.* 丑陋的：unpleasant to look at *adj.* (道德上)可鄙的，卑鄙的：morally despicable or abhorrent

servile [ˈsɜːrvl] *adj.* 低下的，卑屈的：meanly or cravenly <u>submissive</u>: <u>abject</u>

shackle [ˈʃækl] *vt.* 束缚：to deprive of freedom especially of action by means of <u>restrictions</u> or handicaps
vt. 限制，阻碍：to <u>create difficulty</u> for the work or activity of

ramshackle [ˈræmʃækl] *adj.* 摇摇欲坠的：appearing <u>ready to collapse</u>; rickety

tackle [ˈtækl] *vt.* 着手处理：to <u>start work</u> on energetically

heckle [ˈhekl] *vt.* 起哄，使难堪：to <u>harass</u> and try to disconcert with questions, challenges, or gibes

fickle [ˈfɪkl] *adj.* 易变的：<u>likely to change</u> frequently, suddenly, or unexpectedly

trickle [ˈtrɪkl] *vi.* 一滴一滴地流，缓缓地流：to issue or <u>fall in drops</u>

rankle [ˈræŋkl] *vt.* 激怒：to <u>cause anger</u>, irritation, or deep bitterness

hyperbole [haɪˈpɜːrbəli] *n.* 夸张：a figure of speech in which <u>exaggeration</u> is <u>used for emphasis</u> or effect

condole [kənˈdoʊl] *vi.* 表达同情：to express <u>sympathetic</u> sorrow

cajole [kəˈdʒoʊl] *v.* 哄骗：to urge with gentle and repeated appeals, teasing, or flattery; <u>wheedle</u>

rigmarole [ˈrɪgməroʊl] *n.* 混乱而无意义的话：language marked by abstractions, jargon, euphemisms, and circumlocutions; <u>confused or meaningless talk</u>

console [kənˈsoʊl] *vt.* 安慰，慰藉：to <u>alleviate</u> the grief, sense of loss, or trouble of; <u>comfort</u>

disciple [dɪ'saɪpl] *n.* 信徒，追随者：one who accepts and assists in spreading the doctrines of another, follower

rumple ['rʌmpl] *vt.* 打乱，使不整齐：to undo the proper order or arrangement of

crumple ['krʌmpl] *v.* 弄皱：to press, bend, or crush out of shape

supple ['sʌpl] *adj.* 易弯曲的，柔软的：readily bent; pliant

scruple ['skruːpl] *n.* （良心上的）不安：an uneasy feeling about the rightness of what one is doing or going to do

subtle ['sʌtl] *adj.* 微妙的，难以感知的：(so slight as to be)difficult to understand or perceive

dismantle [dɪs'mæntl] *vt.* 分解，分拆：to take to pieces also: to destroy the integrity or functioning of

disgruntle [dɪs'grʌntl] *vt.* 使发怒，使不满意：to make ill-humored or discontented

startle ['stɑːrtl] *vt.* 使吓一跳，使大吃一惊：to frighten or surprise suddenly and usually not seriously

bristle ['brɪsl] *v.* 怒不可遏，咆哮：to express one's anger usually violently

apostle [ə'pɑːsl] *n.* （政策或思想等的）信奉者，支持者：a person who actively supports or favors a cause

bustle ['bʌsl] *n.* 忙乱，喧闹：noisy, energetic, and often obtrusive activity
vi. （快速地）行走，奔忙：to move briskly and often ostentatiously

rustle ['rʌsl] *vi.* 快速地行动：to move or act energetically or with speed; to proceed or move quickly

mettle	[ˈmetl] *n.* 勇气：vigor and strength of spirit or temperament *n.* 毅力，耐力：staying quality: stamina
nettle	[ˈnetl] *vt.* 惹怒：to arouse to sharp but transitory annoyance or anger
brittle	[ˈbrɪtl] *adj.* 易碎的，脆弱的，易坏的：easily broken, cracked, or snapped *adj.* 不热心的，不真心的：lacking in friendliness or warmth of feeling
mottle	[ˈmɑːtl] *vt.* 标记上杂色斑点：to mark with spots or blotches of different shades or colors
ridicule	[ˈrɪdɪkjuːl] *vt.* 嘲笑：to make fun of
minuscule	[ˈmɪnəskjuːl] *adj.* 极小的：very small
embezzle	[ɪmˈbezl] *vt.* 盗用：to appropriate（as property entrusted to one's care）fraudulently to one's own use
guzzle	[ˈɡʌzl] *v.* 狂饮：to drink especially liquor greedily, continually, or habitually
inflame	[ɪnˈfleɪm] *vt.* 使加剧：to make more violent
tame	[teɪm] *adj.* 被驯化的：reduced from a state of native wildness especially so as to be tractable and useful to humans *vt.* 控制，抑制：to keep from exceeding a desirable degree or level（as of expression）
acme	[ˈækmi] *n.* 顶点，极点：the highest point or stage, as of achievement or development
sublime	[səˈblaɪm] *adj.* 崇高的，庄严的：of high spiritual, moral, or intellectual worth
mime	[maɪm] *v.* 模仿：to use（someone or something）as the model for one's speech, mannerisms, or behavior
wholesome	[ˈhoʊlsəm] *adj.* 有益身心健康的：promoting mental, moral, or social health

54

noisome [ˈnɔɪsəm] *adj.* 恶臭的：offensive to the senses and espe-cially to the sense of smell

adj. 非常令人厌恶的：highly obnoxious or objectionable

winsome [ˈwɪnsəm] *adj.* 迷人的，漂亮的：generally pleasing and engaging often because of a childlike charm and innocence

cumbersome [ˈkʌmbərsəm] *adj.* 笨重的，难处理的：difficult to handle because of weight or bulk

lissome [ˈlɪsəm] *adj.* 柔软的：easily bent; supple

adj. 敏捷的，轻盈的：having the ability to move with ease; limber

bane [beɪn] *n.* 有害的物质：a substance that by chemical action can kill or injure a living

urbane [ɜːrˈbeɪn] *adj.* 彬彬有礼的，文雅的：notably polite or finished in manner

hurricane [ˈhɜːrəkən] *n.* 飓风般的事物，引起动荡的事物：something resembling a hurricane especially in its turmoil

arcane [ɑːrˈkeɪn] *adj.* 深奥的，难以理解的：difficult for one of ordinary knowledge or intelligence to understand

mundane [mʌnˈdeɪn] *adj.* 平凡的：relating to, characteristic of, or concerned with commonplaces

profane [prəˈfeɪn] *vt.* 亵渎：to treat (something sacred) with abuse, irreverence, or contempt

germane [dʒɜːrˈmeɪn] *adj.* 有关的，适当的：being at once relevant and appropriate

inane [ɪˈneɪn] *adj.* 空洞的：lacking significance, meaning, or point

wane [weɪn] *vi.* 减少，衰退，降低：to decrease in size, extent, or degree

serene [səˈriːn] *adj.* 安静的：free from disturbing noise or uproar

contravene	[ˌkɑːntrəˈviːn] *vt.* 违反，反对：to <u>violate</u>, to <u>oppose</u> in argument: contradict
convene	[kənˈviːn] *vt.* 召开，召集：to <u>bring together in assembly</u> by or as if by command
refine	[rɪˈfaɪn] *vt.* 改善，改进：to <u>improve or perfect</u> by pruning or polishing
confine	[kənˈfaɪn] *vt.* 限制：to keep within <u>limits</u>
saturnine	[ˈsætərnaɪn] *adj.* 忧郁的，阴沉的：causing or marked by an atmosphere <u>lacking in cheer</u>
pine	[paɪn] *vi.* 渴望，奢望：to <u>yearn</u> intensely and persistently especially for something unattainable

repine [rɪ'paɪn] *vi.* 抱怨，表达不满：to feel or express discontent or dejection
vi. 渴望：to long for something

opine [oʊ'paɪn] *v.* 表达观点；想，认为：to express opinions; to state as an opinion

supine ['suːpaɪn] *adj.* 懒散的，倦怠的，消极的，漠不关心的：showing lethargy, passivity, or blameworthy indifference

saccharine ['sækərɪn] *adj.* 像糖一样的，有甜味的：of, relating to, or resembling that of sugar
adj. 做作的，矫情的：appealing to the emotions in an obvious and tiresome way

elephantine [ˌelɪ'fæntiːn] *adj.* 巨大的：having enormous size or strength
adj. 笨拙的：clumsy, ponderous

quarantine ['kwɔːrəntiːn] *n.* 隔离：enforced isolation or restriction of free movement imposed to prevent the spread of contagious disease

byzantine ['bɪzəntiːn] *adj.* 错综复杂的：complicated or secretive, having many parts or aspects that are usually interrelated

serpentine ['sɜːrpəntiːn] *adj.* 弯曲的：winding or turning one way and another

libertine ['lɪbərtiːn] *n.* 放荡不羁者：one who acts without moral restraint; a dissolute person

57

predestine	[ˌpriːˈdestɪn] *vt.* 预先注定：to determine the fate of in advance
clandestine	[klænˈdestɪn] *adj.* 隐藏的，秘密的：kept or done in secret, often in order to conceal an illicit or improper purpose
philistine	[ˈfɪlɪstiːn] *n.* 市侩(注重物质而鄙视智慧或艺术的人)：a person who is guided by materialism and is usually disdainful of intellectual or artistic values
pristine	[ˈprɪstiːn] *adj.* 纯净的，质朴的，未被文明腐蚀的：remaining in a pure state; uncorrupted by civilization; remaining free from dirt or decay; clean
sanguine	[ˈsæŋgwɪn] *adj.* 乐观的，确信的：having or showing a mind free from doubt
condone	[kənˈdoʊn] *vt.* 宽恕；忽视：to overlook, forgive, or disregard（an offense）without protest or censure
hone	[hoʊn] *vt.* 磨快：to sharpen or smooth with a whetstone
drone	[droʊn] *v.* 低沉单调地说；嗡嗡地叫：to talk in a persistently dull or monotonous tone
chaperone	[ˈʃæpəroʊn] *vt.* 同行，护送：to go along with in order to provide assistance, protection, or companionship
atone	[əˈtoʊn] *v.* 赎罪，弥补：to make amends, as for a sin or fault
jejune	[dʒɪˈdʒuːn] *adj.* 无趣乏味的：not interesting; dull
immune	[ɪˈmjuːn] *adj.* 不易被感染的，有免疫力的：of, relating to, or having resistance to infection *adj.* 不受影响的：not affected by a given influence

58

prune	[pruːn] *vt.* 修剪；修整：to cut off or remove dead or liv-ing parts or branches of (a plant, for example) to improve shape or growth
importune	[ˌɪmpɔːrˈtuːn] *vt.* 恳求，迫切请求：to make a request to (someone) in an earnest or <u>urgent</u> <u>manner</u>
opportune	[ˌɑːpərˈtuːn] *adj.* 合适的，适当的：suitable or <u>convenient</u> for a particular occurrence
attune	[əˈtuːn] *vt.* 使协调，使和谐：to bring <u>into harmony</u>
anodyne	[ˈænədaɪn] *adj.* 无害的：<u>not causing</u> or being capable of causing injury or <u>hurt</u>
agape	[əˈgeɪp] *adj.* 急切盼望的：having or showing signs of <u>eagerly awaiting</u> something
shipshape	[ˈʃɪpʃeɪp] *adj.* 井然有序的：marked by meticulous <u>order</u> and neatness
jape	[dʒeɪp] *v.* 嘲弄：to say or do something jokingly or <u>mockingly</u>
gripe	[graɪp] *vi.* 抱怨：to express <u>dissatisfaction</u>, pain, or resentment usually tiresomely
trope	[troʊp] *n.* 比喻：a word or expression used in a <u>figurative</u> sense *n.* 陈词滥调：an idea or expression that has been <u>used by many people</u>
dupe	[duːp] *n.* 易受骗的人：one that is <u>easily</u> <u>deceived</u> or cheated *vt.* 欺骗：to <u>deceive</u> (an unwary person)
archetype	[ˈɑːkitaɪp] *n.* 典范，榜样：an <u>ideal</u> example of a type
stereotype	[ˈsteriətaɪp] *n.* 成见，老套的理念：a <u>conventional</u>, <u>formulaic</u>, <u>and oversimplified</u> conception, opin-ion, or image
prototype	[ˈproʊtətaɪp] *n.* 原型：an <u>original model</u> on which something is patterned

threadbare	[ˈθredber] *adj.* 陈腐的：overused to the point of being worn out; hackneyed
snare	[sner] *n.* 无法逃脱的困境：something that catches and holds *vt.* 捕捉：to capture by or as if by use of a snare
macabre	[məˈkɑːbrə] *adj.* 恐怖的：suggesting the horror of death and decay; gruesome
mediocre	[ˌmiːdiˈoʊkər] *adj.* 平庸的；质量中等偏下的：moderate to inferior in quality; ordinary
adhere	[ədˈhɪr] *v.* 服从，遵守：to act according to the commands of
sere	[sɪə] *adj.* 干枯的，凋萎的：being dried and withered
austere	[ɔːˈstɪr] *adj.* 朴素的，朴实无华的：markedly simple or unadorned
revere	[rɪˈvɪr] *vt.* (尤指对神)尊崇，尊敬：to offer honor or respect to (someone) as a divine power
persevere	[ˌpɜːrsəˈvɪr] *vi.* 坚持不懈，不屈不挠：to persist in or remain constant to a purpose, idea, or task in the face of obstacles or discouragement
doctrinaire	[ˌdɑːktrəˈner] *adj.* 教条主义的，照本宣科的：given to or marked by the forceful expression of strongly held opinions
dire	[ˈdaɪər] *adj.* 可怕的，恐怖的：causing fear *adj.* 迫切的：needing immediate attention; urgent
backfire	[ˌbækˈfaɪər] *vi.* 产生相反的结果，事与愿违：to have the reverse of the desired or expected effect
mire	[ˈmaɪər] *n.* 困境：a difficult, puzzling, or embarrassing situation from which there is no easy escape

vt. 使陷入困境，拖后腿：to hamper or <u>hold back</u> as if by mire

repertoire [ˈrepərtwɑːr] *n.* (技术、设备或原料等的)详单：the <u>complete list</u> or supply of skills, devices, or ingredients used in a particular field, occupation, or practice

conspire [kənˈspaɪər] *v.* 合谋，密谋：to <u>plan</u> together <u>secretly</u> to commit an illegal or wrongful act or accomplish a legal purpose through illegal action

expire [ɪkˈspaɪər] *v.* 断气，死亡：to breathe one's last breath; <u>die</u>

acquire [əˈkwaɪər] *vt.* 获取，获得：to <u>get as one's own</u>

bore [bɔːr] *n.* 令人厌烦的人或事物：one that <u>causes boredom</u>

underscore [ˌʌndərˈskɔːr] *vt.* 强调：<u>to emphasize</u>; stress

adore [əˈdɔːr] *vt.* 喜爱，因…感到愉悦：to take <u>pleasure</u> in

vt. 宠爱：to feel passion, devotion, or <u>tenderness</u> for

deplore [dɪˈplɔːr] *vt.* 哀悼：to feel or express <u>sorrow</u> for

pore [pɔːr] *vi.* 仔细浏览，仔细研究：to <u>read or study attentively</u> (usually used with over)

sinecure [ˈsaɪnɪkjʊr] *n.* 美差：an office or position that <u>requires little or no work</u> and that usually provides an income

epicure [ˈepɪkjʊr] *n.* 美食家：one with sensitive and <u>discriminating tastes</u> especially in food or wine

procure [prəˈkjʊr] *vt.* 获得，取得：to <u>get possession</u> of

obscure [əbˈskjʊr] *adj.* 含义模糊的：<u>not clearly</u> understood or expressed; having an often intentionally <u>veiled</u> or <u>certain meaning</u>

adj. 平凡的，不知名的：not prominent or famous

vt. 使模糊：to make dark, dim, or indistinct

transfigure [træns'fɪɡjər] *vt.* 使改变外观：to alter the outward appearance of; transform

abjure [əb'dʒʊr] *v.* 发誓放弃：a firm and final rejecting or abandoning often made under oath

v. 抵制，避免：to resist the temptation of

conjure ['kʌndʒər] *vt.* 请求，恳求：to charge or entreat earnestly or solemnly

vt. 在脑海中浮现，想起：to form a mental picture of

allure [ə'lʊr] *vt.* 吸引：to attract or delight as if by magic

immure [ɪ'mjʊr] *vt.* 监禁，禁闭；使闭门不出：to confine within or as if within walls

inure [ɪ'njʊr] *vt.* 使习惯接受不好的东西：to accustom to accept something undesirable

censure ['senʃər] *v.* 公开表示反对，谴责：to express public or formal disapproval of

reassure [ˌriːə'ʃʊr] *vt.* 使安心，打消疑虑：to restore to confidence

caricature ['kærɪkətʃər] *n.* 用讽刺歪曲等手法的夸张，漫画，讽刺画：exaggeration by means of often ludicrous distortion of parts or characteristics

v. 嘲笑性模仿或夸张：to copy or exaggerate (someone or something) in order to make fun of

immature [ˌɪmə'tʃʊr] *adj.* (生理、心理)未完全发展的，未发育成熟的：lacking complete growth, differentiation, or development

stature ['stætʃər] *n.* 高度，身高：natural height (as of a person) in an upright position *n.* 才干，水平：<u>quality</u> or <u>status</u> gained by growth, development, or achievement

fracture [ˈfræktʃər] *n.* 破裂：the act or process of <u>breaking</u>
vt. 打碎，破坏：to cause to <u>separate into pieces</u> usually suddenly or forcibly

conjecture [kənˈdʒektʃər] *n.* 揣测的结果：a <u>conclusion</u> deduced <u>by surmise</u> or guesswork
v. （没有依据地）认为：to <u>form an opinion</u> from little or no evidence

stricture [ˈstrɪktʃər] *n.* 责难，批评：an adverse <u>criticism</u>

divestiture [daɪˈvestɪtʃər] *n.* 剥夺：the act of <u>taking away</u> from a person

rupture [ˈrʌptʃər] *v.* 打破；打碎，破裂：to <u>part</u> by violence

overture [ˈouvərtʃər] *n.* 前言：an <u>introductory</u> section or part, as of a poem; a <u>prelude</u>
n. 序曲：an instrumental composition intended especially as an <u>introduction</u> to an extended work, such as an <u>opera</u> or oratorio

nurture [ˈnɜːrtʃər] *vt.* 培育，培养：to <u>provide</u> (someone) <u>with</u> moral or spiritual <u>understanding</u>

posture [ˈpɑːstʃər] *vi.* 故作姿态，装模作样：to assume an artificial or <u>pretended attitude</u>

suture [ˈsuːtʃər] *n./v.* 缝合：the process of <u>joining</u> two surfaces or edges together along a line by or as if by sewing

abase [əˈbeɪs] *v.* 降低（地位、职位、威望或尊严）：to <u>lower</u> in rank, office, prestige, or esteem

debase [dɪˈbeɪs] *v.* 贬低，贬损：to reduce to a <u>lower standing</u> in one's own eyes or in others' eyes

showcase [ˈʃoukeɪs] *vt.* 展示（优点）：to <u>exhibit</u> especially <u>in an attractive</u> or favorable <u>aspect</u>

chase	[tʃeɪs] *v.* 驱赶：to drive or force out
blasé	[blɑːˈzeɪ] *adj.* （过度放纵之后）厌倦享乐的，腻烦的：apathetic to pleasure or excitement as a result of excessive indulgence or enjoyment
paraphrase	[ˈpærəfreɪz] *v.* 转述，意译，改写：to express something （as a text or statement）in different words
malaise	[məˈleɪz] *n.* 不舒服：a vague feeling of bodily discomfort, as at the beginning of an illness
imprecise	[ˌɪmprɪˈsaɪs] *adj.* 不精确的：not precise
exorcise	[ˈeksɔːrsaɪz] *vt.* 除去：to get rid of （something troublesome, menacing, or oppressive）
paradise	[ˈpærədaɪs] *n.* 快乐，狂喜：a state of overwhelming usually pleasurable emotion
enfranchise	[ɪnˈfræntʃaɪz] *vt.* 给予…权利（例如选举权）：to endow with the rights of citizenship, especially the right to vote *vt.* 解放：to set free（as from slavery）
compromise	[ˈkɑːmprəmaɪz] *v.* 妥协：to adjust or settle by mutual concessions *vt.* 使危险：to place in danger
surmise	[ˈsɜːrmaɪz] *n.* （根据不足的）推测，揣测：a thought or idea based on scanty evidence
despise	[dɪˈspaɪz] *vt.* 极其不喜欢：to dislike strongly
apprise	[əˈpraɪz] *v.* 通知，告知：to give notice to; inform
improvise	[ˈɪmprəvaɪz] *v.* 即兴而作：to invent, compose, or perform with little or no preparation
repulse	[rɪˈpʌls] *vt.* 使厌恶，排斥：to rebuff or reject with rudeness, coldness, or denial
incense	[ɪnˈsens] *vt.* 激怒：to cause to be extremely angry

64

pretense	[ˈpriːtens] *n.* 虚假，伪装：the act of <u>pretending</u>; a false appearance or action intended to <u>deceive</u>
	n. 自大，优越感：an <u>exaggerated sense of one's importance</u> that shows itself in the making of excessive or unjustified claims
verbose	[vɜːrˈboʊs] *adj.* 冗长的，啰嗦的：containing <u>more</u> words <u>than necessary</u>
metamorphose	[ˌmetəˈmɔːrfoʊz] *vt.* (使)变形：to <u>change</u> into a different physical form especially by supernatural means
grandiose	[ˈɡrændioʊs] *adj.* 自命不凡的，浮夸的：characterized by feigned or affected <u>grandeur</u>
lachrymose	[ˈlækrɪmoʊs] *adj.* 催人泪下的，悲伤的：tending to cause tears, <u>mournful</u>
footloose	[ˈfʊtluːs] *adj.* 无拘无束的，自由的：<u>having no attachments</u> or ties; free to do as one pleases
depose	[dɪˈpoʊz] *vi.* 宣誓作证：to <u>testify</u> to under oath or by affidavit
	vt. 废黜，罢免：to <u>remove from a throne</u> or other high position
repose	[rɪˈpoʊz] *n.* (劳作后的)休息：a <u>state of resting</u> after exertion or strain
	vi. 休息：to <u>take a rest</u>
	n. 平静，宁静：a state of <u>freedom from storm</u> or disturbance

compose [kəm'pouz] *vt.* 使镇定：to free from agitation: <u>calm</u>

v. 组成，构成：to <u>form</u> the substance of: <u>constitute</u>

discompose [ˌdɪskəm'pouz] *vt.* 使不安：to <u>disturb</u> the <u>composure</u> or calm of; <u>perturb</u>

vt. 使混乱：to <u>undo</u> the proper <u>order</u> or <u>arrangement</u> of

dispose [dɪ'spouz] *vt.* 使倾向于：to give a <u>tendency</u> to: <u>incline</u>

vi. 处理掉(与 of 连用，dispose of)：to <u>get rid of</u>; <u>throw out</u>

morose [mə'rous] *adj.* 忧郁的：having a <u>sullen</u> and <u>gloomy</u> disposition

lapse [læps] *n.* 小过失：a <u>slight error</u> typically due to forgetfulness or inattention

relapse [rɪ'læps] *vi.* 重蹈覆辙，再犯：to slip or <u>fall back</u> into a former worse state

collapse [kə'læps] *v./n.* 失败：to be <u>unsuccessful</u>; a falling short of one's goals

eclipse [ɪ'klɪps] *vt.* 使声望下降，使黯然失色：to obscure or <u>diminish</u> in <u>importance</u>, fame, or reputation

coarse [kɔːrs] *adj.* 粗糙的，表面不平整的：<u>not</u> having a level or <u>smooth</u> surface

adj. 粗俗的：lacking in delicacy or <u>refinement</u>

sparse [spɑːrs] *adj.* 稀疏的，稀少的：<u>less plentiful</u> than what is normal, necessary, or desirable

terse [tɜːrs] *adj.* 简洁的，简明的：<u>brief</u> and to the point; effectively concise

verse [vɜːrs] *vt.* 使精通，使熟悉：to <u>familiarize</u> by close association, study, or experience

n. 诗歌：a composition using <u>rhythm</u> and often rhyme to create a <u>lyrical effect</u>

66

averse	[əˈvɜːrs] *adj.* 反对的：having a natural <u>dislike</u> for something
traverse	[trəˈvɜːrs] *vt.* 横穿：to travel or <u>pass across</u>, over, or through
endorse	[ɪnˈdɔːrs] *vt.* 公开支持，推崇：to <u>express</u> support or <u>approval</u> of publicly and definitely
remorse	[rɪˈmɔːrs] *n.* 懊悔，悔恨：moral anguish arising from repentance for past misdeeds; <u>bitter regret</u>
largesse	[lɑːrˈdʒes] *n.* 慷慨：<u>liberality</u> in giving or willingness to give
finesse	[fɪˈnes] *n.* 娴熟技巧：mental <u>skill</u> or quickness *v.* (巧妙地)躲避：to get or <u>keep away from</u> (as a responsibility) through cleverness or trickery
applause	[əˈplɔːz] *n.* 鼓掌；认可：<u>approval</u> publicly expressed (as by clapping the hands)
abuse	[əˈbjuːz] *v.* 辱骂，抨击：to <u>condemn or vilify</u> usually unjustly, intemperately, and angrily *v.* 不正当或不合理使用：to put to a <u>wrong or improper use</u>; 过分过量使用：to <u>use excessively</u>
disabuse	[ˌdɪsəˈbjuːz] *vt.* 打消错误念头，纠正：to <u>free from error</u>, <u>fallacy</u>, or <u>misconception</u>
defuse	[ˌdiːˈfjuːz] *vt.* 抚慰，减轻：to <u>make less</u> dangerous, <u>tense</u>, or hostile
diffuse	[dɪˈfjuːs] *adj.* 啰嗦的：being at once <u>verbose</u> and ill-organized [dɪˈfjuːz] *v.* 扩展，散开：to <u>extend</u>, <u>scatter</u>
suffuse	[səˈfjuːz] *vt.* (色彩等)弥漫，染遍，充满：to <u>spread through</u> or over, as with liquid, color, or light
infuse	[ɪnˈfjuːz] *vt.* 灌输，使…充满：to <u>fill</u> or cause to be filled with something
recluse	[ˈrekluːs] *n.* 隐士：a person who <u>lives away</u> from others

67

adj. 隐居的，不爱社交的：marked by <u>withdrawal</u> from society

douse [daʊs] *vt.* 熄灭：to <u>put out</u> (a light or fire)

espouse [ɪˈspaʊz] *vt.* 支持；拥护：to take up and <u>support</u> as a cause

rouse [raʊz] *vt.* 激起，煽动：to <u>stir up</u>
vt. 唤醒：to cause to <u>stop sleeping</u>

carouse [kəˈraʊz] *vi.* 畅饮，狂饮作乐：to <u>drink</u> liquor <u>freely</u> or excessively

ruse [ruːz] *n.* 诡计：a wily <u>subterfuge</u>

peruse [pəˈruːz] *vt.* 细读：to read or <u>examine</u>, typically with <u>great care</u>

abstruse [əbˈstruːs] *adj.* 难以理解的：difficult to comprehend: <u>recondite</u>

obtuse [əbˈtuːs] *adj.* 愚钝的：not having or showing an ability to <u>absorb ideas readily</u>

abate [əˈbeɪt] *v.* 减轻（程度或者强度）：to <u>reduce</u> in <u>degree</u> or <u>intensity</u>
v. 减少(数量)，降低(价值)：to <u>reduce</u> in <u>amount</u> or value

reprobate [ˈreprəbeɪt] *n.* 堕落者，道德败坏的人：a morally <u>unprincipled person</u>
adj. 堕落的，放荡的：<u>morally corrupt</u>

exacerbate [ɪɡˈzæsərbeɪt] *vt.* 使加剧，使恶化：to make more violent, bitter, or <u>severe</u>

incubate [ˈɪŋkjubeɪt] *vt.* 孵化：to <u>cover and warm eggs</u> as the young inside develop
vt. 帮助，培养，促进：to cause or <u>aid</u> the development of

placate [ˈpleɪkeɪt] *vt.* (通过让步以)平息抚慰：to <u>lessen the anger</u> or agitation of

desiccate [ˈdesɪkeɪt] *vt.* 使缺乏活力：to <u>deprive</u> of emotional or intellectual <u>vitality</u>

deprecate	['deprəkeɪt] *vt.* 不喜欢：to hold an <u>unfavorable</u> <u>opinion</u> of *vt.* 贬低，轻视：to <u>express scornfully</u> one's low opinion of
abdicate	['æbdɪkeɪt] *v.* 正式放弃(权力、责任，不干了)：to renounce a <u>throne</u>, to relinquish (power or responsibility) formally
vindicate	['vɪndɪkeɪt] *vt.* 为…平反，为…辩护，使无罪：to <u>free from</u> allegation or <u>blame</u> *vt.* 证明，证实：to <u>give evidence</u> or testimony to the truth or factualness of
adjudicate	[ə'dʒuːdɪkeɪt] *v.* 裁决，判定：to hear and <u>settle</u> (a case, dispute or conflict)
pontificate	[pɑːn'tɪfɪkeɪt] *vi.* 傲慢地做或说：to <u>speak</u> or express opinions in a <u>pompous</u> or dogmatic way
replicate	['replɪkeɪt] *vt.* 复制，复刻：to <u>make an exact</u> <u>likeness</u> of
complicate	['kɑːmplɪkeɪt] *vt.* 使复杂化：to make <u>complex</u> or <u>difficult</u>
supplicate	['sʌplɪkeɪt] *v.* 恳求，乞求：to <u>make a request</u> to (someone) in an <u>earnest or urgent</u> manner
duplicate	['duːplɪkət] *n.* 复制品：either of two things <u>exactly alike</u> and usually produced at the same time or by the same process ['duːplɪkeɪt] *vt.* 复制：to <u>make a copy</u> of
explicate	['eksplɪkeɪt] *vt.* 解释，说明：to give a <u>detailed</u> <u>explanation</u> of
prevaricate	[prɪ'værɪkeɪt] *vi.* 支吾其词，撒谎：to stray from or <u>evade the truth</u>
fabricate	['fæbrɪkeɪt] *vt.* 捏造：to <u>make up</u> for the purpose of deception

lubricate	[ˈluːbrɪkeɪt] vt. 使润滑：to coat (something) with a slippery substance in order to reduce friction
extricate	[ˈekstrɪkeɪt] vt. 使解脱，救出：to free or remove from an entanglement or difficulty
truncate	[ˈtrʌŋkeɪt] vt. 截短；缩短（时间、篇幅等）：to shorten by or as if by cutting off
suffocate	[ˈsʌfəkeɪt] vt. 使窒息：to deprive of oxygen
reciprocate	[rɪˈsɪprəkeɪt] vt. 报答，回报：to return in kind or degree
advocate	[ˈædvəkeɪt] vt. 支持，提倡：to speak, plead, or argue in favor of; support
equivocate	[ɪˈkwɪvəkeɪt] vi. (带有欺骗目的地)模棱两可地说，说谎话：to use equivocal language especially with intent to deceive
bifurcate	[ˈbaɪfərkeɪt] v. (使)分成两支：(to cause) to divide into two branches or parts
obfuscate	[ˈɑːbfʌskeɪt] vt. 使困惑，使模糊：to make so confused or opaque as to be difficult to perceive or understand
sedate	[sɪˈdeɪt] adj. 淡定的，安静的：free from emotional or mental agitation
antedate	[ˌænti ˈdeɪt] vt. 比⋯⋯早，早于：to be of an earlier date than
elucidate	[iˈluːsɪdeɪt] v. 阐明：to make lucid especially by explanation or analysis
consolidate	[kənˈsɑːlɪdeɪt] vt. 加固，使安全：to make firm or secure; strengthen
intimidate	[ɪnˈtɪmɪdeɪt] vt. 威吓：to make timid or fearful, frighten
dilapidate	[dɪˈlæpɪdeɪt] v. (使)荒废：to bring into a condition of decay or partial ruin
inundate	[ˈɪnʌndeɪt] vt. 淹没：to cover with or as if with flood

accommodate [əˈkɑːmədeɪt] *v.* 改变以适应新情况、新场景: to change（something）so as to make it suitable for a new use or situation

vt. 使和谐: to bring to a state free of conflicts, inconsistencies, or differences

permeate [ˈpɜːrmieɪt] *v.* 弥漫, 渗透: to spread throughout

delineate [dɪˈlɪnieɪt] *vt.* 描写, 描绘: to describe, portray, or set forth with accuracy or in detail

nauseate [ˈnɔːzieɪt] *v.*（使）厌恶,（使）作呕: to feel or cause to feel loathing or disgust

propagate [ˈprɑːpəgeɪt] *vt.* 传播, 宣传: to cause to spread out and affect a greater number or greater area; extend

delegate [ˈdelɪgət] *n.* 代理人, 代表: a person authorized to act as representative for another

vt. 移交（权力、任务等）: to put（something）into the possession or safekeeping of another

abnegate [ˈæbnɪgeɪt] *v.* 否认: to deny, renounce

aggregate [ˈægrɪgət] *n.* 集合体: a mass or body of units or parts somewhat loosely associated with one another

[ˈægrɪgeɪt] *v.* 集合, 聚集: to collect or gather into a mass or whole

profligate [ˈprɑːflɪgət] *adj./n.* 挥金如土的, 挥霍的: recklessly wasteful; wildly extravagant

n. 败家子: someone who spends money freely or foolishly

irrigate [ˈɪrɪgeɪt] *vt.* 灌溉: to supply（dry land）with water by means of ditches, pipes, or streams; water artificially

vt. 冲洗: to flush（a body part）with a stream of liquid（as in removing a foreign body or medicating）

mitigate	［ˈmɪtɪɡeɪt］ *vt.* 减轻痛苦，使缓和：to make less severe or painful
castigate	［ˈkæstɪɡeɪt］ *vt.* 强烈（公开）指责：to criticize harshly and usually publicly
instigate	［ˈɪnstɪɡeɪt］ *vt.* 煽动，激起：to goad or urge forward; to stir up
promulgate	［ˈprɑːmlɡeɪt］ *vt.* 正式宣布：to make known openly or publicly
abrogate	［ˈæbrəɡeɪt］ *v.* 官方的正式废除：to abolish by authoritative action, annul *v.* 无视(某事的)存在：to treat as nonexistent
interrogate	［ɪnˈterəɡeɪt］ *vt.* 质问，审问：to question formally and systematically
surrogate	［ˈsɜːrəɡət］ *n.* 替代品：one that takes the place of another
expurgate	［ˈekspərɡeɪt］ *vt.* 净化(书等)，删去(不当处)：to remove erroneous, vulgar, obscene, or otherwise objectionable material from (a book, for example) before publication
subjugate	［ˈsʌbdʒuɡeɪt］ *vt.* 征服，镇压：to bring under control and governance as a subject
emaciate	［ɪˈmeɪʃieɪt］ *vt.* 削弱：to make feeble
depreciate	［dɪˈpriːʃieɪt］ *vt.* 贬低…的价值：to lower the price or estimated value of
enunciate	［ɪˈnʌnsieɪt］ *v.* 清晰地说：to utter articulate sounds *vt.* 公开宣布，宣称：to make known openly or publicly
excruciate	［ɪkˈskruːʃieɪt］ *vt.* 折磨，使痛苦：to inflict severe pain on; torture
mediate	［ˈmiːdieɪt］ *vt.* 调解，调停：to intervene between two or more disputants in order to bring about an agreement, a settlement, or a compromise

72

repudiate	[rɪˈpjuːdieɪt] *vt.* 否认：to <u>declare not to be true</u>
retaliate	[rɪˈtælieɪt] *v.* 报复，反击：to <u>pay back</u> (as an injury) in kind
conciliate	[kənˈsɪlieɪt] *v.* 平息，抚慰：to <u>lessen the anger</u> or agitation of
humiliate	[hjuːˈmɪlieɪt] *vt.* 羞辱，使丧失尊严：to reduce <u>to a lower position</u> in one's own eyes or others' eyes
palliate	[ˈpælieɪt] *vt.* 平息，减轻：to make <u>less severe</u> or <u>intense</u>; mitigate
calumniate	[kəˈlʌmnieɪt] *v.* 诽谤，造谣，中伤：to utter maliciously <u>false statements</u>, charges, or imputations about
expiate	[ˈekspieɪt] *vt.* 赎罪，纠正：to <u>extinguish the guilt</u> incurred by
excoriate	[ˌeksˈkɔːrieɪt] *vt.* 严厉批评：to <u>criticize harshly</u> and usually <u>publicly</u>
appropriate	[əˈprəʊprieɪt] *v.* 私自挪用：to <u>take possession</u> of or make use of exclusively for oneself, often <u>without permission</u> [əˈprəʊpriət] *adj.* 适当的：especially <u>suitable</u> or compatible: <u>fitting</u>
repatriate	[ˌriːˈpeɪtrieɪt] *vt.* 遣返：to restore or <u>return to the country</u> of origin, allegiance, or citizenship
striate	[ˈstraɪeɪt] *vt.* 加条纹：to <u>mark with striations</u> or striae

73

infuriate	[ɪnˈfjʊrieɪt] *vt.* 激怒: to <u>make furious</u>
satiate	[ˈseɪʃieɪt] *vt./adj.* (使)饱足(的), 过分满足(的): to <u>satisfy fully</u> or to excess
initiate	[ɪˈnɪʃieɪt] *vt.* 创始, 发动促进: to <u>cause</u> or fa-cili-tate the <u>beginning</u> of
propitiate	[prəˈpɪʃieɪt] *vt.* 抚慰, 劝解: to conciliate (an offended power); <u>appease</u>
vitiate	[ˈvɪʃieɪt] *v.* 削弱, 损害: to <u>reduce the value</u> or impair the quality of
substantiate	[səbˈstænʃieɪt] *vt.* 证实: to <u>support with proof</u> or evidence
potentiate	[poʊˈtenʃieɪt] *vt.* 激活, 加强: to make effective or active, or more effective or <u>more active</u>
negotiate	[nɪˈgoʊʃieɪt] *v.* 商量, 谈判: to arrange or settle by discussion and <u>mutual agreement</u>
obviate	[ˈɑːbvieɪt] *vt.* 排除, 使不必要: to anticipate and prevent (as a situation) or make <u>unnecessary</u> (as an action)
alleviate	[əˈliːvieɪt] *v.* 缓和, 减轻: <u>relieve</u>, <u>lessen</u>
abbreviate	[əˈbriːvieɪt] *v.* 缩写, 缩短: to make <u>briefer</u>
escalate	[ˈeskəleɪt] *v.* (使)(战争等)升级, 扩大: to increase in extent, volume, number, amount, intensity, or scope
elate	[iˈleɪt] *vt.* 使开心, 使自豪: to <u>fill with joy</u> or pride
correlate	[ˈkɔːrəleɪt] *vt.* 使…相关联: to establish a <u>mutual or reciprocal relation</u> between
conflate	[kənˈfleɪt] *vt.* 混合: to <u>turn into a single mass</u> or entity that is more or less the same throughout
dilate	[daɪˈleɪt] *v.* (使)膨胀, 扩大: to <u>enlarge</u> or <u>expand</u> in bulk or extent; to become <u>wide</u>

74

vacillate [ˈvæsəleɪt] vi. 犹豫不决：to waver in mind, will, or feeling; hesitate in choice of opinions or courses
vi. 摇动，摇摆：to sway from one side to the other; oscillate

oscillate [ˈɑːsɪleɪt] vt. 犹豫，变化：vary between opposing beliefs, feelings, or theories

scintillate [ˈsɪntɪleɪt] vi. 闪耀：to emit sparks

extrapolate [ɪkˈstræpəleɪt] vt. (通过逻辑)推断：to form an opinion or reach a conclusion through reasoning and information

contemplate [ˈkɑːntəmpleɪt] v. 沉思，仔细思索：to view or consider with continued attention

slate [sleɪt] vt. 列入名单，计划，安排：to put (someone or something) on a list

perambulate [pəˈræmbjuleɪt] v. 徒步穿越，走过：to travel over or through especially on foot for exercise or pleasure

discombobulate [ˌdɪskəmˈbɑːbjuleɪt] vt. 使不安，使混乱：upset, confuse

maculate [ˈmækjəleɪt] vt. 使有斑点，弄脏；玷污，损坏：to spot; blemish

immaculate [ɪˈmækjələt] adj. 完美的，没有任何错误的：being entirely without fault or flaw

speculate [ˈspekjuleɪt] v. 推测，揣测：to take to be true on the basis of insufficient evidence

matriculate [məˈtrɪkjuleɪt] v. 录取：to admit or be admitted into a group, especially a college or university

articulate [ɑːrˈtɪkjuleɪt] v. 清晰地表达：to utter clearly and distinctly
[ɑːrˈtɪkjələt] adj. 表达清晰的：able to express oneself clearly and well

adulate	[ˈædʒəleɪt] v. 极度谄媚，拍马屁：to praise too much
coagulate	[koʊˈægjuleɪt] v. (使)凝结，(使)变稠：to (cause to) become viscous or thickened into a coherent mass: curdle, clot
emulate	[ˈemjuleɪt] vt. 效仿并努力超越：to strive to equal or excel, especially through imitation
simulate	[ˈsɪmjuleɪt] vt. 假装，模仿：to have or take on the appearance, form, or sound of: imitate
accumulate	[əˈkjuːmjəleɪt] vi. 逐渐增长：to increase gradually in quantity or number
manipulate	[məˈnɪpjuleɪt] vt. 巧妙处理；暗中操控：to influence or manage shrewdly or deviously
stipulate	[ˈstɪpjuleɪt] v. 规定，特定要求：to specify or arrange in an agreement
insulate	[ˈɪnsəleɪt] vt. 使绝缘，使隔离，不受外界影响：to place in a detached situation
capitulate	[kəˈpɪtʃuleɪt] v. 投降，默许：to give up all resistance; acquiesce; yield
recapitulate	[ˌriːkəˈpɪtʃuleɪt] v./n. 概括，摘要：to make into a short statement of the main points
postulate	[ˈpɑːstʃəleɪt] n. 假定，假设：something taken as being true or factual and used as a starting point for a course of action or reasoning vt. 假定为真：to assume or claim as true, existent, or necessary
expostulate	[ɪkˈspɑːstʃuleɪt] vi. 争论，辩驳：to reason earnestly with a person for purposes of dissuasion or remonstrance
amalgamate	[əˈmælgəmeɪt] v. 合并，混合：to combine into a unified or integrated whole; unite
acclimate	[ˈækləmeɪt] vt. 使适应：to change (something) so as to make it suitable for a new use or situation

animate	[ˈænɪmət] *adj.* 有活力的：having much high-spirited energy and movement [ˈænɪmeɪt] *vt.* 使有活力，支持：to give spirit and support to
inanimate	[ɪnˈænɪmət] *adj.* 无生命的：not having the qualities associated with active, living organisms
intimate	[ˈɪntɪmət] *adj.* 有紧密联系的，亲密无间的：marked by very close association, contact, or familiarity [ˈɪntɪmeɪt] *v.* 间接地沟通：to communicate delicately and indirectly
consummate	[ˈkɑːnsəmət] *adj.* 专业的，有造诣的：extremely skilled and accomplished *adj.* 无纰漏的，完美的：complete in every detail; perfect
alienate	[ˈeɪliəneɪt] *v.* 疏远，离间：to make unfriendly, or indifferent especially where attachment formerly existed
concatenate	[kənˈkætɪneɪt] *v.* 连结，混合：to put or bring together so as to form a new and longer whole
designate	[ˈdezɪgneɪt] *vt.* 任命：to pick（someone）by one's authority for a specific position or duty *vt.* 命名：to give a name to
deracinate	[ˌdiːˈræsɪneɪt] *vt.* 根除：to pull out by the roots; uproot
vaccinate	[ˈvæksɪneɪt] *v.* 预防接种疫苗：to inoculate with a vaccine in order to produce immunity to an infectious disease, such as diphtheria or typhus
fascinate	[ˈfæsɪneɪt] *vt.* 强烈吸引，使入迷：to hold an intense interest or attraction for
subordinate	[səˈbɔːrdɪnət] *adj.* 下级的；次要的：belonging to a lower or inferior class or rank

[səˈbɔːrdɪneɪt] *vt.* 征服：to bring under one's control by force of arms

insubordinate [ˌɪnsəˈbɔːrdɪnət] *adj.* 不服从权威的：not sub-missive to authority

contaminate [kənˈtæmɪneɪt] *vt.* 污染，感染：to soil, stain, corrupt, or infect by contact or association

disseminate [dɪˈsemɪneɪt] *vt.* 散播，传播：to spread abroad; promulgate

incriminate [ɪnˈkrɪmɪneɪt] *vt.* 归罪于：to accuse of a crime or other wrongful act

discriminate [dɪˈskrɪmɪneɪt] *vt.* 区分：to perceive the distin-guishing features of; recognize as distinct
vi. 歧视：to make a difference in treatment or favor on a basis other than individual meri

culminate [ˈkʌlmɪneɪt] *v.* 达到高潮：to bring to a triumphant conclusion

fulminate [ˈfʊlmɪneɪt] *v.* 大声斥责：to issue a thunderous verbal attack or denunciation

abominate [əˈbɑːmɪneɪt] *v.* 痛恨，厌恶：to hate or loathe in-tensely, abhor

germinate [ˈdʒɜːrmɪneɪt] *vi.* 发芽：to begin to grow
vi. 出现：to come into being

exterminate [ɪkˈstɜːrmɪneɪt] *vt.* 根除，消灭：to get rid of completely usually by killing off

illuminate [ɪˈluːmɪneɪt] *vt.* 阐明：to make plain or under-standable

ruminate [ˈruːmɪneɪt] *v.* 反复思考：to go over in the mind repeatedly and often casually or slowly

indoctrinate [ɪnˈdɑːktrɪneɪt] *vt.* 教育，灌输思想：to instruct especially in fundamentals or rudiments

procrastinate [proʊˈkræstɪneɪt] *vi.* （因为懒散）拖延：to put off doing something, especially out of habitual carelessness or laziness

78

obstinate	[ˈɑːbstɪnət] *adj.* 固执的：perversely adhering to an opinion, purpose, or course in spite of reason, arguments, or persuasion
dispassionate	[dɪsˈpæʃənət] *adj.* 客观公正的，不易被情绪或偏见影响的：devoid of or unaffected by passion, emotion, or bias
resonate	[ˈrezəneɪt] *v.* 有重要性：beneficial to the health of body or mind
incarnate	[ɪnˈkɑːrnət] *vt.* 使(思想、理论)具化，体现：to constitute an embodiment or type of
inchoate	[ɪnˈkoʊət] *adj.* 新生的，才开始的：in an initial or early stage
emancipate	[ɪˈmænsɪpeɪt] *vt.* 解放，解除束缚：to free from bondage, oppression, or restraint
dissipate	[ˈdɪsɪpeɪt] *vt.* 驱散：to drive away; disperse *vt.* 浪费：to spend or expend intemperately or wastefully: squander
inculpate	[ɪnˈkʌlpeɪt] *vt.* 归罪于：incriminate
exculpate	[ˈekskʌlpeɪt] *vt.* 声明无罪；开脱，使无罪：to clear from alleged fault or guilt
spate	[speɪt] *n.* 大量：a large number or amount
exhilarate	[ɪgˈzɪləreɪt] *vt.* 使高兴；使兴奋：to make cheerful and excited
disparate	[ˈdɪspərət] *adj.* 迥然不同的：fundamentally distinct or different in kind; entirely dissimilar
calibrate	[ˈkælɪbreɪt] *vt.* 调整，使标准化：to standardize (as a measuring instrument) by determining the deviation from a standard so as to ascertain the proper correction factors
adumbrate	[ˈædəmbreɪt] *vt.* 预示：to give a slight indication of beforehand
desecrate	[ˈdesɪkreɪt] *vt.* 亵渎，玷污：to treat (a sacred place or object) shamefully or with great disrespect

execrate [ˈeksɪkreɪt] *v.* 痛恨：to dislike strongly

dehydrate [diːˈhaɪdreɪt] *vt.* 去除水分，使干燥：to remove water from; make anhydrous

vt. 使失去活力：to deprive of vitality or savor

berate [bɪˈreɪt] *vt.* (长时间)严厉指责：to scold or condemn vehemently and at length

deliberate [dɪˈlɪbərət] *adj.* 深思熟虑的：characterized by or resulting from careful and thorough consideration

reverberate [rɪˈvɜːrbəreɪt] *vi.* 回荡，回响：to continue or be repeated in a series of reflected sound waves

音　频

lacerate	[ˈlæsəreɪt] vt. 使非常痛苦：to cause deep emotional pain to; distress
macerate	[ˈmæsəreɪt] vt. 浸泡（以软化）：to make soft by soaking or steeping in a liquid
moderate	[ˈmɑːdəreɪt] vt. 使缓和：to lessen the intensity or extremeness of [ˈmɑːdərət] adj. 适度的，中庸的：being within reasonable limits; not excessive or extreme
proliferate	[prəˈlɪfəreɪt] vi. 快速繁殖；激增：to grow or multiply by rapidly producing new tissue, parts, cells, or offspring; to increase at a rapid rate
regenerate	[rɪˈdʒenəreɪt] vt. 使重获新生，使焕然一新：to bring back to life, practice, activity or a former condition of vigor
venerate	[ˈvenəreɪt] vt. 尊敬：to regard with reverential respect or with admiring deference
incinerate	[ɪnˈsɪnəreɪt] v. 将…烧成灰烬：to cause to burn to ashes
exonerate	[ɪgˈzɑːnəreɪt] vt. 免除责备：to free from blame
remunerate	[rɪˈmjuːnəreɪt] vt. 支付报酬，补偿：to pay an equivalent to for a service, loss, or expense
temperate	[ˈtempərət] adj. (言行举止)有分寸的：avoiding extremes in behavior or expression adj. 有节制的：given to or marked by restraint in the satisfaction of one's appetites
intemperate	[ɪnˈtempərət] adj. 无节制的，极端的，不温和的：not temperate or moderate

81

exasperate	[ɪg'zæspəreɪt] *vt.* 激怒：to excite the anger of
recuperate	[rɪ'ku:pəreɪt] *v.* 恢复（健康或力量），康复：to recover health or strength
vituperate	[vaɪ'tu:pəreɪt] *vt.* 谩骂，责骂：to abuse or censure severely or abusively
commiserate	[kə'mɪzəreɪt] *vi.* 表示怜悯，同情：to feel or express sympathy
inveterate	[ɪn'vetərət] *adj.* 根深蒂固的：firmly established by long persistence
reiterate	[ri'ɪtəreɪt] *v.* 重申：to say or state again
obliterate	[ə'blɪtəreɪt] *vt.* 除去：to remove from existence
adulterate	[ə'dʌltəreɪt] *vt.* 掺杂，加入低等成分：to corrupt, debase, or make impure by the addition of a foreign or inferior substance or element
grate	[greɪt] *v.* 刮擦（以发出刺耳的声音）：to make a rasping sound *v.* 骚扰，惹恼：to irritate or annoy persistently
emigrate	['emɪgreɪt] *vi.* 移民，移居海外：to leave one's place of residence or country to live elsewhere
denigrate	['denɪgreɪt] *vt.* 诋毁，污蔑：to express scornfully one's low opinion of
irate	[aɪ'reɪt] *adj.* 极其愤怒的：extremely angry
pirate	['paɪrət] *vt.* 盗版，盗用：to take or make use of under a guise of authority but without actual right
elaborate	[ɪ'læbərət] *adj.* 详细的，复杂的：marked by complexity, fullness of detail, or ornament [ɪ'læbəreɪt] *vt.* 详细阐述：to expand something in detail
corroborate	[kə'rɑ:bəreɪt] *vt.* 用证据或权威证实：to support with evidence or authority; make more certain *vt.* 为…提供证据，支持：to provide evidence or information for (as a claim or idea)

perforate [ˈpɜːrfəreɪt] *v.* 打孔，穿透：to make a hole through

invigorate [ɪnˈvɪgəreɪt] *vt.* 使精神，使强壮，鼓舞激励：to impart vigor, strength, or vitality to

ameliorate [əˈmiːliəreɪt] *vt.* 改善，改进：to make or become better; improve

prate [preɪt] *vi.* 闲聊，空谈：to talk long and idly

infiltrate [ˈɪnfɪltreɪt] *vt.* 秘密潜入：to enter or take up positions in gradually or surreptitiously, as for purposes of espionage or takeover

concentrate [ˈkɑːnsntreɪt] *vt.* 浓缩：to make less dilute
v. 聚集：to come together in one body or place

demonstrate [ˈdemənstreɪt] *vt.* （通过证据）证明，表明：to show or make clear by using examples

prostrate [ˈprɑːstreɪt] *adj./vt.* 平躺(的) / 使平躺：lying flat or at full length
adj./v. 衰弱的 / (使)衰竭：to reduce to extreme weakness or incapacitation

obdurate [ˈɑːbdərət] *adj.* 固执的：resistant to persuasion or softening influences
adj. 冷酷无情的：having or showing a lack of sympathy or tender feelings

indurate [ˈɪndjʊreɪt] *adj.* 铁石心肠的，冷酷无情的：having or showing a lack of sympathy or tender feelings
vt. 使变硬：to become physically firm or solid

inaugurate [ɪˈnɔːgjəreɪt] *vt.* 开始：to cause to begin, especially officially or formally

commensurate [kəˈmenʃərət] *adj.* 同样大小的：equal in measure or extent
adj. 相称的，相当的：corresponding in size or degree; proportionate

incommensurate [ˌɪnkəˈmenʃərət] *adj.* 不相称的：too large or too small in relation to something

83

saturate	[ˈsætʃəreɪt] *vt.* 使饱和，浸透：to wet thoroughly with liquid
sate	[seɪt] *vt.* 使饱足，充分满足：to glut; to satisfy (an appetite) fully
dictate	[ˈdɪkteɪt] *vt.* (仗着地位、权力)下令：to request the doing of by virtue of one's authority
resuscitate	[rɪˈsʌsɪteɪt] *vt.* 使复活，使苏醒：to restore consciousness, vigor, or life to
meditate	[ˈmedɪteɪt] *vt.* 思索，沉思：to focus one's thoughts on
premeditate	[ˌpriːˈmedɪteɪt] *vi.* 预先考虑：to, think, consider, or deliberate beforehand
agitate	[ˈædʒɪteɪt] *v.* 煽动，激起：to attempt to arouse public feeling *vt.* 使不安：to excite and often trouble the mind or feelings of: disturb
rehabilitate	[ˌriːəˈbɪlɪteɪt] *vt.* 使复原，使康复：to restore to a former state (as of efficiency, good management, or solvency) or a healthy condition
debilitate	[dɪˈbɪlɪteɪt] *vt.* 使衰弱：to impair the strength of; enfeeble
facilitate	[fəˈsɪlɪteɪt] *vt.* 使变容易，促进：to make easy or easier
precipitate	[prɪˈsɪpɪteɪt] *adj.* 匆忙的：acting or done with excessive or careless speed *vt.* 促使，导致：to cause to happen, especially suddenly or prematurely
irritate	[ˈɪrɪteɪt] *vt.* 刺激，惹恼：to provoke impatience, anger, or displeasure in
potentate	[ˈpoʊtnteɪt] *n.* 有权势的人：one who has the power and position to rule over others
annotate	[ˈænəteɪt] *vt.* 给…作注解：to furnish (a literary

work) with critical <u>commentary or explanatory</u> <u>notes</u>

instate	[ɪn'steɪt] *vt.* 任命：to set or <u>establish</u> in a <u>rank</u> or office
understate	[ˌʌndər'steɪt] *vt.* 保守陈述：to state or present with <u>restraint</u> especially for effect
mutate	['mju:teɪt] *v.* (使)改变，(使)变异：to undergo or cause to <u>undergo mutation</u>
evacuate	[ɪ'vækjueɪt] *vt.* 撤离：to <u>empty or remove</u> the contents of
attenuate	[ə'tenjueɪt] *v.* 降低 (数量、力量、价值)：to <u>lessen</u> the amount, force, magnitude, or value of
extenuate	[ɪk'stenjueɪt] *vt.* 减轻罪过：to lessen or to try to <u>lessen the seriousness</u> or extent of by making partial excuses
infatuate	[ɪn'fætʃueɪt] *vt.* 使迷恋：to <u>inspire</u> with <u>unreasoning love</u> or attachment
accentuate	[ə'ksentʃueɪt] *v.* 强调：to make (something) more <u>noticeable</u>
excavate	['ekskəveɪt] *v.* 挖掘，挖空：to <u>dig out</u> and remove
aggravate	['ægrəveɪt] *vt.* 加重，恶化：to make <u>worse</u>, more <u>serious</u>, or more <u>severe</u>
elevate	['elɪveɪt] *vt.* (在道德、智力、文化水平上)提升：to <u>improve</u> morally, intellectually, or culturally *vt.* 使兴奋：to <u>raise</u> the <u>spirits</u> of
recidivate	[ri:'sɪdəveɪt] *vi.* 回到原先的习惯，尤指重新犯罪：to <u>return</u> to a previous pattern of behavior, especially to <u>return to criminal habits</u>
cultivate	['kʌltɪveɪt] *vt.* 提升，加强：to <u>improve</u> by labor, care, or study *vt.* 种植，培养：to <u>promote</u> the <u>growth</u> of (a biological culture)

motivate ['moʊtɪveɪt] *vt.* 刺激，激发：to provide with an incentive; move to action

captivate ['kæpɪveɪt] *vt.* 吸引：to attract and hold by charm, beauty, or excellence

renovate ['renəveɪt] *vt.* 修复，维修：to restore to a former better state（as by cleaning, repairing, or rebuilding）

enervate ['enərveɪt] *vt.* 使衰弱：to weaken or destroy the strength or vitality of

effete [ɪ'fiːt] *adj.* 衰弱的，衰落的：depleted of vitality, force, or effectiveness

obsolete [ˌɑːbsə'liːt] *adj.* 过时的，被淘汰的：no longer in use or no longer useful

deplete [dɪ'pliːt] *vt.* 耗尽，使衰竭：to decrease the fullness of; to make complete use of

replete [rɪ'pliːt] *adj.* 充满…的，富于…的：possessing or covered with great numbers or amounts of something specified

accrete [æ'kriːt] *v.* 逐渐增长：to grow or increase gradually, as by addition

secrete [sɪ'kriːt] *vt.* 隐藏：to conceal in a hiding place: cache

vt. 分泌：to generate and separate（a substance）from cells or bodily fluids

concrete ['kɑːŋkriːt] *adj.* 事实性的，明确的：existing in fact and not merely as a possibility

discrete [dɪ'skriːt] *adj.* 离散的，不连续的：constituting a separate entity

excrete [ɪk'skriːt] *vt.* 排泄：to separate and discharge（waste matter）from the blood, tissues, or organs

incite [ɪn'saɪt] *vt.* 煽动，激起：to provoke and urge on

expedite [ˈekspədaɪt] *vt.* 加快进程：to speed up the progress of; accelerate

recondite [ˈrekəndaɪt] *adj.* 深奥的，难解的：difficult or impossible for one of ordinary understanding or knowledge to comprehend

erudite [ˈerudaɪt] *adj.* 博学的：characterized by erudition; learned

mite [maɪt] *n.* 微小的东西，很少的钱：a very small object, creature, or particle, a very small sum of money

ignite [ɪɡˈnaɪt] *vt.* 激起，唤起（感情等）：to arouse the passions of

infinite [ˈɪnfɪnət] *adj.* 无尽的，无限的：having no boundaries or limits

respite [ˈrespɪt] *n.* 间歇，休息：an interval of rest or relief

rite [raɪt] *n.* 惯例，仪式：a prescribed form or manner governing the words or actions for a ceremony

sybarite [ˈsɪbəraɪt] *n.* 沉溺于奢侈逸乐者，酒色之徒：a person devoted to pleasure and luxury; a voluptuary

trite [traɪt] *adj.* 陈腐的，陈词滥调的：hackneyed or boring from much use, not fresh or original

contrite [kənˈtraɪt] *adj.* （因为有罪孽或过错而感到）后悔悲痛的：feeling or showing sorrow and remorse for a sin or shortcoming

requisite [ˈrekwɪzɪt] *n.* 必需品：something necessary, indispensable, or unavoidable
adj. 必不可少的，必备的：essential, necessary

prerequisite [ˌpriːˈrekwəzɪt] *n.* 先决条件，前提：something that is necessary to an end or to the carrying out of a function

perquisite	[ˈpɜːrkwɪzɪt] *n.* 额外的好处：something <u>given in addition</u> to what is ordinarily expected or owed
exquisite	[ɪkˈskwɪzɪt] *adj.* 精致精巧的：having qualities that appeal to a <u>refined taste</u>
apposite	[ˈæpəzɪt] *adj.* 相关的，合适的：highly <u>pertinent</u> or <u>appropriate</u>: apt
requite	[rɪˈkwaɪt] *vt.* 酬谢，报答：to <u>make repayment</u> or return for *vt.* 报仇：to <u>punish in kind</u> the wrongdoer responsible for
svelte	[svelt] *adj.* (女人)体态苗条的，优雅的：slender or graceful in figure or outline; <u>slim</u>
dilettante	[ˌdɪləˈtænti] *n./adj.* 业余爱好者(对艺术或知识领域涉猎浅薄者)/ 缺乏专业技术的：a person having a <u>superficial interest</u> in an art / <u>lacking</u> or showing a lack of <u>expert skill</u>

音 频

anecdote	[ˈænɪkdoʊt] *n.* 短小有趣的故事，段子：a usually <u>short narrative</u> of an <u>interesting</u>, <u>amusing</u>, or biographical incident
demote	[ˌdiːˈmoʊt] *vt.* 降职，降级：to reduce to <u>a lower grade</u> or rank
rote	[roʊt] *n.* 死记硬背：a memorizing process <u>using routine or repetition</u>, often without full attention or comprehension
forte	[fɔːrt] *n.* 优势，长处：something for which a person shows a <u>special talent</u>
lambaste	[læmˈbeɪst] *vt.* 严厉斥责：to <u>scold sharply</u>; berate
vignette	[vɪnˈjet] *n.* 简介，短文：a <u>vivid representation</u> in words of someone or something
coquette	[koʊˈket] *v.* 调情；不认真对待：to flirt; to deal with something <u>playfully</u> rather than seriously
tribute	[ˈtrɪbjuːt] *n.* 称颂，颂词：a gift, payment, <u>declaration</u>, or other acknowledgment of <u>gratitude</u>, respect, or admiration
acute	[əˈkjuːt] *adj.* 敏锐的：marked by <u>keen discern-ment</u> or intellectual perception especially of subtle distinctions, penetrating *adj.* (程度、影响)极强的：<u>extreme</u> in degree, or effect
persecute	[ˈpɜːrsɪkjuːt] *vt.* 迫害，折磨：to <u>cause</u> persis-tent <u>suffering</u> to

refute	[rɪˈfjuːt] *vt.* 否认：to declare not to be true
dilute	[daɪˈluːt] *vt.* 稀释 / *adj.* 经稀释的：to make thinner or less concentrated by adding a liquid such as water/of relatively low strength or concentration
absolute	[ˈæbsəluːt] *adj.* 专制的：unconstrained by constitutional or other provisions *adj.* 无限的：unqualified in extent or degree; total *adj.* 完美的，纯净不掺杂的：free from imperfection; free or relatively free from mixture *adj.* 不容置疑的，确凿的：positive, unquestionable
resolute	[ˈrezəluːt] *adj.* 坚定的：marked by firm determination
dissolute	[ˈdɪsəluːt] *adj.* 放荡的，无节制的：lacking moral restraint; indulging in sensual pleasures or vices
mute	[mjuːt] *adj.* 不说话的，缄默的：deliberately refraining from speech
minute	[maɪˈnjuːt] *adj.* 仔细的，谨小慎微的：characterized by careful scrutiny and close examination *adj.* 小的，不重要的：very small or of small importance
repute	[rɪˈpjuːt] *n.* (尤指好的) 名声，名誉：a good reputation
substitute	[ˈsʌbstɪtuːt] *n.* 取代者，替代品：a person or thing that takes the place or function of another *vt.* 取代，替代：to take the place of
institute	[ˈɪnstɪtuːt] *vt.* 创立，制定：to establish, organize, and set in operation

90

constitute	[ˈkɑːnstətuːt] *vt.* 指派，任命：to <u>appoint</u> to an office, function, or dignity *vt.* 构成：<u>make up</u>, form, compose
reconstitute	[ˌriːˈkɑːnstətuːt] *vt.* 重建，(尤其是通过加水)使复原：to constitute again or anew; to <u>restore</u> to a former condition, especially <u>by adding water</u>
astute	[əˈstuːt] *adj.* 机敏的，有洞察力的：having or showing <u>shrewdness</u> and <u>perspicacity</u>
neophyte	[ˈniːəfaɪt] *n.* 初学者，新手：a <u>beginner</u> or novice
subdue	[səbˈduː] *vt.* 使顺从；征服：to <u>conquer</u> and bring into subjection; to bring under one's control by force of arms
residue	[ˈrezɪduː] *n.* 剩余物：something that <u>remains</u> after a part is taken, separated, or designated
undue	[ˌʌnˈdjuː] *adj.* 过度的，过多的：<u>going beyond a normal</u> or acceptable limit in degree or amount
plague	[pleɪɡ] *n.* 瘟疫：a <u>widespread disease</u> resulting in a high rate of death *v.* 折磨，使…痛苦：to <u>cause persistent suffering</u>
vague	[veɪɡ] *adj.* 表达不清的：<u>not clearly expressed</u> *adj.* 轮廓不清晰的：<u>lacking definite shape</u>, form, or character
intrigue	[ˈɪntriːɡ] *n.* 阴谋：<u>a secret plan</u> for accomplishing evil or unlawful ends [ɪnˈtriːɡ] *vt.* 激起…的兴趣：to <u>arouse</u> the interest, desire, or <u>curiosity</u> of
fatigue	[fəˈtiːɡ] *n.* 疲惫：<u>weariness or exhaustion</u> from labor, exertion, or stress
harangue	[həˈræŋ] *v./n.* (发表)长篇大论：a <u>long pompous</u> speech, especially one delivered before a gathering

pedagogue [ˈpedəgɑːg] *n.* 教育者，老师：a person whose occupation is to give formal instruction in a school

demagogue [ˈdeməgɑːg] *n.* 蛊惑民心的政客：a leader who makes use of popular prejudices and false claims and promises in order to gain power

epilogue [ˈepɪlɔːg] *n.* 文学作品的结局：a concluding section that rounds out the design of a literary work

monologue [ˈmɑːnəlɔːg] *n.* 独白：a dramatic sketch performed by one actor

prologue [ˈproʊlɔːg] *n.* 序言：the preface or introduction to a literary work

venue [ˈvenjuː] *n.* 场地：the area or space occupied by or intended for something

opaque [oʊˈpeɪk] *adj.* 晦涩的：so obscure as to be unintelligible

oblique [əˈbliːk] *adj.* 斜的：inclined or twisted to one side

pique [piːk] *vt.* 激起，刺激：to excite or arouse especially by a provocation, challenge, or rebuff

baroque [bəˈroʊk] *adj.* 装饰华丽的，过分雕琢的，复杂的：characterized by extravagance, complexity, or flamboyance

burlesque [bɜːrˈlesk] *n./v.* 夸张滑稽地模仿以嘲弄他人的文学艺术作品，恶搞：to copy or exaggerate (someone or some-thing) in order to make fun of

grotesque [groʊˈtesk] *adj.* 难看的：unpleasant to look at

rue [ruː] *n.* 后悔，遗憾：the feeling of regret, remorse, or sorrow for

misconstrue [ˌmɪskənˈstruː] *vt.* 误解，曲解：to mistake the meaning of

ensue	[ɪn'suː] *vi.* 紧随其后：to take place <u>afterward</u> or as a result
issue	['ɪʃuː] *n.* (有争议的)话题，议题：a <u>matter that is in dispute</u> between two or more parties *v.* (使)流出：to (cause to) go, come, or <u>flow out</u>
cleave	[kliːv] *vi.* 紧贴，坚持：to <u>adhere</u> firmly and closely or loyally and unwaveringly *vt.* 分隔，割裂，劈开：to <u>divide</u> by or as if by a cutting blow
rave	[reɪv] *vi.* 狂热赞扬：to make an <u>exaggerated display of affection</u> or enthusiasm *vi.* (发疯般地)怒吼：to <u>talk</u> irrationally and wildly in or <u>as if in delirium</u>
crave	[kreɪv] *vt.* 热望：to have an <u>intense desire</u> for
peeve	[piːv] *vt.* 打扰，惹恼：to <u>disturb</u> the peace of mind of (someone) especially by repeated disagreeable acts
grieve	[griːv] *vt.* (使)感到悲伤：to (cause to) feel <u>deep sadness</u> or mental pain
aggrieve	[ə'griːv] *vt.* 使苦恼，使悲痛：to give <u>pain</u> or <u>trouble</u> to, <u>distress</u>
reprieve	[rɪ'priːv] *vt.* 对…暂缓处刑，免罪：to <u>postpone or cancel</u> the <u>punishment</u> of
retrieve	[rɪ'triːv] *vt.* 寻回，找回：to <u>get back again</u>
naïve	[naɪ'iːv] *adj.* 天真纯朴的：<u>lacking worldly experience</u> and understanding, simple and guileless
conducive	[kən'duːsɪv] *adj.* 有益的，有促进作用的：tending to <u>promote</u> or assist
hive	[haɪv] *n.* 忙碌之地：a place swarming with activity *v.* 储备，积累：to <u>store up</u>；accumulate

connive	[kəˈnaɪv] *vi.* 暗中合作，共谋：to cooperate secretly or have a secret understanding; collude
rive	[raɪv] *v.* 撕开：to wrench open or tear apart or to pieces
cohesive	[koʊˈhiːsɪv] *adj.* 有粘性的；有凝聚力的：exhibiting or producing cohesion or coherence
compulsive	[kəmˈpʌlsɪv] *adj.* 不能自拔的：caused by or suggestive of an irresistible urge
expansive	[ɪkˈspænsɪv] *adj.* 健谈的，外向的：open and communicative; talkative or effusive
apprehensive	[ˌæprɪˈhensɪv] *adj.* 知晓的，理解的：having specified facts or feelings actively impressed on the mind *adj.* 恐惧的，害怕的：anxious or fearful about the future
pensive	[ˈpensɪv] *adj.* 沉思的，(尤指)哀思的：given to or marked by long, quiet and often musingly sad thinking
responsive	[rɪˈspɑːnsɪv] *adj.* 反应的；敏感的：quick to respond or react appropriately or sympathetically
corrosive	[kəˈroʊsɪv] *adj.* 腐蚀性的：tending to destroy slowly by chemical action *adj.* 讽刺性的：bitingly sarcastic
discursive	[dɪsˈkɜːrsɪv] *adj.* (谈话内容) 杂乱的：moving from topic to topic without order
excursive	[ɪkˈskɜːrsɪv] *adj.* 离题的；散漫的：passing from one topic to another
impassive	[ɪmˈpæsɪv] *adj.* 冷漠的，无感情的：giving no sign of feeling or emotion
recessive	[rɪˈsesɪv] *adj.* 内向的，内敛的：not comfortable around people

94

aggressive	[ə'gresɪv] *adj.* 好斗的：having a quality of anger and determination that makes it ready to attack others
	adj. 强有力的，强烈的：marked by or uttered with forcefulness
submissive	[səb'mɪsɪv] *adj.* 服从的，顺从的，恭顺的：submitting to others
effusive	[ɪ'fjuːsɪv] *adj.* 感情泛滥的 / 溢于言表的；感情表达不节制的 / 过度的；过分多情的：unrestrained or excessive in emotional expression
inconclusive	[ˌɪnkən'kluːsɪv] *adj.* 没有定论的：not showing that something is certainly true
obtrusive	[əb'truːsɪv] *adj.* 扎眼的，难看显眼的：noticeable in an unpleasant way
prerogative	[prɪ'rɑːgətɪv] *n.* 特权，权力：an exclusive or special right, power, or privilege
lucrative	['luːkrətɪv] *adj.* 有利可图的：yielding a profit
imperative	[ɪm'perətɪv] *adj.* 命令的，强制性的：forcing one's compli-ance or participation by or as if by law
	adj. 迫切的：needing immediate attention
pejorative	[pɪ'dʒɔːrətɪv] *adj.* 轻蔑的，贬低的：disparaging; belittling
restorative	[rɪ'stɔːrətɪv] *adj.* 有益健康的：beneficial to the health of body or mind
figurative	['fɪgərətɪv] *adj.* 比喻的：expressing one thing in terms normally denoting another with which it may be regarded as analogous
tentative	['tentətɪv] *adj.* 暂时性的，尝试的：not fully worked out or developed
hortative	['hɔːrtətɪv] *adj.* 鼓励的：giving exhortation
putative	['pjuːtətɪv] *adj.* 推测的，假定的：generally regarded as such

derivative	[dɪˈrɪvətɪv] *adj.* 非原创的：lacking originality: banal
innovative	[ˈɪnəveɪtɪv] *adj.* 创新性的：characterized by, tending to, or introducing innovations
conservative	[kənˈsɜːrvətɪv] *adj.* 守旧的，不愿改变的：favoring traditional views and values; tending to oppose change
	adj. 不招摇的，低调的：not excessively showy
retroactive	[ˌretrouˈæktɪv] *adj.* 有追溯效力的：extending in scope or effect to a prior time or to conditions that existed or originated in the past
retrospective	[ˌretrəˈspektɪv] *adj.* 回顾的：looking back on, contemplating, or directed to the past
invective	[ɪnˈvektɪv] *adj.* 侮辱性的：of, relating to, or characterized by insult or abuse
vindictive	[vɪnˈdɪktɪv] *adj.* 复仇的，有寻仇倾向的：disposed to seek revenge
distinctive	[dɪˈstɪŋktɪv] *adj.* 完全不同的：being not of the same kind
disjunctive	[dɪsˈdʒʌŋktɪv] *adj.* 分离的：marked by breaks or disunity
counterproductive	[ˌkaʊntərprəˈdʌktɪv] *adj.* 反效果的，阻碍预期目标的：not producing or tending to hinder the attainment of a desired goal
prohibitive	[prəˈhɪbətɪv] *adj.* （价格高得）抑制购买的：so high or burdensome as to discourage purchase or use
primitive	[ˈprɪmətɪv] *adj.* 原始的：belonging to or characteristic of an early level of skill or development
acquisitive	[əˈkwɪzətɪv] *adj.* 贪婪的：strongly desirous of acquiring and possessing

音 频

inquisitive	[ɪnˈkwɪzətɪv] *adj.* 过分好奇的：inordinately or improperly curious about the affairs of others
intuitive	[ɪnˈtuːɪtɪv] *adj.* 直觉的：knowing or perceiving by intuition
substantive	[səbˈstæntɪv] *adj.* 本质的，关键的：of or relating to the essence or substance
incentive	[ɪnˈsentɪv] *n.* 刺激，诱因：something that incites or has a tendency to incite to determination or action
retentive	[rɪˈtentɪv] *adj.* 记性好的：having the ability or capacity to retain knowledge or information with ease
plaintive	[ˈpleɪntɪv] *adj.* 悲伤的：expressing suffering or sadness
perceptive	[pərˈseptɪv] *adj.* 敏锐的：able to sense slight impressions or differences
assertive	[əˈsɜːrtɪv] *adj.* 自信的：inclined to bold or confident assertion; aggressively self-assured
furtive	[ˈfɜːrtɪv] *adj.* 鬼鬼祟祟的；秘密的：done by stealth
restive	[ˈrestɪv] *adj.* 急躁的，忧虑的：marked by impatience or uneasiness
diminutive	[dɪˈmɪnjətɪvl] *adj.* 极小的：of a size that is less than average
revive	[rɪˈvaɪv] *vi.* 再获新生：to become active or flourishing again

salve	[sælv] v. 减轻，缓解：quiet, <u>assuage</u>
delve	[delv] v. 探究，钻研：to make a careful or <u>detailed search for</u> information
absolve	[əb'zɑːlv] v. 使无罪，解除责任：to set <u>free from</u> an obligation or the consequences of <u>guilt</u>, <u>exculpate</u>
dissolve	[dɪ'zɑːlv] v. 溶解，融化：to cause to pass into <u>solution</u>; to reduce (solid matter) to liquid form; <u>melt</u> v. 解散：to <u>break into</u> component <u>parts</u>; <u>disintegrate</u>
behoove	[bɪ'huːv] vt. 对…有利：to be <u>necessary</u>, <u>proper</u> or <u>advantageous</u> for
groove	[gruːv] v. 享受，极其满意，过得快活：to <u>take pleasure in</u>
reprove	[rɪ'pruːv] vt. 温和地责备，警告：to <u>scold</u> or correct usually <u>gently</u> or with kindly intent
disprove	[ˌdɪs'pruːv] vt. 反驳，证明为假：to <u>prove to be false</u> or wrong
nerve	[nɜːrv] n. （坚强的）意志，勇气：<u>power of endurance</u> or control; strength of mind to carry on in spite of danger vt. 给予勇气，鼓励：to <u>give</u> strength or <u>courage</u> to
verve	[vɜːrv] n. 活力，热情：<u>vitality</u>, liveliness
swerve	[swɜːrv] vi. 突然改变方向：to <u>turn aside abruptly</u> from a straight line or course
awe	[ɔː] n./v. 敬畏：an emotion variously combining <u>dread</u>, <u>veneration</u>, and <u>wonder</u> that is inspired by authority or by the sacred or sublime

faze	[feɪz] *vt.* 打扰，使尴尬：to <u>disturb the com-posure</u> of: disconcert, dismay
glaze	[ɡleɪz] *vt.* 给…上釉，妆点：to <u>coat</u> with or as if with a <u>glaze</u>
raze	[reɪz] *vt.* 摧毁，粉碎：to <u>destroy completely</u> by or as if by knocking down or breaking to pieces
ostracize	[ˈɑːstrəsaɪz] *vt.* 驱逐：to <u>exclude</u> from a group
aggrandize	[əˈɡrændaɪz] *vt.* 增加、提高(力量、财富、地位、声誉)等：to <u>enhance</u> the power, wealth, position, or reputation of
eulogize	[ˈjuːlədʒaɪz] *vt.* 称赞；颂扬：to <u>speak</u> or write in high praise of
demoralize	[dɪˈmɔːrəlaɪz] *vt.* 使士气低落：to undermine the confidence or morale of; <u>dishearten</u> *vt.* 贬低，使堕落：to <u>lower in character</u>, dignity, or quality
neutralize	[ˈnuːtrəlaɪz] *vt.* 使无效：to <u>make inoperative or</u> ineffective usually by means of an opposite force, influence, or effect
tantalize	[ˈtæntəlaɪz] *vt.* 激起，挑逗，引诱：to <u>excite</u> (another) by exposing something desirable while keeping it out of reach
fertilize	[ˈfɜːrtəlaɪz] *vt.* 使肥沃，使多产：to <u>make fertile</u>
monopolize	[məˈnɑːpəlaɪz] *vt.* 垄断，主宰：to have <u>complete control</u> over
minimize	[ˈmɪnɪmaɪz] *vt.* 将…减到最少：to <u>reduce to</u> the <u>smallest</u> possible amount, extent, size, or degree *vt.* 刻意低估：to <u>underestimate</u> intentionally
victimize	[ˈvɪktɪmaɪz] *vt.* 使受骗：to <u>subject to deception</u> or fraud
epitomize	[ɪˈpɪtəmaɪz] *vt.* 代表，体现，是…的典型范例：to <u>represent</u> in visible form; to be <u>a typical example of</u>

galvanize ['gælvənaɪz] *vt.* (好似用电击)刺激：to stimulate or excite as if by an electric shock

homogenize [hə'mɑːdʒənaɪz] *vt.* 使统一化：to make agree with a single established standard or model

scrutinize ['skruːtənaɪz] *vt.* 仔细检查：to examine or observe with great care

agonize ['ægənaɪz] *v.* (使)非常痛苦：to (cause to) feel deep sadness or mental pain

antagonize [æn'tægənaɪz] *vt.* 与…敌对，反对：to act in opposition to: counteract

vt. 激怒：to incur or provoke the hostility of

lionize ['laɪənaɪz] *vt.* 追捧，把…捧为名人：to look on or treat (a person) as a celebrity

canonize ['kænənaɪz] *vt.* 使崇高，使神圣：to assign a high status or value to

patronize ['peɪtrənaɪz] *vt.* 赞助：to provide aid or support for

vt. 以高人一等的态度对待：to adopt an air of condescension toward: treat haughtily or coolly

plagiarize ['pleɪdʒəraɪz] *v.* 剽窃，抄袭：to steal and pass off (the ideas or words of another) as one's own

polarize ['poʊləraɪz] *vt.* 使分开对立，使两极分化：to break up into opposing factions or groupings

particularize [pər'tɪkjələraɪz] *vt.* 详述：to go into or give details or particulars

pulverize ['pʌlvəraɪz] *vt.* 将…彻底摧毁：to pound, crush or grind to powder or dust; to bring to a complete end the physical soundness, existence, or usefulness of

satirize ['sætəraɪz] *vt.* 讽刺：to ridicule or attack by means of satire

valorize	[ˈvæləraɪz] *v.* 提升，赞美：to <u>enhance</u> or try to enhance the price, value, or status
vaporize	[ˈveɪpəraɪz] *vt.* 彻底消灭：to <u>destroy</u> by or as if by converting into vapor
temporize	[ˈtempəraɪz] *vi.* 行动躲躲闪闪以争取时间、躲避争论等，打哈哈：to <u>act evasively</u> in order to gain time, avoid argument, or postpone a decision
extemporize	[ɪkˈstempəraɪz] *v.* 即兴表现：to do or perform (something) <u>without prior preparation</u> or practice
idolatrize	[aɪˈdɑːlətraɪz] *vt.* (通常盲目)崇拜：<u>admires intensely</u> and often blindly
stigmatize	[ˈstɪgmətaɪz] *vt.* 使蒙上污名：to characterize or brand as <u>disgraceful or ignominious</u>
proselytize	[ˈprɑːsələtaɪz] *v.* (使)改变信仰：to persuade to <u>change</u> to one's <u>religious faith</u>
doze	[doʊz] *vi./n.* 小憩：to sleep <u>lightly</u> or briefly
catalyze	[ˈkætəlaɪz] *vt.* 成为…的导火索，导致：to <u>be the cause of</u> (a situation, action, or state of mind)
oaf	[oʊf] *n.* 愚蠢的人：a <u>stupid person</u>
chaff	[tʃæf] *v.* 开玩笑：to <u>make jokes</u>
quaff	[kwæf] *vt.* 大口地喝：to <u>drink</u> (a beverage) <u>heartily</u>
miff	[mɪf] *vt.* 使恼怒：to cause to become offended or <u>annoyed</u>
tiff	[tɪf] *n./v.* 小争吵：a <u>petty quarrel</u>
stiff	[stɪf] *adj.* 僵硬的，无法弯曲的：<u>lacking</u> in suppleness or flexibility *adj.* 艰苦的，费力的：<u>requiring</u> considerable physical or mental <u>effort</u>
scoff	[skɔːf] *v.* 嘲笑：to treat or address with <u>derision</u>: <u>mock</u>

doff	[dɑːf] *vt.* 脱下：to take off; remove
rebuff	[rɪ'bʌf] *vt.* 严词拒绝：to reject or criticize sharply
scuff	[skʌf] *v.* (使)磨损：to become scratched, chipped, or roughened by wear
bluff	[blʌf] *adj.* 直率的，(说话)直截了当的：being or characterized by direct, brief, and potentially rude speech or manner *vt.* 欺骗：to cause to believe what is untrue; deceive
aloof	[ə'luːf] *adj.* 高冷的：removed or distant either physically or emotionally
spoof	[spuːf] *n.* 轻松幽默的模仿，小恶搞：a work that imitates and exaggerates another work for comic effect
reproof	[rɪ'pruːf] *n.* 批评，反对：criticism for a fault, rebuke
foolproof	['fuːlpruːf] *adj.* 十分简单以至于不会失败的：so simple, plain, or reliable as to leave no opportunity for error, misuse, or failure
windbag	['wɪndbæg] *n.* 健谈的人：an exhaustively talkative person
gag	[gæg] *n.* 笑话；玩笑之举：a laugh-provoking remark or act; a joke
lag	[læg] *vi.* 缓慢行走：to proceed or develop with comparative slowness *vi.* 萎靡，失去活力：to lose bodily strength or vigor
flag	[flæg] *vi.* 变得衰弱：to become unsteady, feeble, or spiritless

snag	[snæg] *n.* 障碍：a danger or difficulty that is hidden or not easily recognized
wag	[wæg] *v.* 摆动：to move to and fro or up and down especially with quick jerky motions
bracing	['breɪsɪŋ] *adj.* 令人振奋的，给人带来活力的：giving strength, vigor, or freshness
padding	['pædɪŋ] *n.* 夸张，废话：the representation of something in terms that go beyond the facts
plodding	['plɑːdɪŋ] *adj.* 无聊的，单调乏味的：characterized by dullness and monotony; lacking variety or excitement
abiding	[ə'baɪdɪŋ] *vt.* 持久的：lasting for a long time; enduring
demanding	[dɪ'mændɪŋ] *adj.* 难取悦的，难满足的：not easily satisfied or pleased *adj.* 费时间花心思的：requiring much time, effort, or careful attention
condescending	[ˌkɑːndɪ'sendɪŋ] *adj.* 摆出高人一等的姿态的：displaying a patronizingly superior attitude
impending	[ɪm'pendɪŋ] *adj.* 即将发生的：being soon to appear or take place
heartrending	['hɑːrtˌrendɪŋ] *adj.* 令人心碎的：causing intense sorrow or distress
astounding	[ə'staʊndɪŋ] *adj.* 令人吃惊的，出乎意料的：causing astonishment or amazement
unflagging	[ˌʌn'flægɪŋ] *adj.* 不懈的，不知疲倦的：not declining in strength or vigor
obliging	[ə'blaɪdʒɪŋ] *adj.* 乐于助人的：willing to do favors
bewitching	[bɪ'wɪtʃɪŋ] *adj.* 迷人的，令人着迷的：having an often mysterious or magical power to attract
dashing	['dæʃɪŋ] *adj.* 爱好冒险的，大胆的：inclined or willing to take risks

103

refreshing [rɪˈfreʃɪŋ] *adj.* 令人身心振奋的，提神的：having a <u>renewing effect</u> on the state of the body or mind

scathing [ˈskeɪðɪŋ] *adj.* 尖酸刻薄的：marked by the use of wit that is intended to <u>cause hurt feelings</u>

painstaking [ˈpeɪnzteɪkɪŋ] *adj.* 煞费苦心的：taking pains：expending, showing, or involving <u>diligent care</u> and effort

appealing [əˈpiːlɪŋ] *adj.* 吸引人的：<u>attractive</u>, <u>inviting</u>

cling [klɪŋ] *vi.* 紧贴；支持：to <u>adhere</u> as if glued firmly

List 14

音 频

piddling [ˈpɪdlɪŋ] *adj.* 微不足道的：so trifling or trivial as to be beneath one's consideration

grueling [ˈgruːəlɪŋ] *adj.* 费时间花心思的：requiring much time, effort, or careful attention

trifling [ˈtraɪflɪŋ] *adj.* 细微的，不重要的：lacking in significance or solid worth

fledgling [ˈfledʒlɪŋ] *n.* 新手：a person who is just starting out in a field of activity

smuggling [ˈsmʌglɪŋ] *n.* 走私，私运：secret importation or exportation contrary to the law and especially without paying duties imposed by law

unavailing [ˌʌnəˈveɪlɪŋ] *adj.* 徒劳的，无果的：producing no results

inkling [ˈɪŋklɪŋ] *n.* 轻微暗示，小提示：a slight indication or suggestion

compelling [kəmˈpelɪŋ] *adj.* 极具说服力的：having the power to persuade

telling [ˈtelɪŋ] *adj.* 有效的，显著的：effective expressive

sterling [ˈstɜːrlɪŋ] *adj.* 优秀的：of the very best kind

sling [slɪŋ] *vt.* 投掷：to send through the air especially with a quick forward motion of the arm

dazzling [ˈdæzlɪŋ] *adj.* 炫目的，耀眼的：giving off or reflecting much light

teeming [ˈtiːmɪŋ] *adj.* 大量的：possessing or covered with great numbers or amounts of something specified

overweening [ˌouvərˈwiːnɪŋ] *adj.* 傲慢的，专横的：having a feeling of superiority that shows itself in an overbearing attitude

cunning [ˈkʌnɪŋ] *adj.* 狡猾的：marked by or given to artful subtlety and deceptiveness

overbearing [ˌouvərˈberɪŋ] *adj.* 专横傲慢的：domineering in manner; arrogant

sparing [ˈsperɪŋ] *adj.* 节俭的，节约的：marked by or practicing careful restraint（as in the use of resources）

sweltering [ˈsweltərɪŋ] *adj.* 酷热的：oppressively hot

smattering [ˈsmætərɪŋ] *n.* 少量：a small scattered number or amount

jarring [ˈdʒɑːrɪŋ] *adj.* 刺耳的：harsh or discordant

hamstring [ˈhæmstrɪŋ] *vt.* 使无效，使无力：to make ineffective or powerless

imposing [ɪmˈpouzɪŋ] *adj.* 宏伟壮丽的：impressive in size, bearing, dignity, or grandeur

prepossessing [ˌpriːpəˈzesɪŋ] *adj.* 给人好感的，有魅力的：serving to impress favorably

self-defeating [ˌselfdɪˈfiːtɪŋ] *adj.* 适得其反的，自我拆台的：causing more problems than it solves

ingratiating [ɪnˈɡreɪʃieɪtɪŋ] *adj.* 讨人喜欢的：capable of winning favor
adj. 逢迎的，意在奉承的：intended or adopted in order to gain favor

self-perpetuating [ˌselfpərˈpetʃueɪtɪŋ] *adj.* 自续的，能使自身永久存在的：continuing or prevailing without any external intervention

exacting	[ɪɡ'zæktɪŋ] *adj.* 严格的，苛求的：making severe demands; <u>rigorous</u> *adj.* 费时间的，花心思的：<u>requiring</u> much <u>time</u>, <u>effort</u>, or careful <u>attention</u>
fleeting	['fliːtɪŋ] *adj.* 稍纵即逝的，短暂的：<u>lasting only for a short time</u>; passing swiftly
riveting	['rɪvɪtɪŋ] *adj.* 吸引人的，极迷人的：wholly <u>absorbing</u> or <u>engrossing</u> one's attention
wanting	['wɑːntɪŋ] *adj.* 未出现的，缺少的：<u>not present</u> or in evidence *adj.* 未达到要求的：<u>not being up to standards</u> or expectations
everlasting	[ˌevər'læstɪŋ] *adj.* 永恒的，持久的：lasting <u>forever</u>; eternal
arresting	[ə'restɪŋ] *adj.* 吸引人的：<u>attracting</u> and holding the attention; <u>striking</u>
earsplitting	[ɪr'splɪtɪŋ] *adj.* 震耳欲聋的：<u>distressingly loud</u> or shrill
unremitting	[ˌʌnrɪ'mɪtɪŋ] *adj.* 连续不断的：going on and on <u>without any interruptions</u>
unwitting	[ʌn'wɪtɪŋ] *adj.* 不知道的，未觉察的：not knowing, <u>unaware</u>
misbehaving	[ˌmɪsbɪ'heɪvɪŋ] *adj.* 调皮的，行为不端的：engaging in or marked by <u>childish misbehavior</u>
misgiving	[ˌmɪs'ɡɪvɪŋ] *n.* 担忧，疑虑：a feeling of <u>doubt</u> or suspicion especially concerning a future event
taxing	['tæksɪŋ] *adj.* 繁重的，费力的：<u>requiring much time</u>, <u>effort</u>, or careful attention
cloying	['klɔɪɪŋ] *adj.* 甜得发腻的；感情用事的：excessively <u>sweet</u>; <u>sentimental</u>
headlong	['hedlɔːŋ] *adj.* 鲁莽的，草率的：<u>without deliberation</u>

prolong	[prə'lɔːŋ] *vt.* 延长，拖延：to <u>lengthen</u> in extent, scope, or range
throng	[θrɔːŋ] *v./n.* 大量聚集：to <u>crowd</u> together in <u>great numbers</u>
unsung	[ˌʌn'sʌŋ] *adj.* 被埋没的；不知名的：<u>not cele-brated</u> or praised (as in song or verse)
hangdog	['hæŋdɔːg] *adj.* 伤心的，沮丧的：<u>sad</u>, <u>dejected</u>
agog	[ə'gɑːg] *adj.* 极度感兴趣的：showing <u>urgent desire or interest</u>
jog	[dʒɑːg] *vt.* 唤起：to <u>rouse</u> or stimulate
clog	[klɑːg] *n.* 阻碍物：<u>something</u> that makes <u>move-ment</u> or <u>progress difficult</u> *v.* 阻碍：to create <u>difficulty</u> for the work or activity of
humbug	['hʌmbʌg] *n.* 骗子：a willfully false, <u>deceptive</u>, or insincere person
lug	[lʌg] *vt.* 费力搬运：to carry <u>laboriously</u>
smug	[smʌg] *adj.* 自大的，自鸣得意的：having too high an <u>opinion of oneself</u>
shrug	[ʃrʌg] *vt.* 轻视，忽略：to <u>dismiss</u> as of little importance
pariah	[pə'raɪə] *n.* 被排斥或鄙视的人：one that is <u>despised or rejected</u>, outcast
breach	[briːtʃ] *v.* 违背：to <u>fail to keep</u>
preach	[priːtʃ] *vi.* 传道，布道：to deliver a <u>sermon</u>
stomach	['stʌmək] *vt.* 容忍：to <u>bear</u> without overt reaction or resentment
poach	[poʊtʃ] *vt.* 水煮：to <u>cook in a liquid</u> heated to the point that it gives off steam
broach	[broʊtʃ] *vt.* 提出讨论：to <u>present</u> or bring forward for discussion
reproach	[rɪ'proʊtʃ] *n.* 令人羞愧的事物，耻辱：one that <u>causes shame</u>, rebuke or blame

108

detach [dɪ'tætʃ] *vt.* 使分离：to separate or unfasten；disconnect

beseech [bɪ'siːtʃ] *vt.* (急切地)恳求：to beg for urgently or anxiously

squelch [skweltʃ] *vt.* 压制，镇压(运动)：to put a stop to (something) by the use of force

drench [drentʃ] *vt.* 使湿透，浸透：to wet thoroughly

retrench [rɪ'trentʃ] *vi.* 削减开支：to curtail expenses

stench [stentʃ] *n.* 臭气，恶臭：a strong, foul odor

quench [kwentʃ] *vt.* 熄灭：to put out (a fire , for example); extinguish
vt. 使满足：to put a complete end to (a physical need or desire)

inch [ɪntʃ] *v.* (使) 慢慢移动：to move or cause to move slowly or by small degrees

flinch [flɪntʃ] *vi.* 畏缩；退缩：to draw back in fear, pain, or disgust

staunch [stɔːntʃ] *adj.* 忠 诚 的 , 坚 定 的 ：steadfast in loyalty or principle

monarch ['mɑːnərk] *n.* 君主，帝王：one who rules over a people with a sole, supreme, and usually hereditary authority

parch [pɑːrtʃ] *v.* 炽，烤；烤干：to make extremely dry, especially by exposure to heat

besmirch [bɪ'smɜːrtʃ] *vt.* 诽谤，玷污：to detract from the honor or luster of

scorch [skɔːrtʃ] *v.* 炙烤，烘干：to burn on the surface; to make dry

lurch [lɜːrtʃ] *vi.* 蹒 跚 ： to move forward while swaying from side to side

dispatch [dɪ'spætʃ] *n.* 迅速：promptness and efficiency in performance or transmission *vt.* 发送，派遣：to cause to go or be taken from one place to another

etch [etʃ] *v.* 留下深刻印象，铭记：to produce a vivid impression of

glitch [glɪtʃ] *n.* 小故障：a minor malfunction, mishap, or technical problem

stitch [stɪtʃ] *n.* 突然剧痛：a sharp unpleasant sensation usually felt in some specific part of the body

scotch [skɑːtʃ] *vt.* 停止：to put an abrupt end to

notch [nɑːtʃ] *vt.* 通过努力获得：to obtain (as a goal) through effort

crutch [krʌtʃ] *n./v.* 支撑，支柱：something that supports or sustains

slouch [slaʊtʃ] *vi.* 缓慢行走：to go or move slowly or reluctantly

retouch [ˌriːˈtʌtʃ] *v.* 润饰，改进：to improve or change (a photographic negative or print)

vouch [vaʊtʃ] *v.* 担保，声称为真：to declare (something) to be true or genuine; to give a guarantee

inveigh [ɪnˈveɪ] *vi.* 激烈抗议，表示强烈不满：to protest or complain bitterly or vehemently

bash [bæʃ] *vt.* 抨击，严厉批评：to criticize harshly and usually publicly

abash [əˈbæʃ] *vt.* 使尴尬，使羞愧：to destroy the self-possession or self-confidence of, disconcert, embarrass

slapdash [ˈslæpdæʃ] *adj.* 马虎的：to do things carelessly without much thinking or planning

balderdash [ˈbɔːldərdæʃ] *n.* 胡言乱语，废话，无意义的话：words or language having no meaning or conveying no intelligible ideas; nonsense

110

rehash [ˈriːhæʃ] *v.* 重复，老调重弹：to present (something) again in a slightly different form

lash [læʃ] *v.* 猛击，撞击：to strike against with force or violence

mash [mæʃ] *vt.* 捣碎：to cause to become a pulpy mass

rash [ræʃ] *adj.* 草率的，仓促的：marked by or proceeding from undue haste or lack of deliberation or caution

brash [bræʃ] *adj.* 愚勇的，鲁莽的：foolishly adventurous or bold

quash [kwɔːʃ] *vt.* 镇压，阻止：to put a stop to (something) by the use of force

awash [əˈwɔːʃ] *adj.* (如洪水般)泛滥的：filled, covered, or completely overrun as if by a flood

mesh [meʃ] *v.* 诱捕：to catch or hold as if in a net

snobbish [ˈsnɑːbɪʃ] *adj.* 谄上傲下的，自大的：being or characteristic of a person who has an offensive air of superiority and tends to ignore or disdain anyone regarded as inferior

outlandish [aʊtˈlændɪʃ] *adj.* 古怪的，奇异的：strikingly out of the ordinary; bizarre

brandish [ˈbrændɪʃ] *vt.* (带有威胁性地)挥舞：to shake or wave (as a weapon) menacingly

prudish [ˈpruːdɪʃ] *adj.* 过分守礼的：marked by prudery

音频

List 15

raffish	[ˈræfɪʃ] *adj.* 低俗的：marked by or suggestive of flashy vulgarity or <u>crudeness</u>
offish	[ˈɔːfɪʃ] *adj.* 冷淡的：inclined to be distant and reserved; <u>aloof</u>
sluggish	[ˈslʌgɪʃ] *adj.* 缓慢的，迟缓的：markedly <u>slow in movement</u>, flow, or growth
rakish	[ˈreɪkɪʃ] *adj.* 放荡，行为不检点的：having or showing <u>lowered moral character</u> or standards; dissolute
puckish	[ˈpʌkɪʃ] *adj.* 淘气的，顽皮的：<u>mischievous</u>; <u>impish</u>
mawkish	[ˈmɔːkɪʃ] *adj.* 过度伤感的：excessively and objectionably <u>sentimental</u>
relish	[ˈrelɪʃ] *n.* 喜好，偏好： an appetite for something; a strong <u>appreciation or liking</u> *vt.* 享受，喜欢：to <u>take</u> keen or zestful <u>pleasure</u> in
ticklish	[ˈtɪklɪʃ] *adj.* 易怒的：<u>easily offended</u> or upset; touchy *adj.* 棘手的，对技巧要求高的：requiring <u>exceptional skill or caution</u> in performance or handling
churlish	[ˈtʃɜːrlɪʃ] *adj.* 粗鲁无礼的：having or showing crudely insensitive or <u>impolite manners</u>
mulish	[ˈmjuːlɪʃ] *adj.* 固执的：un reasonably and inflexibly <u>obstinate</u>

squeamish [ˈskwiːmɪʃ] *adj.* 恶心的，晕船的：affected with nausea

blemish [ˈblemɪʃ] *n.* 缺点，污点：a noticeable imperfection
vt. 损害，玷污：to reduce the soundness, effectiveness, or perfection of

banish [ˈbænɪʃ] *vt.* 驱逐出境：to require by authority to leave a country
vt. 赶出：to drive or force out

replenish [rɪˈplenɪʃ] *vt.* 补充：to fill or make complete again; add a new stock or supply to

diminish [dɪˈmɪnɪʃ] *v.* (使)变小，(使)减少：to (cause to) become smaller or less
v. 轻视，贬低：to lessen the authority, dignity, or reputation of: belittle

admonish [ədˈmɑːnɪʃ] *v.* 建议：to give advice to
v. 责备：to reprove gently but earnestly

tarnish [ˈtɑːrnɪʃ] *vt.* 玷污：to affect slightly with something morally bad or undesirable

varnish [ˈvɑːrnɪʃ] *vt.* 粉饰(令人不悦的东西)：to cover or conceal (as something unpleasant) with something that gives an attractive appearance

burnish [ˈbɜːrnɪʃ] *v.* 擦亮，磨光：to make smooth or glossy usually by repeatedly applying surface pressure

clownish [ˈklaʊnɪʃ] *adj.* 滑稽可笑的：acting in a silly or funny way

garish [ˈɡerɪʃ] *adj.* 过于鲜艳的，过于张扬的：marked by strident color or excessive ornamentation

perish [ˈperɪʃ] *vi.* 死亡，消亡：to become destroyed or ruined: cease to exist

boorish [ˈbʊrɪʃ] *adj.* 粗鲁无礼的：having or showing crudely insensitive or impolite manners

flourish [ˈflɜːrɪʃ] *vi.* 茂盛；繁荣：to grow luxuriantly; to achieve success

nourish [ˈnɜːrɪʃ] *vt.* 培养，促进：to help the growth or development of

coltish [ˈkoʊltɪʃ] *adj.* 爱开玩笑的：given to good-natured joking or teasing

skittish [ˈskɪtɪʃ] *adj.* 容易受到惊吓的，胆小的：easily frightened

adj. 善变的，多变的：likely to change frequently, suddenly, or unexpectedly

loutish [ˈlaʊtɪʃ] *adj.* 粗鲁的：having the characteristics of a lout；awkward, stupid, and boorish

languish [ˈlæŋgwɪʃ] *vi.* 变得衰弱：to be or become feeble, weak, or enervated

extinguish [ɪkˈstɪŋgwɪʃ] *vt.* 熄灭：to put out（a fire, for example）; quench

cliquish [ˈkliːkɪʃ] *adj.* 小集团的：bound together by feelings of very close association

vanquish [ˈvæŋkwɪʃ] *vt.* 打败，征服：to defeat in a conflict or contest

relinquish [rɪˈlɪŋkwɪʃ] *vt.* 放弃（职位、权力等）：to give up（as a position of authority）formally

lavish [ˈlævɪʃ] *adj.* 奢侈的，大量的，无节制的：characterized by or produced with extravagance and profusion

vt. 挥霍，浪费：to give readily and in large quantities; to use up carelessly

ravish [ˈrævɪʃ] *vt.* 使陶醉，使沉迷：to overcome with emotion（as wonder or delight）

dovish [ˈdʌvɪʃ] *adj.* 鸽派的，爱好和平的：inclined to live in peace and to avoid war

114

harsh	[hɑːrʃ] *adj.* 严厉的：unduly <u>exacting</u>, given to exacting standards of discipline and self-restraint
gush	[gʌʃ] *v.* (使)感情强烈外溢：to make an <u>exaggerated display</u> of affection or enthusiasm
lush	[lʌʃ] *adj.* 多产的：<u>producing abundantly</u>
flush	[flʌʃ] *adj.* 大量的：marked by <u>abundance</u> *vi.* 冲洗：to <u>pour liquid</u> over or through in order to cleanse
plush	[plʌʃ] *adj.* 奢华的，豪华的：<u>notably luxurious</u>
polymath	[ˈpɑːlimæθ] *n.* 学识渊博的人，博学者：a person of <u>encyclopedic learning</u>
loath	[loʊθ] *adj.* 不情愿的，讨厌的：unwilling or <u>reluctant</u>; disinclined
zenith	[ˈzenɪθ] *n.* 最高点，巅峰：<u>culminating</u> point
stealth	[stelθ] *adj.* 秘密的：intended <u>not to attract attention</u>
labyrinthine	[ˌlæbəˈrɪnθaɪn] *adj.* 迷宫似的，复杂曲折的：of, relating to, resembling, or constituting a labyrinth：<u>extremely complex</u> or tortuous in <u>structure</u>
sloth	[sloʊθ] *n.* 怠惰，懒惰：<u>disinclination to action</u> or labor: indolence
dearth	[dɜːrθ] *n.* 供应不足：an <u>inadequate</u> supply
mirth	[mɜːrθ] *n.* 欢乐，欢笑：<u>gladness</u> or gaiety as shown by or accompanied with <u>laughter</u>
uncouth	[ʌnˈkuːθ] *adj.* 粗俗的，没有品位的：<u>lacking in refinement</u> or good taste
outgrowth	[ˈaʊtɡroʊθ] *n.* 结果，后果：a condition or occurrence <u>traceable to a cause</u>

alibi ['æləbaɪ] *n.* 不在场的证明；托辞，借口：an ex-cuse usually intended to avert blame or punishment (as for failure or negligence)

illuminati [ɪˌluːmiˈnɑːtiː] *n.* 智者：persons who claim to be unusually enlightened

ennui [ɑːnˈwiː] *n.* 倦怠；缺乏兴趣：listlessness and dissatisfaction resulting from lack of interest

cloak [kloʊk] *vt.* 遮掩，隐藏：to change the dress or looks of so as to conceal true identity

soak [soʊk] *vt.* 使…湿透：to make thoroughly wet or saturated by or as if by placing in liquid

hack [hæk] *n.* 雇佣文人：a writer who aims solely for commercial success
v. 乱砍；开辟：to cut or chop with repeated and irregular blows

slack [slæk] *adj.* 松弛的：not tightly fastened, tied, or stretched
adj. 疏忽的，大意的：failing to give proper care and attention

knack [næk] *n.* 诀窍，聪明的做法：a clever trick or stratagem; a clever way of doing something

quack [kwæk] *n.* 骗子医生，江湖郎中：a pretender to medical skill

bedeck [bɪˈdek] *vt.* 装饰，点缀：to make more attractive by adding something that is beautiful or be coming

check [tʃek] *vt.* 使突然停止，阻止：to arrest the motion abruptly
v. 同意，一致：to be in agreement on every point

peck [pek] *n.* 大量：a considerable amount
v. (不情愿地)小口咬：to eat reluctantly and in small bites

speck [spek] *n.* 小点，少量：a very small amount: bit

nitpick ['nɪtpɪk] *v.* 吹毛求疵：to criticize by nit-picking

goldbrick [ˈɡouldbrɪk] *v.* 逃避工作和责任：to shirk one's assigned duties or responsibilities

maverick [ˈmævərɪk] *n.* 特立独行之人：a person who does not conform to generally accepted standards or customs

adj. 标新立异的，不合常规的：deviating from commonly accepted beliefs or practices

deadlock [ˈdedlɑːk] *n.* 僵局：a state of inaction or neutralization resulting from the opposition of equally powerful uncompromising persons or factions

vt. 使陷入僵局，使停顿：to bring or come to a deadlock

flock [flɑːk] *vi.* 聚集，集体行动：to congregate or travel in a flock or crowd

interlock [ˌɪntərˈlɑːk] *vi.* 连锁，连结：to become united or joined closely, as by hooking or dovetailing

stock [stɑːk] *adj.* 普通的，常备的：commonly used or brought forward

buck [bʌk] *v.* 阻止，反对：to refuse assent, to refuse to give in to

pluck [plʌk] *n.* 敢于面对困难的勇气：resourceful courage and daring in the face of difficulties

sleek [sliːk] *adj.* 时髦的，优美的：stylish and attractive

meek [miːk] *adj.* 顺从的：easily imposed on; submissive

balk [bɔːk] *vt.* 阻碍：to check or stop by or as if by an obstacle

v. 不愿接受，拒绝：to show unwillingness to accept, do, engage in, or agree to

milk	[mɪlk] *vt.* 榨取（财富、信息等）: to draw or coerce profit or advantage from illicitly or to an extreme degree
sulk	[sʌlk] *vi.* 生气，愠怒: to be sullenly aloof or withdrawn, as in silent resentment or protest
dank	[dæŋk] *adj.* 阴湿的: slightly or moderately wet
lank	[læŋk] *adj.* 细长瘦弱的: long and lean *adj.* 不僵硬的，柔软松弛的: long, straight, and limp; not stiff in structure
shrink	[ʃrɪŋk] *vi.* （在数量或价值方面）降低，减小: to become reduced in amount or value: dwindle
hoodwink	['hʊdwɪŋk] *vt.* 欺骗: to take in by deceptive means; deceive
debunk	[ˌdiːˈbʌŋk] *vt.* 揭穿…的真面目: to reveal the true nature of
brook	[brʊk] *vt.* 忍受，容许: to stand for, tolerate
crook	[krʊk] *vt.* 使弯曲: to cause to turn away from a straight line
debark	[diˈbɑːrk] *v.* （使）下船(飞机、车等); 卸(客、货): to unload, as from a ship or an airplane; disembark
embark	[ɪmˈbɑːrk] *vi.* 开始从事: to make a start
hallmark	['hɔːlmɑːrk] *n.* 典型的特征: a conspicuous feature or characteristic
irk	[ɜːrk] *vt.* 使烦恼，使厌倦: to cause to be irritating, wearisome, or vexing to
shirk	[ʃɜːrk] *v.* 逃避，规避: to get or keep away from (as a responsibility) through cleverness or trickery
smirk	[smɜːrk] *vi.* （自鸣得意地）笑: to smile in an affected, often offensively self-satisfied manner

| patchwork | [ˈpætʃwɜːrk] *n./adj.* 混合物(的)：an unorganized collection or <u>mixture of various things</u> |

patchwork [ˈpætʃwɜːrk] *n./adj.* 混合物(的)：an unorganized collection or <u>mixture of various things</u>

lurk [lɜːrk] *vi.* 潜伏：to <u>lie in wait</u> in a place of concealment especially for an evil purpose

brisk [brɪsk] *adj.* 充满生机的，有活力的：marked by much life, movement, or <u>activity</u>

husk [hʌsk] *vt.* 剥去：to <u>remove</u> the natural covering of

methodical [məˈθɑːdɪkl] *adj.* 井然有序的，有条理的：arranged or proceeding in regular, <u>systematic order</u>

periodical [ˌpɪriˈɑːdɪkl] *adj.* 周期性的，有固定间隔的：occurring or recurring at <u>regular intervals</u>

pedagogical [ˌpedəˈgɑːdʒɪkl] *adj.* 教学的；教师的：of, relating to, or befitting a <u>teacher or education</u>

pathological [ˌpæθəˈlɑːdʒɪkl] *adj.* 不正常的，病态的：being such to a degree that is extreme, excessive, or <u>markedly abnorma</u>

hierarchical [ˌhaɪəˈrɑːrkɪkl] *adj.* 分等级的，等级制的：<u>classified</u> according to various criteria into successive levels or layersl

音频

List 16

inimical	[ɪ'nɪmɪkl] *adj.* 带有敌意的：reflecting or indicating hostility
ecumenical	[ˌiːkjuː'menɪkl] *adj.* 世界范围的，普遍性的：worldwide or general in extent, influence, or application
empirical	[ɪm'pɪrɪkl] *adj.* 基于观察、实验的：based on observation or experiment
categorical	[ˌkætə'gɔːrɪkl] *adj.* 没有例外的；绝对的：being without exception or qualification; absolute
rhetorical	[rɪ'tɔːrɪkl] *adj.* 言辞华丽(却往往无内涵)的：full of fine words and fancy expressions but mostly meaningless words and phrases
theatrical	[θi'ætrɪkl] *adj.* 做作的，夸张的，矫揉造作的：marked by exaggerated self-display and unnatural behavior
asymmetrical	[ˌeɪsɪ'metrɪkl] *adj.* 不平衡的，不对称的：having no balance or symmetry
whimsical	['wɪmzɪkl] *adj.* 反复无常的：prone to sudden illogical changes of mind, ideas, or actions
commonsensical	[ˌkɑːmən'sensɪkl] *adj.* 符合常识的，有依据的：displaying common sense, based on sound reasoning or information
metaphysical	[ˌmetə'fɪzɪkl] *adj.* 哲学上的，理论上的：dealing with or expressing a quality or idea *adj.* 非尘世的：of, relating to, or being part of a reality beyond the observable physical universe

120

antithetical [ˌæntɪˈθetɪkl] *adj.* 完全对立的，相反的：being in direct and unequivocal opposition

heretical [həˈretɪkl] *adj.* 异教的，异端邪说的：departure from established beliefs or standards

hypocritical [ˌhɪpəˈkrɪtɪkl] *adj.* 虚伪的：not being or expressing what one appears to be or express

elliptical [ɪˈlɪptɪkl] *adj.* 含糊不清的：of or relating to deliberate obscurity（as of literary or conversational style）
adj. 椭圆的：of, relating to, or shaped like an ellipse

nautical [ˈnɔːtɪkl] *adj.* 航海的：of, relating to, or characteristic of ships, shipping, sailors, or navigation on a body of water

univocal [ˌjuːnɪˈvoʊkl] *adj.* 含义明确的：so clearly expressed as to leave no doubt about the meaning

soft-pedal [sɔːftˈpedl] *v.* 降低…的力度：to reduce in apparent importance

conceal [kənˈsiːl] *v.* 隐藏，隐瞒：to prevent disclosure or recognition of

ordeal [ɔːrˈdiːl] *n.* 严峻的考验：a severe trial or experience

congeal [kənˈdʒiːl] *v.* 凝固，固化：to change from a fluid to a solid state by or as if by cold

repeal [rɪˈpiːl] *vt.* 撤销，废除（法律等）：to rescind or annul by authoritative act

appeal [əˈpiːl] *n.* 申请：an application（as to a recognized authority）for corroboration, vindication, or decision
n. 起诉：to charge with a crime：accuse

ethereal [iˈθɪriəl] *adj.* 轻巧精致的：resembling air in lightness, highly refined; delicate

121

adj. 非物质的，精神(上)的：not of this world；spiritual; not composed of matter

corporeal ［kɔːrˈpɔːriəl］ *adj.* 肉体的：not spiritual
adj. 有形的，实体的：not immaterial or intangible

zeal ［ziːl］ *n.* 热心，热诚：enthusiastic devotion to a cause, ideal, or goal and tireless diligence in its furtherance

prodigal ［ˈprɑːdɪgl］ *adj.* 挥霍的：recklessly spendthrift
n. 败家子：someone who spends money freely or foolishly

frugal ［ˈfruːgl］ *adj.* 节约的：characterized by or reflecting economy in the use of resources

apocryphal ［əˈpɑːkrɪfl］ *adj.* 假的：of doubtful authenticity: spurious

lethal ［ˈliːθl］ *adj.* 非常有害的，致命的：extremely harmful; devastating

glacial ［ˈgleɪsiəl］ *adj.* 极冷的：extremely cold
adj. 冷漠的，无感情的：devoid of warmth and cordiality

superficial ［ˌsuːpərˈfɪʃl］ *adj.* 表面的，肤浅的：lacking in depth, solidity, and comprehensiveness

provincial ［prəˈvɪnʃl］ *adj./n.* 狭隘（的）：limited in perspective; narrow and self-centered

crucial ［ˈkruːʃl］ *adj.* 非常重要的，决定性的：extremely significant or important

cordial ［ˈkɔːrdʒəl］ *adj.* 热情的，友好的：showing a natural kindness and courtesy especially in social situations
adj. 令人振奋的，令人焕然一新的：having a renewing effect on the state of the body or mind

primordial ［praɪˈmɔːrdiəl］ *adj.* 原始的，最初的：being or happening first in sequence of time

parochial [pə'roʊkiəl] *adj.* 狭隘的：<u>not broad</u> or open in views or opinions

genial ['dʒiːniəl] *adj.* 和蔼亲切的：having an <u>easy-going</u> and pleasing manner especially in social situations

congenial [kən'dʒiːniəl] *adj.* 和善的，友好的：having or marked by <u>agreement</u> in feeling or action

menial ['miːniəl] *adj.* 卑贱的，低下的：showing, expressing, or offered in a <u>spirit of humility or unseemly submissiveness</u>

venial ['viːniəl] *adj.* 可宽恕的：<u>easily excused</u> or forgiven

imperial [ɪm'pɪriəl] *adj.* 巨大的，令人惊叹的：large and <u>impressive in size</u>, grandeur, extent, or conception

immaterial [ˌɪmə'tɪriəl] *adj.* 无关的，不重要的：of <u>no</u> importance or relevance

immemorial [ˌɪmə'mɔːriəl] *adj.* 古老的：dating or surviving <u>from the distant past</u>

sartorial [sɑːr'tɔːriəl] *adj.* 裁缝匠的，裁缝的：of or relating to a tailor or tailored <u>clothes</u>

mercurial [mɜːr'kjʊriəl] *adj.* （情绪）善变的：characterized by rapid and unpredictable <u>changeableness of mood</u>

ambrosial [æm'broʊziəl] *adj.* （食物）特别美味的；香的：something <u>extremely pleasing</u> to taste or smell

palatial [pə'leɪʃl] *adj.* 宫殿般奢华的：of the nature of a palace, as in spaciousness or <u>ornateness</u>

substantial [səb'stænʃl] *adj.* 物质的：of, relating to, or <u>having substance</u>
adj. 有重大意义的：<u>considerable in importance</u>, value, degree, amount, or extent

providential [ˌprɑːvɪ'denʃl] *adj.* 天意，幸运(的)：happening as if through <u>divine intervention</u>

torrential	[təˈrenʃl] *adj.* 急流的：caused by or resulting from action of rapidstreams
inconsequential	[ɪnˌkɑːnsɪˈkwenʃl] *adj.* 不重要的：of no significance
partial	[ˈpɑːrʃl] *adj.* 偏袒的，偏爱的：inclined to favor one party more than the other: biased *adj.* 部分的，不完整的：lacking some necessary part
trivial	[ˈtrɪviəl] *adj.* 无足轻重的，不重要的：of little worth or importance
jovial	[ˈdʒoʊviəl] *adj.* 愉快的：markedly good-humored especially as evidenced by jollity and conviviality
abysmal	[əˈbɪzməl] *adj.* （程度）很深的；极端的：immeasurably great
cataclysmal	[kætəˈklɪzəməl] *adj.* 灾难性的：bringing about ruin or misfortune
banal	[bəˈnɑːl] *adj.* 非原创的，陈腐的：lacking originality, freshness, or novelty; trite
phenomenal	[fəˈnɑːmɪnl] *adj.* 不寻常的，非凡的：being out of the ordinary; extraordinary; outstanding
venal	[ˈviːnl] *adj.* 贪污受贿的：open to corrupt influence and especially bribery
signal	[ˈsɪgnəl] *adj.* （在重要性、成就方面）非同寻常的：standing above others in rank, importance, or achievement *v.* 给出信号：to direct or notify by a movement or gesture
cardinal	[ˈkɑːrdɪnl] *adj.* 主要的，非常重要的：of foremost importance; paramount
original	[əˈrɪdʒənl] *adj.* 创新的：independent and creative in thought or action: inventive

124

adj. 最初的，最早的：coming <u>before</u> all others in time or order

marginal [ˈmɑːrdʒɪnl] *adj.* 不重要的：<u>not of central importance</u>

seminal [ˈsemɪnl] *adj.* 创新的：of, relating to, or having the power to originate; <u>creative</u>

subliminal [ˌsʌbˈlɪmɪnl] *adj.* 下意识的，潜在意识的：<u>below</u> the threshold of conscious <u>perception</u>

nominal [ˈnɑːmɪnl] *adj.* 不重要的：so small or <u>unimportant</u> as to warrant little or no attention

provisional [prəˈvɪʒənl] *adj.* 临时的：provided or serving only for the time being; <u>temporary</u>

rational [ˈræʃnəl] *adj.* 合乎逻辑的：consistent with or based on reason; <u>logical</u>
adj. 理性的：<u>based on</u> sound <u>reasoning</u> or information

conditional [kənˈdɪʃənl] *adj.* 有条件的，受制约的：subject to, implying, or <u>dependent</u> upon a condition

exceptional [ɪkˈsepʃənl] *adj.* 例外的，特别的，非凡的：being an exception; <u>uncommon</u>; extraordinary

carnal [ˈkɑːrnl] *adj.* 肉体的，物质的：relating to the <u>physical</u>
adj. 世俗的：<u>worldly</u>

eternal [ɪˈtɜːrnl] *adj.* 永恒的：having <u>infinite duration</u>; <u>everlasting</u>; <u>perpetual</u>

diurnal [daɪˈɜːrnl] *adj.* 白天发生或行动的：occurring or active during the <u>daytime</u> rather than at night

nocturnal [nɑːkˈtɜːrnl] *adj.* 夜间的：of, relating to, or occurring <u>in the night</u>

shoal [ʃoʊl] *adj.* 浅的：having <u>little depth</u>: shallow

liberal [ˈlɪbərəl] *adj.* 思想前卫的：<u>not bound</u> by traditional ways or beliefs
adj. 慷慨的，大方的：marked by <u>generosity</u>

principal	[ˈprɪnsəpl] *adj.* 主要的，重要的：first, highest, or foremost in importance, rank, worth, or degree
feral	[ˈferəl] *adj.* 野生的：not domesticated or cultivated
peripheral	[pəˈrɪfərəl] *adj.* 辅助性的：available to supply something extra when needed
ephemeral	[ɪˈfemərəl] *adj.* 短暂的：lasting a very short time
integral	[ˈɪntɪgrəl] *adj.* 完整的：not lacking any part or member that properly belongs to it
sepulchral	[səˈpʌlkrəl] *adj.* 阴沉的；丧葬的：causing or marked by an atmosphere lacking in cheer; funereal
temporal	[ˈtempərəl] *adj.* 世俗的，尘世的：of or relating to earthly life
preternatural	[ˌpriːtərˈnætʃrəl] *adj.* 超乎寻常的：surpassing the normal or usual
rehearsal	[rɪˈhɜːrsl] *n.* 排练，彩排：the act of practicing in preparation for a public performance
colossal	[kəˈlɑːsl] *adj.* 巨大的：of a size, extent, or degree that elicits awe or taxes belief; immense
accidental	[ˌæksɪˈdentl] *adj.* 意外发生的，偶然的：occurring unexpectedly or by chance
pivotal	[ˈpɪvətl] *adj.* 最关键的，最为重要的：of the greatest possible importance
distal	[ˈdɪstl] *adj.* 远离中心的,(神经)末梢的：situated away from the point of attachment or origin or a central point
residual	[rɪˈzɪdʒuəl] *adj.* 剩余的，残存的：of, relating to, or characteristic of a residue
perpetual	[pərˈpetʃuəl] *adj.* 永恒的，不断的：continuing forever; everlasting

126

coeval	[koʊˈiːvl] *adj.* 同时代的，同龄的：of the same or equal age, antiquity, or duration
avowal	[əˈvaʊəl] *n.* 承认，公开宣布：a solemn and often public declaration of the truth or existence of something
peel	[piːl] *vi.* 脱去(衣服等)：to take off one's clothes
reel	[riːl] *vi.* 感到眩晕：to be in a confused state as if from being twirled around
genteel	[dʒenˈtiːl] *adj.* 有教养的，不粗俗的：free from vulgarity or rudeness
yokel	[ˈjoʊkl] *n.* 乡下人，天真纯朴的人：a naive or gullible inhabitant of a rural area or small town
enamel	[ɪˈnæml] *vt.* 装饰：to adorn with a brightly colored surface
channel	[ˈtʃænl] *vt.* 将…导向，投入：to cause to move to a central point or along a restricted pathway
repel	[rɪˈpel] *vt.* 使厌恶：to cause aversion in: disgust

音 频

mongrel	[ˈmʌŋɡrəl] *adj.* 杂种的，混血儿的：of <u>mixed origin</u> or character
wastrel	[ˈweɪstrəl] *n.* 肆意挥霍的人，败家子：one who <u>expends</u> resources foolishly and <u>self-indulgently</u>
sequel	[ˈsiːkwəl] *n.* 结果：a <u>result</u> or consequence
ravel	[ˈrævl] *vt.* 解开，松开：to <u>separate</u> the various <u>strands</u> of *vt.* 阐明：to <u>clarify by separating</u> the aspects of *vt.* 使纠缠，使复杂化：to <u>tangle</u> or complicate
revel	[ˈrevl] *v.* 享乐，陶醉：to <u>take intense pleasure</u> or satisfaction
drivel	[ˈdrɪvl] *n.* 胡言乱语：unintelligible or <u>mean-ingless talk</u> *v.* 胡言乱语，说傻话：to <u>talk stupidly</u> and care-lessly
novel	[ˈnɑːvl] *adj.* 新奇的：strikingly <u>new</u>, unusual, or different
grovel	[ˈɡrɑːvl] *vi.* 卑躬屈膝：to <u>draw back</u> or crouch down in <u>fearful submission</u>
marvel	[ˈmɑːrvl] *n.* 令人惊奇的事物：one that evokes <u>surprise, admiration, or wonder</u> *v.* （因为壮观、美丽等而）表示惊讶：to <u>feel amazement</u> or bewilderment at or about
blackmail	[ˈblækmeɪl] *n./vt.* 敲诈，勒索：<u>extortion of money</u> or something else of value from a person

by the threat of exposing a criminal act or discreditable information

rail [reɪl] *vi.* 怒骂，猛烈抨击：to revile or scold in harsh, insolent, or abusive language

frail [freɪl] *adj.* 虚弱的：physically weak
adj. （意志）薄弱的：easily led astray; morally weak

assail [əˈseɪl] *vt.* 抨击，严厉批评：to criticize harshly and usually publicly

entail [ɪnˈteɪl] *v.* 牵连；导致：If one thing entails another, it involves it or causes it.

curtail [kɜːrˈteɪl] *vt.* 缩短，削减：to make less in extent or duration

quail [kweɪl] *vi.* 胆怯，畏缩：to shrink back in fear; cower

travail [ˈtræveɪl] *n./v.* 辛苦劳动：work, especially when arduous or involving painful effort

countervail [ˈkaʊntərveɪl] *vt.* 抗衡，抵消：to exert force against; counteract

nil [nɪl] *n.* 不存在，零：nothing; zero

recoil [ˈriːkɔɪl] *vi.* 退却，畏缩：to shrink back, as under pressure or in fear or repugnance

foil [fɔɪl] *vt.* 挫败：to prevent from being successful; defeat

turmoil [ˈtɜːrmɔɪl] *n.* 骚动，混乱：a state or condition of extreme confusion, agitation, or commotion

roil [rɔɪl] *vt.* 激怒：to displease or disturb

cavil [ˈkævl] *v.* 挑剔，吹毛求疵：to find fault unnecessarily; raise trivial objections: quibble

daredevil [ˈderdevl] *adj./n.* 大胆鲁莽的(人)：foolishly adventurous or bold

windfall [ˈwɪndfɔːl] *n.* 好运，幸事：an unexpected, unearned, or sudden gain or advantage

pitfall	[ˈpɪtfɔːl] *n.* 陷阱：a pit flimsily covered or camouflaged and used to <u>capture and hold animals</u> or men
gall	[ɡɔːl] *vt.* (使)焦躁，激怒：<u>irritate</u>, vex
pall	[pɔːl] *vi.* 失去兴趣：to lose in <u>interest</u> or <u>attraction</u>
appall	[əˈpɔːl] *vt.* 使惊恐：to overcome with <u>consternation</u>, shock, or dismay
enthrall	[ɪnˈθrɔːl] *vt.* （像用魔咒般）吸引：to <u>hold the attention</u> of as if by a spell
forestall	[fɔːrˈstɔːl] *vt.* 预先阻止：to delay, hinder, or <u>prevent</u> by taking precautionary measures <u>beforehand</u>
squall	[skwɔːl] *v.* 尖叫：t o <u>scream</u> or cry loudly and harshly
stonewall	[ˌstoʊnˈwɔːl] *v.* 拒绝(合作)，阻挠：to be <u>uncooperative</u>, <u>obstructive</u>, or evasive
quell	[kwel] *vt.* 压制：to put down forcibly; <u>suppress</u> *vt.* 使平静，使安静：to <u>pacify</u>; quiet
thrill	[θrɪl] *n.* 强烈的兴奋感，快感：a <u>pleasurably intense stimulation</u> of the feelings *vt.* 使兴奋，使激动：to cause to experience a sudden sharp feeling of <u>excitement</u>
distill	[dɪˈstɪl] *vt.* 对…用蒸馏法提高纯度：to <u>increase</u> the concentration of, separate, or <u>purify</u> by or as if by distillation
instill	[ɪnˈstɪl] *vt.* 灌输：to <u>impart</u> gradually
loll	[lɑːl] *vi.* 偷懒，打发时间：to spend time <u>doing nothing</u>
gull	[ɡʌl] *vt.* 欺骗：to cause to believe what is <u>untrue</u>
lull	[lʌl] *n.* 相对平静时期，间隙：a <u>momentary halt</u> in an activity

vt. 使镇静，使安心：to free from distress or disturbance

idyll ['aɪdl] *n.* 无忧无虑的生活：a carefree episode or experience

gambol ['gæmbl] *vi.* 欢跳，雀跃：to leap about playfully

protocol ['proʊtəkɔːl] *n.* 正确的礼仪规范：a code of correct conduct

extol [ɪk 'stoʊl] *vt.* 赞美；吹捧：to praise highly；glorify

snarl [snɑːrl] *v.* 纠缠，纠结：to twist together into a usually confused mass

caterwaul ['kætərwɔːl] *v.* 嚎叫：to make a very loud and unpleasant sound

resourceful [rɪ 'sɔːrsfl] *adj.* 有创造力的，机智的：able to act effectively or imaginatively, especially in difficult situations

baleful ['beɪlfl] *adj.* 有害的： harmful or malignant in intent or effect

fateful ['feɪtfl] *adj.* 意义重大的：involving momentous consequences

fanciful ['fænsɪfl] *adj.* 不切实际的，荒谬的：conceived or made without regard for reason or reality

willful ['wɪlfl] *adj.* 固执的，倔强的：obstinately and often perversely self-willed

mournful ['mɔːrnfl] *adj.* 悲伤的：feeling or expressing sorrow or grief

fretful ['fretfl] *adj.* 易怒的，烦躁的：inclined to be vexed or troubled

fitful ['fɪtfl] *adj.* 断断续续的：having an erratic or intermittent character

wistful ['wɪstfl] *adj.* (带着忧伤而)渴望的，怀念的：full of yearning or desire tinged with melancholy

playful [ˈpleɪfl] *adj.* 爱开玩笑的，好打闹的：given to good-natured joking or teasing

annul [əˈnʌl] *vt.* 宣告无效，取消：to declare or make legally invalid or void

scrawl [skrɔːl] *vt.* 乱涂，潦草地写：to write or draw awkwardly, hastily, or carelessly

drawl [drɔːl] *v.* 慢吞吞地说：to speak slowly with vowels greatly prolonged

sprawl [sprɔːl] *v.* 杂乱无序地发展；蔓生，蔓延：to grow, develop, or spread irregularly and without apparent design or plan

scowl [skaʊl] *vi.* 皱眉（表现出不高兴）：to contract the brow in an expression of displeasure

prowl [ˈpraʊl] *v.* 巡游以猎取食物；徘徊：to roam through stealthily, as in search of prey or plunder

gleam [gliːm] *v.* 闪光：to shoot forth bursts of light

ream [riːm] *vt.* 怒斥，训斥：to criticize (someone) severely or angrily especially for personal failings

sham [ʃæm] *v.* 掩饰，假装：to present a false appearance of
adj. 虚假的：not genuine; fake

epigram [ˈepɪgræm] *n.* 机智的短诗，警句：a short, witty poem expressing a single thought or bservation

redeem [rɪˈdiːm] *vt.* 改过自新：to make better in behavior or character

esteem [ɪˈstiːm] *n./v.* 尊重：to regard with respect; prize

stratagem [ˈstrætədʒəm] *n.* 谋略，策略：an artifice or trick in war for deceiving and outwitting the enemy

paradigm [ˈpærədaɪm] *n.* 典范，模范：one that serves as a pattern or model

132

acclaim [əˈkleɪm] *n.* 称赞：public acknowledgment or admiration for an achievement

vt. 赞扬，赞颂：to declare enthusiastic approval of

proclaim [prəˈkleɪm] *vt.* 宣告，使…公之于众：to declare publicly, typically insistently, proudly, or defiantly and in either speech or writing

brim [brɪm] *n.* 边缘，边界：an upper or outer margin

vi. 充满：to be or become full often to overflowing

interim [ˈɪntərɪm] *n.* 中间过渡时期，间隔：an interval of time between one event, process, or period and another

adj. 暂时的：serving in a position for the time being

verbatim [vɜːrˈbeɪtɪm] *adv.* 逐字地，一字不差地：in the exact words

vim [vɪm] *n.* 活力，精力：robust energy and enthusiasm

balm [bɑːm] *n.* 香油，止痛膏；安慰物：a sweet-smelling oil that heals wounds or reduce pain; things that soothe the mind

qualm [kwɑːm] *n.* 担忧，不安：a sudden uneasy feeling about the rightness

overwhelm [ˌoʊvərˈwelm] *vt.* 淹没：to cover with or as if with a flood

random [ˈrændəm] *adj.* 随机的，随意的：lacking a definite plan, purpose, or pattern

fathom [ˈfæðəm] *vt.* 彻底理解，弄懂：to penetrate and come to understand

venom [ˈvenəm] *n.* 恶意，恶毒的用心：the desire to cause pain for the satisfaction of doing harm

doom [duːm] *v.* 注定（倒霉）：to determine the fate of suffering in advance

maelstrom [ˈmeɪlstrɑːm] *n.* 混乱、动荡的局势：a violent or turbulent situation

accustom [əˈkʌstəm] *vt.* 使习惯：to make familiar with something through use or experience

disarm [dɪsˈɑːrm] *vt.* 使息怒，平息，抚慰：to lessen the anger or agitation of

affirm [əˈfɜːrm] *vt.* 声称…为真，肯定…属实：to assert (as a judgment or decree) as valid or confirmed

infirm [ɪnˈfɜːrm] *adj.* 虚弱的：weak in body, especially from old age or disease
adj. 不果断的，优柔寡断的：lacking firmness of will, character, or purpose

conform [kənˈfɔːrm] *vt.* 使协调：to bring into harmony or accord
vi. 遵照，遵从：to be obedient or compliant

sarcasm [ˈsɑːrkæzəm] *n.* 讽刺，轻蔑：a sharp and often satirical or ironic utterance designed to cut or give pain

chasm [ˈkæzəm] *n.* 分歧，(意见、利益或忠诚上的)明显差异：a pronounced difference of opinion, interests, or loyalty

syllogism [ˈsɪlədʒɪzəm] *n.* 由一般到个别的推理，演绎：reasoning from the general to the specific; deduction

schism [ˈskɪzəm] *n.* 不一致：a lack of agreement or harmony

sophism [ˈsɑːfɪzəm] *n.* 假推理，诡辩：deceptive or fallacious argumentation

teetotalism [ˌtiːˈtoʊtlizəm] *n.* 禁酒：the principle or practice of complete abstinence from alcoholic drinks

euphemism [ˈjuːfəmɪzəm] *n.* 婉言，委婉的说法：the substitution of an agreeable or inoffensive expression for one that may offend or suggest something unpleasant

sectarianism [sekˈterɪənɪzəm] *n.* 宗派主义，顽固：stubborn or intolerant adherence to one's opinions or prejudices

hedonism [ˈhiːdənɪzəm] *n.* 享乐主义：the doctrine that pleasure or happiness is the sole or chief good in life

anachronism [əˈnækrənɪzəm] *n.* 不合时代的人或事物；过时现象：something or someone that is not in its correct historical or chronological time, especially a thing or person that belongs to an earlier time

n. 时代错误，年代误植(指所叙人、事与时代不符的错误)：an error in chronology in which a person, object, event, etc., is assigned a date or period other than the correct one

音频

List 18

aphorism	['æfərɪzəm] *n.* 格言，警句：a <u>short witty</u> sentence which expresses a general truth or comment
favoritism	['feɪvərɪtɪzəm] *n.* 偏爱，偏袒：the showing of <u>special favor</u>
truism	['truːzəm] *n.* 陈词滥调：an idea or expression that has been <u>used by many people</u>
altruism	['æltruɪzəm] *n.* 利他主义，无私：<u>unselfish</u> regard for or devotion to the welfare of others
cronyism	['krouniːzəm] *n.* 任人唯亲，对好朋友的偏袒：<u>favoritism</u> shown to old <u>friends</u> without regard for their qualifications
paroxysm	['pærəksɪzəm] *n.* (政治、社会领域的)大动荡：a violent <u>disturbance</u> (as of the political or social order)
modicum	['mɑːdɪkəm] *n.* 少量：a <u>small portion</u>; a limited quantity
compendium	[kəm'pendiəm] *n.* 摘要：a brief <u>summary</u> of a larger work or of a field of knowledge：<u>abstract</u>
odium	['oudiəm] *n.* 憎恶，讨厌：<u>strong dislike</u>, contempt, or aversion
premium	['priːmiəm] *adj.* 高端的：of <u>superior quality or value</u>
encomium	[en'koumiəm] *n.* 赞颂之词：glowing and warmly enthusiastic <u>praise</u>
pandemonium	[ˌpændə'mouniəm] *n.* 喧嚣，骚动：wild uproar or <u>noise</u>

equilibrium [ˌiːkwɪˈlɪbrɪəm] *n.* 均势，平衡：a condition in which opposing forces are equal to one another

delirium [dɪˈlɪrɪəm] *n.* 精神错乱；极度兴奋，发狂：an acute mental disturbance characterized by confused thinking and disrupted attention usually accompanied by disordered speech and hallucinations; frenzied exitement

moratorium [ˌmɔːrəˈtɔːrɪəm] *n.* 延期，暂缓施行：a suspension of activity

effluvium [ɪˈfluːvɪəm] *n.* 难闻的气味：an offensive exhalation or smell

asylum [əˈsaɪləm] *n.* 收容所，保护所：an inviolable place of refuge and protection giving shelter to criminals and debtors/something（as a building）that offers cover from the weather or protection from danger

interregnum [ˌɪntəˈregnəm] *n.* 过渡期：break in continuity

humdrum [ˈhʌmdrʌm] *adj.* 无聊的，乏味的：lacking variety or excitement

conundrum [kəˈnʌndrəm] *n.* 无法解决的问题，迷：a paradoxical, insoluble, or difficult problem; a dilemma

spectrum [ˈspektrəm] *n.* 光谱；范围：a broad sequence or range of related qualities, ideas, or activities

tantrum [ˈtæntrəm] *n.* 勃然大怒，发脾气：a fit of bad temper

momentum [moʊˈmentəm] *n.* 动力；冲力，势头：impetus of a physical object in motion; impetus of a nonphysical process, such as an idea or a course of events

pseudonym [ˈsuːdənɪm] *n.* 假名，笔名：a fictitious name

paean [ˈpiːən] *n.* 欢乐颂，赞扬：a joyous song or hymn of praise, tribute, thanksgiving, or triumph

glean	[gliːn] *v.* 收集：to collect bit by bit
mean	[miːn] *adj.* 卑贱的：ignoble; base *adj.* 吝啬的：giving or sharing as little as possible
protean	['prəʊtiən] *adj.* 善变的；多才多艺的：displaying great diversity or variety; versatile
patrician	[pə'trɪʃn] *n.* 贵族，名门望族：a man or woman of high birth or social position *adj.* 贵族的，地位高的：of high birth, rank, or station
quotidian	[kwəʊ'tɪdiən] *adj.* 每日的；平凡的：everyday; commonplace
guardian	['gɑːrdiən] *n.* 保护者，捍卫者：The guardian of something is someone who defends and protects it.
plebeian	[plə'biːən] *adj.* 平民的，社会下层的：belonging to the class of people of low social or economic rank
stygian	['stɪdʒiən] *adj.* 极阴暗的：extremely dark, gloomy, or forbidding
bohemian	[bəʊ'hiːmiən] *n.* 特立独行之人：a person (as an artist) who has an unconventional life-style that often reflects protest against or indifference to convention
draconian	[drə'kəʊniən] *adj.* 极其残酷的；十分严厉的：exceedingly harsh; very severe
sectarian	[sek'teriən] *adj.* 狭隘的：not broad or open in views or opinions
egalitarian	[iˌgælɪ'teriən] *adj.* 平等主义的：affirming, promoting, or characterized by belief in equal political, economic, social, and civil rights for all people

138

stentorian	[stenˈtɔːriən] *adj.* 声音洪亮的：extremely <u>loud</u>
pedestrian	[pəˈdestriən] *adj.* 平庸无奇的，令人厌倦的：<u>causing weariness</u>, restlessness, or lack of interest
antediluvian	[ˌæntidɪˈluːviən] *adj.* 非常古老的；过时的：<u>extremely old</u> and <u>antiquated</u>
clan	[klæn] *n.* (有共同爱好的)团体，帮派：a group <u>united by a common interest</u> or common characteristics
pan	[pæn] *vt./n.* 严厉批评：a <u>harsh criticism</u>
deadpan	[ˈdedpæn] *n.* 无趣的，无生气的，不活泼的：marked by <u>impassively</u> matter-of-fact, as in style, behavior, or expression
veteran	[ˈvetərən] *n.* 老兵；有丰富经验的人：an old soldier; one having <u>knowledge</u> or ability gained <u>through long experience</u> *adj.* 经验丰富的，资深的：having or showing exceptional <u>knowledge</u>, <u>experience</u>, or skill in a field of endeavor
diocesan	[daɪˈɑːsɪsn] *adj.* 主教管辖区的：of or relating to a <u>diocese</u>
partisan	[ˈpɑːrtəzn] *n.* 有偏见的人 *adj.* 偏袒的：inclined to favor <u>one side</u> over another
charlatan	[ˈʃɑːrlətən] *n.* 骗子，装懂的人：a person who makes elaborate, <u>fraudulent</u>, and often voluble claims to skill or knowledge; a quack or fraud
cosmopolitan	[ˌkɑːzməˈpɑːlɪtən] *adj.* 有世界性眼光的，包容的：having <u>worldwide</u> rather than limited or provincial scope or bearing
spartan	[ˈspɑːrtn] *adj.* 简朴的，节约的：marked by <u>simplicity</u>, frugality, or avoidance of luxury and comfort

gargantuan	[gɑːrˈɡæntʃuən] *adj.* 巨大的：tremendous in size, volume, or degree
wan	[wæn] *adj.* 苍白的，病态的：suggestive of poor health
sodden	[ˈsɑːdn] *adj.* 湿透的：containing, covered with, or thoroughly penetrated by water *vt.* 使…湿透：to wet thoroughly with liquid
embolden	[ɪmˈboʊldən] *vt.* 鼓励，使大胆：to instill with boldness or courage
beholden	[bɪˈhoʊldən] *adj.* 欠他人人情的：owing something, such as gratitude, to another
spleen	[spliːn] *n.* 怒气，怨恨：feelings of anger or ill will often suppressed
careen	[kəˈriːn] *vi.* 蹒跚而行，不稳地行走：to lurch or swerve while in motion
screen	[skriːn] *n.* 掩护物，屏障：something that shelters, protects, or hides
green	[ɡriːn] *adj.* 无经验的：deficient in training, knowledge, or experience
preen	[priːn] *vt.* 打扮修饰：to dress or groom (oneself) with elaborate care
ken	[ken] *n.* 视野范围：the range of vision
liken	[ˈlaɪkən] *vt.* 显示相似，把…比作：to see, mention, or show as similar; compare
hearken	[ˈhɑːrkən] *vi.* 倾听，关注：to give respectful attention
crestfallen	[ˈkrestfɔːlən] *adj.* 垂头丧气的，沮丧的：dispirited and depressed; dejected
sullen	[ˈsʌlən] *adj.* 闷闷不乐的：causing or marked by an atmosphere lacking in cheer
regimen	[ˈredʒɪmən] *n.* (政治上的)统治：lawful control over the affairs of a political unit (as a nation)

140

| acumen | ['ækjəmən] *n.* 不同寻常的洞察力和鉴别力：exceptional discernment and judgment especially in practical matters |

| ripen | ['raɪpən] *v.* 使成熟，变成熟：to make or become ripe or riper |

| dampen | ['dæmpən] *vt.* 抑制，压抑(感情、精力等)，泼冷水：to check or diminish the feeling, activity or vigor of |

| barren | ['bærən] *adj.* 不产生结果的，无效的：producing no results; unproductive |
| | *adj.* 贫瘠的：deficient in production of vegetation and especially crops |

| moth-eaten | ['mɔːθ,iːtn] *adj.* 过时的：having passed its time of use or usefulness |

| enlighten | [ɪn'laɪtn] *vt.* 使知道，启发：to give information to; inform or instruct |

| hearten | ['hɑːrtn] *vt.* 给予鼓励，鼓舞：to give strength, courage, or hope to; encourage |

| dishearten | [dɪs'hɑːrtn] *vt.* 使沮丧，使失去信心：to cause to lose spirit or morale |

| hasten | ['heɪsn] *vt.* 促进：to speed up; accelerate |

| glisten | ['glɪsn] *vi.* 闪光：to shine by reflection with a sparkling luster |

| hard-bitten | [hɑːrd'bɪtn] *adj.* 顽强的，经受得住困境、压力的：able to withstand hardship, strain, or exposure |

| leaven | ['levn] *vt.* 在…中加入轻松、活泼或变更的因素：to mingle or permeate with some modifying, alleviating, or vivifying element |

| haven | ['heɪvn] *n.* 安全的地方：a place of safety |

| maven | ['meɪvn] *n.* 专家：one who is experienced or knowledgeable: expert |

141

craven	[ˈkreɪvn] *adj.* 非常懦弱的，因胆小而遭人鄙视的：lacking the least bit of courage；contemptibly fainthearted
doyen	[ˈdɔɪən] *n.* 有经验的人，资深人士，老司机：a person considered to be knowledgeable or uniquely skilled as a result of long experience in some field of endeavor
brazen	[ˈbreɪzn] *adj.* 蛮横大胆的，厚颜无耻的：marked by contemptuous boldness *v.* 大胆自信地去面对或从事：to face or undergo with bold self-assurance
wizen	[ˈwaɪzn] *v.* （使）凋谢，（使）枯萎：to become dry, shrunken, and wrinkled often as a result of aging or of failing vitality *adj.* 凋谢的，枯萎的：shriveled or dried up
cozen	[ˈkʌzn] *v.* 诱骗：to mislead by means of a petty trick or fraud; deceive
condign	[kənˈdaɪn] *adj.* 应得的，恰当的：deserved, appropriate
deign	[deɪn] *vi.* （不情愿地）屈尊，俯就：to condescend reluctantly and with a strong sense of the affront to one's superiority that is involved
feign	[feɪn] *vt.* 制造假象，装出…的样子：to give a false appearance of
reign	[reɪn] *n.* 统治权：the right or means to command or control others *vi.* 占统治地位或盛行：to be predominant or prevalent
align	[əˈlaɪn] *vt.* 调准，校准：to adjust to produce a proper relationship or orientation
malign	[məˈlaɪn] *adj.* 恶意的：having or showing a desire to cause someone pain or suffering for the sheer enjoyment of it

vt. 诽谤：to <u>utter injuriously</u> misleading or false reports about: speak evil of

benign [bɪˈnaɪn] *adj.* 无害的：<u>not causing</u> or being capable of causing injury or <u>hurt</u>

resign [rɪˈzaɪn] *vt.* 辞职，放弃(职位)：to <u>give up</u> one's job or <u>office</u>

consign [kənˈsaɪn] *vt.* 转交，转移（给他人）：to give, transfer, or deliver into the hands or <u>control of</u> <u>another</u>

impugn [ɪmˈpjuːn] *vt.* 责难，抨击：to <u>attack as false</u> or questionable; challenge in argument

disdain [dɪsˈdeɪn] *vt.* 轻视，鄙视：to look on with <u>scorn</u>

bargain [ˈbɑːrɡən] *n.* 协议：an <u>agreement</u> between parties settling what each gives or receives in a transaction
vi. 讨价还价：to <u>negotiate</u> over the terms of a purchase

constrain [kənˈstreɪn] *vt.* 限制：to force by imposed stricture, <u>restriction</u>, or limitation

detain [dɪˈteɪn] *vt.* 拘留，扣留：to <u>hold</u> or <u>keep</u> in or as if in custody

pertain [pərˈteɪn] *vi.* 有关联：to <u>have a relation</u> or connection; relate

音频

List 19

abstain	[əbˈsteɪn] v. 自我克制，主动戒绝：to refrain from something by one's own choice
distain	[dɪsˈteɪn] vt. 贬损，伤害(某人的)名誉：to cause to lose honor, respect, or reputation
rein	[reɪn] n. 抑制，限制：the act or practice of keeping something（as an activity）within certain boundaries vi. 抑制，控制：to keep from exceeding a desirable degree or level（as of expression）
maudlin	[ˈmɔːdlɪn] adj. 过于感伤的：effusively or tearfully sentimental
purloin	[pɜːrˈlɔɪn] vt. 偷窃：to steal, often in a violation of trust
grin	[grɪn] v. 咧嘴笑，咧嘴笑着表示：to express an emotion（as amusement）by curving the lips upward
chagrin	[ʃəˈgrɪn] n. 沮丧，懊恼：disquietude or distress of mind caused by humiliation, disappointment, or failure
damn	[dæm] vt.（在道德上）谴责：to declare to be morally wrong or evil
condemn	[kənˈdem] vt. 谴责（…为不道德的、邪恶的）：to declare to be reprehensible, wrong, or evil usually after weighing evidence and without reservation
hymn	[hɪm] n. 赞歌，赞美诗：a song of praise or joy v. 赞美：to proclaim the glory of

144

don [dɑːn] *vt.* 穿上：to put on (an article of clothing)

abandon [ə'bændən] *v./n.* 放纵：carefree, freedom from constraint
v. 放弃：to withdraw from often in the face of danger or encroachment

curmudgeon [kɜːr'mʌdʒən] *n.* 脾气坏的、爱抱怨的人：an irritable and complaining person

burgeon ['bɜːrdʒən] *vi.* 迅速成长扩大，蓬勃发展：to grow and expand rapidly; flourish

chameleon [kə'miːliən] *n.* 变色龙，善变的人：a person who dexterously and expediently changes or adopts opinions

paragon ['pærəgɑːn] *n.* 优秀模范：a model of excellence or perfection of a kind; a peerless example
vt. 把…比作；显示相似：to compare with; parallel

jargon ['dʒɑːrgən] *n.* 行业术语：the specialized or technical language of a trade, profession, or similar group

legion ['liːdʒən] *adj.* 大量的：many, numerous

rapscallion [ræp'skæliən] *n.* 流氓，恶棍：a mean, evil, or unprincipled person

champion ['tʃæmpiən] *vt.* 支持：to fight for, defend, or support as a champion

clarion ['klæriən] *adj.* 清楚响亮的：loud and clear

revision [rɪ'vɪʒn] *n.* 修订：he act, process, or result of making different

convulsion [kən'vʌlʃn] *n.* 骚乱：a violent disturbance

apprehension [ˌæprɪ'henʃn] *n.* 忧虑，恐惧：suspicion or fear especially of future evil
n. 理解：the knowledge gained from the process of coming to know or understand something

misapprehension [ˌmɪsæprɪˈhenʃn] *n.* 错误的理解、判断：a failure to understand correctly; a wrong judgement

dissension [dɪˈsenʃn] *n.* 意见不合：difference of opinion; disagreement

aspersion [əˈspɜːrʒn] *n.* 诽谤，中伤：a false or misleading charge meant to harm someone's reputation

incursion [ɪnˈkɜːrʒn] *n.* 入侵：a hostile entrance into a territory

scission [ˈsɪʒən] *n.* 切断，分离，分裂：a division or split in a group or union: schism

profusion [prəˈfjuːʒn] *n.* 丰富，大量：the state of being profuse; abundance

delusion [dɪˈluːʒn] *n.* 错觉，妄想：a false idea

approbation [ˌæprəˈbeɪʃn] *n.* 同意：an expression of warm approval

nullification [ˌnʌlɪfɪˈkeɪʃn] *n.* (尤指法律条文等正式的)废除，废弃：the doing away with something by formal action

ramification [ˌræmɪfɪˈkeɪʃn] *n.* 影响，结果：something that is the result of an action, decision

vocation [voʊˈkeɪʃn] *n.* 职业：the work in which a person is regularly employed

trepidation [ˌtrepɪˈdeɪʃn] *n.* 恐惧，战栗：the emotion experienced in the presence or threat of danger; apprehension

negation [nɪˈɡeɪʃn] *n.* 否定：the opposite or absence of something regarded as actual, positive, or affirmative

revelation [ˌrevəˈleɪʃn] *n.* 爆料，揭示：the act of making known something previously unknown or concealed

146

ratiocination [ˌreɪʃiˌoʊsɪˈneɪʃn] *n.* 推理: the thought processes that have been established as leading to valid solutions to problems

hallucination [həˌluːsɪˈneɪʃn] *n.* 错觉: a false idea or belief

machination [ˌmæʃɪˈneɪʃn] *n.* 诡计: a scheming or crafty action or artful design intended to accomplish some usually evil end

disinclination [ˌdɪsˌɪnklɪˈneɪʃn] *n.* 不喜欢，厌恶，不情愿: a lack of willingness or desire to do or accept something; a lack of willingness or desire to do or accept something

divination [ˌdɪvɪˈneɪʃn] *n.* 预言: the art or practice of foretelling future events by interpreting omens

coronation [ˌkɔːrəˈneɪʃn] *n.* 加冕，加冕礼: the act or ceremony of crowning a sovereign or the sovereign's consort

consternation [ˌkɑːnstərˈneɪʃn] *n.* 惊愕, 恐慌, 恐惧: a state of paralyzing dismay

preoccupation [priˌɑːkjuˈpeɪʃn] *n.* 非常关心，全神贯注: extreme or excessive concern with something

ration [ˈræʃn] *vt.* 按比例分配: to give as a share or portion

conflagration [ˌkɑːnfləˈɡreɪʃn] *n.* 武装冲突，战争: a state of armed violent struggle between states, nations, or groups

deterioration [dɪˌtɪriəˈreɪʃn] *n.* 恶化；堕落: a gradual sinking and wasting away of mind or body

ministration [ˌmɪnɪˈstreɪʃn] *n.* 帮助: the act or process of serving or aiding

sensation [senˈseɪʃn] *n.* 轰动事件: a state of intense public interest and excitement

cessation [seˈseɪʃn] *n.* 终止，暂停: the stopping of a process or activity

affectation	[ˌæfek'teɪʃn] *n.* 虚伪，做作：the act of taking on or displaying an attitude or mode of behavior <u>not natural</u> to oneself or <u>not genuinely felt</u>
imitation	[ˌɪmɪ'teɪʃn] *n.* 仿制品：something that is made to look exactly <u>like something else</u>
precipitation	[prɪˌsɪpɪ'teɪʃn] *n.* 沉积物，尤指降水：something precipitated as a <u>deposit</u> on the earth of hail, mist, <u>rain</u>, sleet, or <u>snow</u> *n.* 仓促：excited and often showy or <u>disorderly speed</u>
palpitation	[ˌpælpɪ'teɪʃn] *n.* (有节奏的)舒张收缩：a rhythmic <u>expanding and contracting</u>
incantation	[ˌɪnkæn'teɪʃn] *n.* 咒语：a spoken word or set of words believed to have <u>magic power</u>
deportation	[ˌdiːpɔːr'teɪʃn] *n.* 放逐：the <u>removal from a country</u> of an alien whose presence is unlawful or prejudicial
salutation	[ˌsæljuː'teɪʃn] *n.* 赞扬：a formal expression of <u>praise</u>
privation	[praɪ'veɪʃn] *n.* 缺乏，穷困：<u>lack</u> of what is needed for existence
deprivation	[ˌdeprɪ'veɪʃn] *n.* 匮乏：the condition of being deprived; <u>privation</u>
faction	['fækʃn] *n.* 派系：<u>a party</u> or group (as within a government) <u>that is often contentious</u> or self-seeking
infraction	[ɪn'frækʃn] *n.* 违背，违犯：a <u>failure to uphold the requirements</u> of law, duty, or obligation
predilection	[ˌpredl'ekʃn] *n.* 爱好，偏袒：a partiality or <u>dis-position</u> in <u>favor</u> of something
valediction	[ˌvælɪ'dɪkʃn] *n.* 告别词：an <u>address</u> or statement of <u>farewell</u> or leave-taking

affliction [əˈflɪkʃn] *n.* 痛苦，悲伤，折磨：a state of great suffering of body or mind

friction [ˈfrɪkʃn] *n.* 摩擦：the rubbing of one object or surface against another

n. 冲突，不和：the clashing between two persons or parties of opposed views

conviction [kənˈvɪkʃn] *n.* 深信，确信：the state of being convinced

n. 证明有罪：state of being found or proved guilty

sanction [ˈsæŋkʃn] *vt.* 批准，同意，认可：to make valid or binding usually by a formal procedure (as ratification)

compunction [kəmˈpʌŋkʃn] *n.* 焦虑，内疚，良心不安：anxiety arising from awareness of guilt

discretion [dɪˈskreʃn] *n.* 谨慎：the quality of being discreet; circumspection

n. 自制，节制：the checking of one's true feelings and impulses when dealing with others

demolition [ˌdeməˈlɪʃn] *n.* 破坏，毁坏：the act or process of wrecking or destroying, especially destruction by explosives

volition [vəˈlɪʃn] *n.* 意志，自愿选择的行为：the act or power of making one's own choices or decisions

apparition [ˌæpəˈrɪʃn] *n.* 鬼魂，幽灵：a ghostly figure

disquisition [ˌdɪskwɪˈzɪʃn] *n.* 专题论文：a systematic search for the truth or facts about something

supposition [ˌsʌpəˈzɪʃn] *n.* 猜想，推测：an opinion or judgment based on little or no evidence

petition [pəˈtɪʃn] *n.* 请愿，正式的申请；申请书：a solemn supplication or request to a superior authority; an entreaty *v.* (尤指正式地)请求：to make a request, especially a formal written one

partition [pɑːrˈtɪʃn] *n.* 分割，划分：the act or process of dividing something into parts

convention [kənˈvenʃn] *n.* 常规，习俗：general agreement on or acceptance of certain practices or attitudes

n. 大会，集会：a coming together of a number of persons for a specified purpose

commotion [kəˈmoʊʃn] *n.* 骚乱：an agitated disturbance

inception [ɪnˈsepʃn] *n.* 开端，开始：an act, process, or instance of beginning

prescription [prɪˈskrɪpʃn] *n.* 规定，传统的规矩：something prescribed as a rule; especially an inherited or established way of thinking, feeling, or doing

retribution [ˌretrɪˈbjuːʃn] *n.* 报偿，报应：the dispensing or receiving of reward or punishment especially in the hereafter

prosecution [ˌprɑːsɪˈkjuːʃn] *n.* 实行，执行：the doing of an action

circumlocution [ˌsɜːrkəmləˈkjuːʃn] *n.* 冗长：the use of too many words to express an idea

restitution [ˌrestɪˈtuːʃn] *n.* 补偿，赔偿：a making good of or giving an equivalent for some injury

summon [ˈsʌmən] *vt.* 召集，召唤：to call together

sermon [ˈsɜːrmən] *n.* 布道，说教：public speech usually by a member of the clergy for the purpose of giving moral guidance or uplift

canon [ˈkænən] *n.* 准则，标准：a basis for judgment; a standard or criterion

n. 真经，正典：the authentic works of a writer

150

boon [buːn] *n.* 恩惠，福利：benefit, favor
adj. 喜欢集体行动的：likely to seek or enjoy the company of others

tycoon [taɪˈkuːn] *n.* 大亨，巨头：a person of rank, power, or influence in a particular field

balloon [bəˈluːn] *v.* 迅速增加：to increase rapidly

lampoon [læmˈpuːn] *n.* 讽刺：a harsh satire usually directed against an individual

croon [kruːn] *v.* 低声歌唱或说话：to sing or speak in a gentle murmuring manner

oxymoron [ˌɑːksɪˈmɔːrɑːn] *n.* 矛盾修饰法：a combination of contradictory or incongruous words

jettison [ˈdʒetɪsn] *vt.* 丢弃，投弃：to cast overboard or off

simpleton [ˈsɪmpltən] *n.* (缺乏常识的)笨蛋：a person lacking in common sense; a stupid person

glutton [ˈɡlʌtn] *n.* 贪吃者：a person who eats or consumes immoderate amounts of food and drink

halcyon [ˈhælsiən] *adj.* 宁静的，平静的：free from storms or physical disturbance

blazon [ˈbleɪzn] *vt.* 使知名：to make known openly or publicly
v. 修饰，装扮：to make more attractive by adding something that is beautiful or becoming

discern [dɪˈsɜːrn] *v.* 识别，辨别差异：to perceive with the eyes or intellect; detect

音频

List 20

scorn	[skɔːrn] *vt.* 轻蔑，鄙视，不屑：to reject or dismiss as contemptible or unworthy
timeworn	[ˈtaɪmˌwɔːrn] *adj.* 陈腐的：hackneyed, stale
careworn	[ˈkerwɔːrn] *adj.* 忧心忡忡的，焦虑的：showing the effect of grief or anxiety
shopworn	[ˈʃɑːpwɔːrn] *adj.* 陈旧的：worn-out, as from overuse: trite
adjourn	[əˈdʒɜːrn] *vi.* 延期，休会：to suspend a session indefinitely or to another time or place
spurn	[spɜːrn] *vt.* 摈弃，拒绝：to reject with disdain or contempt
taciturn	[ˈtæsɪtɜːrn] *adj.* 沉默寡言的，话少的：temperamentally disinclined to talk
shun	[ʃʌn] *vt.* 避开，避免：to avoid deliberately; keep away from
fawn	[fɔːn] *vi.* 阿谀奉承：to seek favor or attention by flattery and obsequious behavior
placebo	[pləˈsiːboʊ] *n.* 安慰性的事物：something of no intrinsic remedial value that is used to appease or reassure another
fiasco	[fiˈæskoʊ] *n.* 大失败：a complete failure
bravado	[brəˈvɑːdəʊ] *n.* 假装勇敢：a pretense of bravery *n.* 虚张声势：blustering swaggering conduct
crescendo	[krəˈʃendoʊ] *n.* （渐强之后到达的）顶峰：the peak of a gradual increase

152

vertigo [ˈvɜːrtɪɡoʊ] *n.* 眩晕：a dizzy confused state of mind

embargo [ɪmˈbɑːrɡoʊ] *n.* 贸易禁止令：a legal prohibition on commerce

imbroglio [ɪmˈbroʊlioʊ] *n.* 困境，复杂的局面：an intricate or complicated situation

boo [ˈbuː] *n./v.* 嘘（以表示不满或嘲笑）：a sound uttered to show contempt, scorn, or disapproval

typo [ˈtaɪpoʊ] *n.* 打字错误：an error in typed or typeset material

tyro [ˈtaɪroʊ] *n.* 新手，业余爱好者：a beginner in learning；novice

virtuoso [ˌvɜːrtʃuˈoʊsoʊ] *n.* 艺术鉴赏家，专家：a person with masterly skill or technique in the arts
adj. 经验丰富的，技艺精湛的：having or showing exceptional knowledge, experience, or skill in a field of endeavor

veto [ˈviːtoʊ] *n./vt.* 否决，禁止：to forbid or prohibit authoritatively

madcap [ˈmædkæp] *n.* 热爱冒险的人：a person who seeks out very dangerous or foolhardy adventures with no apparent fear
adj. 大胆的，鲁莽的：behaving or acting impulsively or rashly; foolishly adventurous or bold

mishap [ˈmɪshæp] *n.* 不幸之事：an unfortunate accident

overlap [ˌoʊvərˈlæp] *v.* （与…）部分重叠：to occupy the same area in part

kidnap [ˈkɪdnæp] *vt.* 绑架勒索：to seize and detain by unlawful force or fraud and often with a demand for ransom

scrap [skræp] *vt.* 抛弃：to get rid of as useless or unwanted

entrap [ɪn'træp] *vt.* 诱骗：to lure into a compromising statement or act

sap [sæp] *vt.* 削弱：to weaken or exhaust the energy or vitality of
n. 健康，活力：active strength of body or mind

wiretap ['waɪərtæp] *n./vt.* 偷听，窃听：to tap a telephone or telegraph wire in order to get information

peep [piːp] *n.* 一瞥：a brief and sometimes furtive look

creep [kriːp] *vi./n.* 缓慢地行进：to go very slowly

steep [stiːp] *adj.* 陡峭的：having an incline approaching the perpendicular
adj. 过分的，过高的：going beyond a normal or acceptable limit in degree or amount

sidestep ['saɪdstep] *vt.* （通过逃避而）不遵守：to avoid having to comply with （something）especially through cleverness

showmanship ['ʃoʊmənʃɪp] *n.* 擅于表演、展示的技巧：the skill or ability of an individual who has a sense or knack for dramatically effective presentation

nip [nɪp] *n.* 少量：a very small amount
vi. 小口吃喝：to sip （alcoholic liquor）in small amounts

strip [strɪp] *vt.* 脱衣，剥去：to remove clothing, covering, or surface matter from

skimp [skɪmp] *adj.* 缺乏的，不足的：less plentiful than what is normal, necessary, or desirable
vi. 节省花费，吝啬：to give insufficient or barely sufficient attention or effort to or funds for

limp	[lɪmp] *adj.* 柔软的，松散的：lacking firm texture, substance, or structure *adj.* 软弱的，没有精神的：lacking strength or firmness; weak or spiritless *vi.* 跛行，艰难地行走：to move or proceed haltingly or unsteadily
scrimp	[skrɪmp] *vi.* 节俭：to avoid unnecessary waste or expense
primp	[prɪmp] *v.* 精心打扮：to dress, adorn, or arrange in a careful or finicky manner
plump	[plʌmp] *adj.* 丰满的：well-rounded and full in form *v.* 鼎力支持，赞不绝口：to give full support or praise
slump	[ˈslʌmp] *n./v.* 暴跌，急剧下降：to decline suddenly as in activity, prices, or business
coop	[kuːp] *vt.* 监禁，困于…之中：to confine in a restricted and often crowded area
eavesdrop	[ˈiːvzdrɑːp] *vi.* 偷听：to listen secretly to the private conversation of others
sop	[sɑːp] *n.* 安慰物：something yielded to placate or soothe
carp	[kɑːrp] *vi.* 对小事吹毛求疵，挑剔，表现不满：to make often peevish criticisms or objections about matters that are minor, unimportant, or irrelevant; to express dissatisfaction, pain, or resentment usually tiresomely
warp	[wɔːrp] *vt.* 曲解：to change so much as to create awrong impression or alter the meaning of
usurp	[juˈzɜːrp] *vt.* 篡夺，篡位：to seize and hold (the power or rights of another, for example) by force and without legal authority

155

clasp [klæsp] *n./v.* 紧握：the act or manner of <u>holding</u>

forebear [ˈfɔːrber] *n.* 祖先：a person from whom one is descended; <u>an ancestor</u>

gear [gɪr] *v.* 调整（以配合）：to <u>adjust</u> or adapt so as to make suitable

swear [swer] *vi.* 咒骂：to use profane or obscene language: <u>curse</u>
v. 宣誓：to promise or pledge with a solemn <u>oath</u>; vow

vulgar [ˈvʌlgər] *adj.* 粗俗的，无教养的：morally <u>crude</u>, undeveloped, or unregenerate

verisimilar [ˌverɪsɪˈmɪlər] *adj.* 似乎真实的：<u>appearing to be true</u> or real

vernacular [vərˈnækjələr] *n.* 方言：a <u>nonstandard language</u> or dialect of a place, region, or country
adj. 非正式的，口头的：used in or <u>suitable for speech</u> and not formal writing

secular [ˈsekjələr] *adj.* 世俗的，尘世的：of or relating to the <u>worldly or temporal</u>

jocular [ˈdʒɑːkjələr] *adj.* 搞笑的，欢乐的：characterized by <u>joking, playful</u>

cellular [ˈseljələr] *adj.* 多孔的：containing cavities; having a <u>porous</u> texture

insular [ˈɪnsələr] *adj.* （观念、想法等）孤立狭隘的，村里来的：being, having, or reflecting a <u>narrow provincial viewpoint</u>

mar [mɑːr] *vt.* 破坏，削弱：to <u>impair</u> the soundness, perfection, or integrity of; spoil

jabber [ˈdʒæbər] *vi.* 快而不清楚地说：to <u>talk rapidly, indistinctly</u>, or unintelligibly

limber [ˈlɪmbər] *adj.* 可塑的，柔软的：capable of being shaped: <u>flexible</u>

somber [ˈsɑːmbər] *adj.* 悲伤的，不愉快的：causing or marked by an atmosphere <u>lacking in cheer</u>

156

encumber	[ɪn'kʌmbər] *vt.* 阻碍；妨碍：to impede or hamper the function or activity of
lumber	['lʌmbər] *vi.* 笨拙地行动：to walk or move with heavy clumsiness *vt.* 使负担(从而拖累)：to place a weight or burden on
slumber	['slʌmbər] *vi.* 睡着：to be in a state of sleep
sober	['soʊbər] *adj.* 严肃的：marked by seriousness, gravity, or solemnity of conduct or character *adj.* 节制的：given to or marked by restraint in the satisfaction of one's appetites
dodder	['dɑːdər] *vi.* 蹒跚，颤巍巍地行进：to progress feebly and unsteadily
embroider	[ɪm'brɔɪdər] *v.* (时常伴有夸张和想象内容地)详细说明：to give an elaborate account of, often with florid language and fictitious details
solder	['sɑːdər] *v.* 连接，联合：to join or unite
meander	[mi'ændər] *vi.* 闲逛，漫步：to move aimlessly and idly without fixed direction
squander	['skwɑːndər] *vt.* 浪费：to spend wastefully or extravagantly
engender	[ɪn'dʒendər] *vt.* 引起，使发展：to cause to exist or to develop
surrender	[sə'rendər] *vt.* 交出，放弃，投降：to give (something) over to the control or possession of another usually under duress
tender	['tendər] *vt.* 正式提出：to offer formally *adj.* 考虑周到的，关心同情的：having or marked by sympathy and consideration for others
faultfinder	[fɔːlt'faɪndər] *n.* 吹毛求疵的人：one who is given to petty criticism and constant complaint
blunder	['blʌndər] *n.* 过失 *v.* 犯错误：a gross error or mistake resulting usually from stupidity, ignorance, or carelessness

157

founder	[ˈfaʊndər] *n.* 建立者：<u>one</u> that founds or establishes *vi.* 完败：to <u>fail utterly</u>
flounder	[ˈflaʊndər] *vi.* 笨拙地行动，挣扎：to proceed or <u>act clumsily</u> or ineffectually
sunder	[ˈsʌndər] *vt.* 分裂，分离：to <u>break apart</u> or in two
asunder	[əˈsʌndər] *adv.* 分离地：<u>apart</u> from each other in position
leer	[lɪr] *vi.* 一瞥，斜眼看：to cast a <u>sidelong</u> glance
veneer	[vəˈnɪr] *vt.* 粉饰（不好的东西）：to cover over with a veneer; especially to <u>conceal</u>（as a <u>defect</u> of character）under a superficial and deceptive attractiveness
domineer	[ˌdɑːməˈnɪr] *vt.* 专制统治：to exercise arbitrary or <u>overbearing control</u>
pioneer	[ˌpaɪəˈnɪr] *n.* 扩荒者，先驱者：one of the <u>first to</u> <u>settle</u> in a territory *vt.* 开创，创造：to <u>open up</u>（an area）or prepare（a way）
sneer	[snɪr] *vt.*（轻蔑地）嘲笑：to speak in a <u>scornful</u>, contemptuous, or derisive manner
peer	[pɪr] *n.* 同等地位的人，同辈：a person who has <u>equal</u> standing with others *vi.* 好奇地凝视：to <u>look</u> narrowly or curiously
veer	[vɪr] *v.*（使）转向，（使）改变航线：to <u>change</u> <u>direction</u> or course
defer	[dɪˈfɜːr] *v.* 推迟，延期：to put off; <u>postpone</u>; defer *vi.* 遵从：to submit to another's wishes, opinion, or governance usually through deference or <u>respect</u>

proffer [ˈprɑːfər] *v./n.* 献出，提供：to <u>offer</u> for acceptance; tender

pilfer [ˈpɪlfər] *vt.* 偷窃：to <u>steal</u> stealthily in small amounts

meager [ˈmiːgər] *adj.* 贫乏的：<u>deficient</u> in quantity, fullness, or extent; scanty

badger [ˈbædʒər] *vt.* 不断纠缠或骚扰：to <u>harass</u> or annoy <u>persistently</u>

swagger [ˈswægər] *vi.* 自夸，吹嘘：to <u>boast</u>, brag

harbinger [ˈhɑːrbɪndʒər] *n.* 预言者：one that <u>presages</u> or foreshadows what is to come

linger [ˈlɪŋgər] *vi.* 磨蹭，闲荡：to <u>proceed slowly</u>; saunter

malinger [məˈlɪŋgər] *vi.* 装病以逃避工作：to <u>pretend</u> or exaggerate incapacity or <u>illness</u> (as to avoid duty or work)

warmonger [ˈwɔːrmʌŋgər] *n.* 好战者：one who <u>urges</u> or attempts to stir up <u>war</u>

cipher [ˈsaɪfər] *n.* 密码：a method of transforming a text in order to <u>conceal</u> its meaning

音频

List 21

decipher	[dɪˈsaɪfər] *vt.* 破译：to read or interpret (ambiguous, obscure, or illegible matter) *vt.* 对…有清晰想法，理解，解读：to have a clear idea of
usher	[ˈʌʃər] *v.* 开启：to mark or observe the beginning of
weather	[ˈweðər] *vt.* 安全度过（危机等），经受住：to come through (something) safely
tether	[ˈteðər] *vt.* (用绳、铁链)拴系，束缚：to fasten or restrain by or as if by a tether
bellwether	[ˈbelweðə] *n.* 领导者，带头人：one that takes the lead or initiative
wither	[ˈwɪðər] *vi.* 枯萎，凋谢：to become dry and sapless
smother	[ˈsmʌðər] *vt.* 抑制（表达、说出），压制：to refrain from openly showing or uttering
cavalier	[ˌkævəˈlɪr] *n.* 有骑士精神的人，彬彬有礼的绅士：one having the spirit or bearing of a knight; a courtly gentleman *adj.* 傲慢的：having a feeling of superiority that shows itself in an overbearing attitude
hanker	[ˈhæŋkər] *v./n.* 向往，渴望：to have a strong or persistent desire: yearn
tinker	[ˈtɪŋkər] *v.* 乱修，乱调整：to handle thoughtlessly, ignorantly, or mischievously

160

stickler [ˈstɪklər] *n.* 坚持细节的人，一丝不苟的人：one who insists on exactness or completeness in the observance of something

gossamer [ˈgɑːsəmər] *n.* 虚无缥缈的东西：something light, delicate, or insubstantial

adj. 轻薄的；薄弱的：extremely light, delicate, or tenuous

hammer [ˈhæmər] *v.* 屡次重申：to make repeated efforts especially：to reiterate an opinion or attitude

stammer [ˈstæmər] *vi.* 口吃，结巴：to speak with involuntary pauses or repetitions

retainer [rɪˈteɪnər] *n.* 家仆：a person attached or owing service to a household

practitioner [prækˈtɪʃənər] *n.* 职业人士：one who practices a profession

taper [ˈteɪpər] *v.* 逐渐减少，减弱：to diminish or lessen gradually

damper [ˈdæmpər] *n.* 抑制因素：one that deadens, restrains, or depresses

hamper [ˈhæmpər] *vt.* 阻碍：to restrict the movement of by bonds or obstacles：impede

tamper [ˈtæmpər] *v.* 恶意窜改，损害：to handle thoughtlessly, ignorantly, or mischievously

dapper [ˈdæpər] *adj.* 衣冠整洁的：being strikingly neat and trim in style or appearance

deter [dɪˈtɜːr] *vt.* 吓住，威慑：to prevent or discourage from acting, as by means of fear or doubt

teeter [ˈtiːtər] *vi.* 蹒跚，不稳定地行走：to move unsteadily：wobble

vi. 犹豫不决：to show uncertainty about the right course of action

perimeter [pəˈrɪmɪtər] *n.* 边界，界限：the line or relatively narrow space that marks the outer limit of something

161

reconnoiter	[ˌrekəˈnɔɪtə] *vt.* 侦察，勘查：to make a preliminary inspection of, especially in order to gather military information
falter	[ˈfɔːltər] *vi.* 蹒跚：to walk unsteadily *vi.* 犹豫，踌躇：to be unsteady in purpose or action, as from loss of courage or confidence
palter	[ˈpɔːltər] *vi.* 欺骗；讨价还价：to act insincerely or deceitfully; haggle, chaffer
welter	[ˈweltər] *n.* 混乱，动乱：a state of wild disorder
filter	[ˈfɪltər] *v.* 过滤：to pass through a filter
kilter	[ˈkɪltər] *n.* 平衡：state of being or fitness
banter	[ˈbæntər] *n./v.* 幽默、打趣的（地）谈话：good humored, playful conversation
inter	[ɪnˈtɜːr] *vt.* 埋葬：to place in a grave or tomb
pointer	[ˈpɔɪntər] *n.* 忠告，建议：a useful suggestion or hint usually from an expert
disinter	[ˌdɪsɪnˈtɜːr] *vt.* （从墓地里）掘出：to take out of the grave or tomb
saunter	[ˈsɔːntər] *vi.* 闲逛，漫步：to travel by foot for exercise or pleasure
barter	[ˈbɑːrtər] *v.* 以物换物：to trade (goods or services) without the exchange of money
fester	[ˈfestər] *v.* 感染，溃烂，腐烂：to infect, inflame, or corrupt
sequester	[sɪˈkwestər] *vt.* 使隔绝，分离：to set apart: segregate
bolster	[ˈboʊlstər] *n./v.* 支撑(物)：a structural part designed to eliminate friction or provide support or bearing *vt.* 鼓励，使有精力：to give a boost to
foster	[ˈfɔːstər] *vt.* 促进，鼓励，培养：to help the growth or development of *vt.* 养育：to bring to maturity through care and education

| filibuster | ['fɪlɪbʌstər] *n./v.* 拖延议事：the use of obstructionist tactics, especially prolonged speechmaking, for the purpose of delaying legislative action |

| bluster | ['blʌstər] *v.* 狂妄自大地大声说：to speak in a loudly arrogant or bullying manner
n. 喧闹的状态：a state of noisy, confused activity |

| cluster | ['klʌstər] *n.* 一群人：a usually small number of persons considered as a unit |

| fluster | ['flʌstər] *vt.* 使慌乱：to put into a state of agitated confusion |

| lackluster | ['læklʌstər] *adj.* 黯淡无光泽的：lacking brightness, luster, or vitality |

| flatter | ['flætər] *vt.* 拍马屁，奉承，讨好：to praise excessively especially from motives of self-interest |

| fetter | ['fetər] *vt.* 束缚：to restrain from motion, action, or progress |

| splutter | ['splʌtər] *vi.* 急切而不清楚地说：to speak hastily and incoherently, as when confused or angry |

| mutter | ['mʌtər] *vi.* 低声抱怨：to murmur complainingly or angrily |

| beleaguer | [bɪ'liːgər] *vt.* 包围，围攻：to surround (as a fortified place) with armed forces for the purpose of capturing or preventing commerce and communication |

| aver | [ə'vɜːr] *v.* 声称为真：to state as a fact usually forcefully |

| palaver | [pə'lævər] *n.* 对话，交流：an exchange of views for the purpose of exploring a subject or deciding an issue
vi. 闲聊：to talk profusely or idly |

pushover	[ˈpʊʃoʊvər] *n.* 容易做的工作；易如反掌的事：something that is easy to do
maneuver	[məˈnuːvər] *vt.* 巧妙地操纵：to guide with adroitness and design or to bring about or secure as a result of skillful management
outmaneuver	[ˌaʊtməˈnuːvər] *vt.* 以策略取胜：to overcome (an opponent) by artful, clever maneuvering
cower	[ˈkaʊər] *vi.* 畏缩：to cringe in fear
glower	[ˈɡlaʊər] *vi.* 怒目而视：to look or stare with sullen annoyance or anger
soothsayer	[ˈsuːθseɪər] *n.* 预言家：one who predicts future events or developments
debonair	[ˌdebəˈner] *adj.* 无忧无虑的，不在乎的：having or showing freedom from worries or troubles *adj.* 风度翩翩的：having or showing very polished and worldly manners
nadir	[ˈneɪdɪr] *n.* 最低点：the lowest point
belabor	[bɪˈleɪbər] *vt.* (当众) 严厉批评：to criticize harshly and usually publicly *vt.* 就…作过度的说明，喋喋不休：to explain or insist on excessively
harbor	[ˈhɑːrbər] *vt.* 心怀，牢记：to keep in one's mind or heart
succor	[ˈsʌkər] *vt.* 救援，援助：to go to the aid of
rancor	[ˈræŋkər] *n.* 敌意，深仇：a bitter deep-seated ill will
candor	[ˈkændər] *n.* 坦白，直率，诚挚：unreserved, honest, or sincere expression
vendor	[ˈvendər] *n.* 小贩，商贩：one that sells or vends
ardor	[ˈɑːrdər] *n.* 狂热：strong enthusiasm or devotion; zeal

164

abhor	[əbˈhɔːr] *vt.* 深恶痛绝，极度厌恶: to regard with <u>extreme repugnance</u>
metaphor	[ˈmetəfər] *adj.* 暗喻: a word or phrase for one thing that is <u>used to refer to another thing</u> in order to show or suggest that they are <u>similar</u>
anterior	[ænˈtɪriər] *adj.* 前面的: coming <u>before</u> in time or development
clamor	[ˈklæmər] *n.* 喧闹，喧哗，噪声: <u>loud</u>, confused, and usually <u>inharmonious</u> sound
humor	[ˈhjuːmə] *vt.* 迎合，迁就: to <u>comply with</u> the wishes or ideas of
donor	[ˈdoʊnər] *n.* 捐赠人，给体: one that gives, <u>donates</u>, or presents something
torpor	[ˈtɔːrpər] *n.* 缺乏兴趣: <u>lack of interest</u> or concern *n.* (肉体或精神上的)迟钝，懒散: physical or mental <u>inertness</u>
stupor	[ˈstuːpər] *n.* 迟钝，麻痹，无知觉: a condition of greatly dulled or completely <u>suspended sense</u> or sensibility
furor	[ˈfjʊrɔːr] *n.* 喧闹，狂怒；激动，狂热: a general commotion; public disorder or uproar; a state of <u>intense excitement</u> or ecstasy
censor	[ˈsensər] *vt.* 审查并删除不良的东西: to <u>examine</u> in order to suppress or <u>delete</u> anything considered objectionable
precursor	[priːˈkɜːrsər] *n.* 先驱者，先导: one that pre- cedes and indicates the approach of another
predecessor	[ˈpredəsesər] *n.* 前任，先辈: a person who has <u>previously occupied</u> a position or office to which another has succeeded

intercessor	[ˌɪntərˈsesər] *n.* 调停者：one that <u>mediates</u>
spectator	[ˈspekteɪtər] *n.* 观众，目击者，旁观者：one who looks on or <u>watches</u>
mentor	[ˈmentɔːr] *vt.* 教导，指导：to <u>give advice</u> and instructionregarding the course or process to be followed
impostor	[ɪmˈpɑːstər] *n.* 冒充者，骗子：one that <u>assumes false identity</u> or title for the purpose of deception
languor	[ˈlæŋgər] *n.* 懒惰：physical or mental <u>inertness</u> *n.* 衰弱：<u>weakness</u> or <u>weariness</u> of body or mind
endeavor	[ɪnˈdevər] *n.* 努力，奋斗：a <u>conscientious or concerted effort</u> toward an end *vt.* 努力做，拼搏：to <u>devote serious and sustained effort</u>
concur	[kənˈkɜːr] *vi.* 同意：to express <u>agreement</u> *vi.* 同一时间发生、存在：to occur or exist at the <u>same time</u> *vi.* 团结合作：to participate or assist in a <u>joint</u> effort to accomplish an end
grandeur	[ˈgrændʒər] *n.* 宏伟，壮丽：the quality or condition of being <u>grand</u>; magnificence
poseur	[poʊˈzɜːr] *n.* 故作姿态、不真诚的人：an <u>affected</u> or <u>insincere</u> person
connoisseur	[ˌkɑːnəˈsɜːr] *n.* 鉴赏家（尤指艺术领域）：a person who enjoys <u>with discrimination</u> and <u>appreciation</u> of subtleties and details especially in matters of culture or art *n.* 专家：a person with a <u>high level of knowledge</u> or skill in a field
hauteur	[hɔːˈtɜːr] *n.* 傲慢，自大：haughtiness in bearing and attitude; <u>arrogance</u>

augur	['ɔːɡər] *n.* 预言家 *vt.* 预言：to tell of or describe beforehand
blur	[blɜːr] *v.* (使)变得朦胧，(使)变得不清楚：to (cause sth. to) become vague or indistinct *vt.* 使不易理解：to make (something) unclear to the understanding
slur	[slɜːr] *n.* 耻辱：a mark of guilt or disgrace *vt.* 疏忽，忽略：to slide or slip over without due mention, consideration, or emphasis
demur	[dɪ'mɜːr] *n./vi.* 表示异议，反对：to voice opposition; object
murmur	['mɜːrmər] *vi.* 低声抱怨，发牢骚：to complain in low mumbling tones; grumble
scour	['skaʊər] *vt.* 搜查：to look through (as a place) carefully or thoroughly in an effort to find or discover something
dour	['daʊər] *adj.* 严厉的：harsh and threatening in manner or appearance
misdemeanour	[ˌmɪsdɪ'miːnər] *n.* 轻罪：a crime less serious than a felony
detour	['diːtʊr] *n.* 偏离正常标准：a turning away from a course or standard
spur	[spɜːr] *n.* 刺激物：something that arouses action or activity *n.* 支撑物：a structure that holds up or serves as a foundation for something else *vt.* 刺激，激励：to incite or stimulate

167

List 22

fracas	[ˈfreɪkəs] *n.* 争吵，吵闹：a <u>physical dispute</u> between opposing individuals or groups；a rough and often <u>noisy fight</u> usually involving several people
ethics	[ˈeθɪks] *n.* 道德规范：rules or standards <u>governing</u> the <u>conduct</u> of a person or the members of a profession
scads	[skædz] *n.* 许多，大量：a <u>large number</u> or quantity
debris	[dəˈbriː] *n.* 废墟：<u>discarded</u> or <u>useless</u> <u>material</u>
hubris	[ˈhjuːbrɪs] *n.* 狂妄自大：<u>exaggerated pride</u> or <u>self-confidence</u>
parenthesis	[pəˈrenθəsɪs] *n.* 间断：an <u>interruption</u> of continuity; an interval
synthesis	[ˈsɪnθəsɪs] *n.* 合成，综合：the <u>combination</u> of parts or elements so as to form a whole
symbiosis	[ˌsɪmbaɪˈoʊsɪs] *n.* 共生关系：the <u>living together</u> in more or less intimate association or close union of two dissimilarl
prognosis	[prɑːgˈnoʊsiːz] *n.* 预兆：a declaration that <u>something will happen in the future</u>
synopsis	[sɪˈnɑːpsɪs] *n.* 摘要，概要：a brief <u>outline</u> or general view; an <u>abstract</u> or a <u>summary</u>
catharsis	[kəˈθɑːrsiːs] *n.* 情绪的宣泄、释放：<u>elimination of a complex</u> by bringing it to consciousness and affording it expression

doldrums	['douldrəmz] *n.* 低迷，中断：a state or period of <u>inactivity</u>, stagnation, or slump
kudos	['ku:dɑ:s] *n.* 名望，名声：<u>fame</u> and renown resulting from an act or achievement *n.* 夸奖，赞扬：<u>acclaim or praise</u> for exceptional achievement
ethos	['i:θɑ:s] *n.* 道德准则：the <u>code of good conduct</u> for an individual or group
apropos	[ˌæprə'pou] *adj.* 相关的：being both <u>relevant</u> and opportune *prep.* 关于，有关：<u>having to do with</u>
jitters	['dʒɪtərz] *n.* 紧张，不安：a sense of <u>panic</u> or extreme <u>nervousness</u>
encompass	[ɪn'kʌmpəs] *vt.* 组成，包含：to constitute or <u>include</u>
surpass	[sər'pæs] *vt.* 超越，强于：to <u>become better</u>, greater, or stronger than
trespass	['trespəs] *vi.* 非法侵入；违反，冒犯：to <u>enter unlawfully</u> upon the land of another; to commit an <u>offense</u>
harass	['hærəs] *vt.* 烦扰：to <u>irritate</u> or torment per-sistently
crass	[kræs] *adj.* 粗俗的，愚钝的：so crude and <u>unrefined</u> as to be in discrimination and sensibility
embarrass	[ɪm'bærəs] *vt.* 使尴尬：to cause to <u>experience</u> a state of self-conscious <u>distress</u>
canvass	['kænvəs] *v.* 仔细检查，详尽讨论：to <u>examine carefully or discuss thoroughly</u>; scrutinize *v.* 游说，去(一个地区)的各处或找到(个人)来拉选票或订单：to go through (a region) or go to (persons) to <u>solicit votes or orders</u>

groundless [ˈɡraʊndləs] *adj.* 没有依据的：having no basis in reason or fact

featureless [ˈfiːtʃərləs] *adj.* 缺乏特征的：lacking distinguishing characteristics or features

ruthless [ˈruːθləs] *adj.* 没有怜悯心的，残忍的：having no pity

pitiless [ˈpɪtɪləs] *adj.* 没有同情心的：devoid of or unmoved by pity

feckless [ˈfekləs] *adj.* 无成果的，没有价值的：having no real worth or purpose
adj. 粗心不负责任的：careless and irresponsible

reckless [ˈrekləs] *adj.* 不考虑后果的，大胆鲁莽的：careless of consequences; foolishly adventurous or bold

tactless [ˈtæktləs] *adj.* 不机智的，笨拙的：bluntly inconsiderate or indiscreet

shiftless [ˈʃɪftləs] *adj.* 胸无大志的，懒惰的：lacking in ambition or incentive: lazy

relentless [rɪˈlentləs] *adj.* 残酷的，无情的：showing or promising no abatement of severity, intensity, strength, or pace
adj. 固执的，不肯妥协的：showing no signs of slackening or yielding in one's purpose

bootless [ˈbuːtləs] *adj.* 无用的：useless, unprofitable, futile

restless [ˈrestləs] *adj.* 不平静的：marked by or causing a lack of quiet, repose, or rest

drollness [ˈdroʊlnəs] *n.* 搞笑，逗逼：the amusing quality or element in something

harness [ˈhɑːrnɪs] *vt.* 利用：utilize

regress [rɪˈɡres] *vi.* 退化，恶化：to become worse or of less value

170

digress [daɪˈgres] *v.* 脱离主题：to <u>turn aside</u> especially from the <u>main subject</u> of attention or course of argument

transgress [trænzˈgres] *vt.* 违背；犯错：to <u>fail to keep</u>；to <u>commit an offense</u>

repress [rɪˈpres] *vt.* 镇压：to <u>put down by force</u>, usually before total control has been lost; quell
vt. 阻止(正常的表达、活动或发展等)：to <u>prevent</u> the natural or normal <u>expression</u>, activity, or development of

compress [kəmˈpres] *vt.* 压缩(体积)：to <u>reduce</u> in <u>size</u> or volume as if by squeezing

suppress [səˈpres] *vt.* 用暴力终止，镇压：to <u>put a stop to</u>(something) by the use of <u>force</u>
v. 封锁，删除：to <u>put a stop to</u>(something) by the use of <u>force</u>

buttress [ˈbʌtrɪs] *vt.* 为…提供支撑的证据或者信息：to <u>provide evidence or information for</u> (as a claim or idea)

obsess [əbˈses] *vt.* 迷住；使困扰：to <u>haunt</u> or excessively preoccupy the mind of

assess [əˈses] *v.* 评估(重要性、尺寸、价值等)：to <u>determine</u> the importance, size, or <u>value</u> of
v. 征收费用(如罚款)：to establish or apply as a <u>charge</u> or <u>penalty</u>

prowess [ˈpraʊəs] *n.* 英勇，勇敢：<u>superior</u> strength, <u>courage</u>, or daring, especially in battle

bliss [blɪs] *n.* 极度快乐：extreme happiness; <u>ecstasy</u>

remiss [rɪˈmɪs] *adj.* 疏忽的，不留心的：exhibiting <u>carelessness</u> or slackness

emboss [ɪmˈbɔːs] *vt.* 装饰：to raise the surface of into bosses; especially to <u>ornament with raised work</u>

gloss [glɑːs] *n.* 简短解释：a <u>brief explanation</u> of a difficult or <u>obscure</u> word or expression *v.* 敷衍潦草做事（甚至忽略）: to deal with (a subject or problem) <u>too lightly</u> or not at all

engross [ɪnˈɡroʊs] *vt.* 使全神贯注: to <u>occupy exclu-sively</u>

syllabus [ˈsɪləbəs] *n.* 提纲，摘要；课文、演讲或研究课题的概要或提纲: an outline or a <u>summary</u> of the main points of a text, lecture, or course of study

exodus [ˈeksədəs] *n.* 大批离去: a mass <u>departure</u>

bogus [ˈboʊɡəs] *adj.* 伪造的，假冒的: <u>being such in appearance only</u> and made or manufactured with the intention of committing fraud

nonplus [ˌnɑːnˈplʌs] *vt.* 使迷惑，使困窘: to put at a loss as to what to say, think, or do: <u>perplex</u>

animus [ˈænɪməs] *n.* 敌意: a usually prejudiced and often <u>spiteful</u> or <u>malevolent</u> ill will, enmity

terminus [ˈtɜːrmɪnəs] *n.* 终点，终点站: the final point; the <u>end</u>

viscous [ˈvɪskəs] *adj.* 粘稠的，粘的: <u>viscid</u>; sticky

tremendous [trəˈmendəs] *adj.* 极大的: unusually <u>large</u>

hideous [ˈhɪdiəs] *adj.* 非常丑陋的: exceedingly <u>ugly</u>

outrageous [aʊtˈreɪdʒəs] *adj.* 过分的，难以容忍的: <u>exceed-ing the limits</u> of what is normal or tolerable
adj. 极坏的，极可怕的: enormously or flagrantly <u>bad or horrible</u>

extraneous [ɪkˈstreɪniəs] *adj.* 无关的，不重要的: having <u>no relevance</u>

spontaneous [spɑːnˈteɪniəs] *adj.* 自发的，不经思索的: acting or activated <u>without apparent thought</u> or deliberation

courteous [ˈkɜːrtiəs] *adj.* 礼貌的，谦恭有礼的: marked by <u>polished manners</u>, gallantry, or ceremonial usage of a court

analogous [ə'næləgəs] *adj.* 相似的，可比较的：having qualities in <u>common</u>

amorphous [ə'mɔːrfəs] *adj.* 无固定形状的：having no <u>de-finite</u> form: <u>shapeless</u>

dubious ['duːbiəs] *adj.* 充满不定性的，值得怀疑的：giving rise to <u>uncertainty</u>; <u>questionable</u> or suspect as to true nature or quality

efficacious [ˌefɪ'keɪʃəs] *adj.* 有效的：having the power to <u>produce a desired effect</u>

perspicacious [ˌpɜːrspɪ'keɪʃəs] *adj.* 极敏锐的，有洞察力的：having or showing <u>penetrating mental discernment</u>; clear-sighted

mendacious [men'deɪʃəs] *adj.* 撒谎的，虚假的：telling or containing <u>lies</u>

audacious [ɔː'deɪʃəs] *adj.* 大胆的，(但往往)愚勇的：<u>fear-lessly</u>, often <u>recklessly</u> daring; bold

fallacious [fə'leɪʃəs] *adj.* 谬误的，不合逻辑的：<u>containing</u> or based on a <u>fallacy</u>

contumacious [ˌkɑːntu'meɪʃəs] *adj.* 不服从的，倔强的：<u>stubbornly disobedient</u>; rebellious

tenacious [tə'neɪʃəs] *adj.* 顽固的，不屈不挠的：<u>persistent</u> in maintaining something valued or habitual

pertinacious [ˌpɜːrtn'eɪʃəs] *adj.* 顽固的，固执地坚持的：<u>sticking</u> to an opinion, purpose, or course of action in spite of reason, arguments, or persuasion

rapacious [rə'peɪʃəs] *adj.* 贪婪的：excessively grasping or <u>covetous</u>

veracious [və'reɪʃəs] *adj.* 诚实的，说实话的：being in the habit of <u>telling the truth</u>

voracious [və'reɪʃəs] *adj.* 有很大食量的，贪吃的：having a <u>huge appetite</u>

173

adj. 贪婪的，如饥似渴的：having or marked by an <u>insatiable</u> appetite for an activity or pursuit

loquacious [ləˈkweɪʃəs] *adj.* 话多的：given to fluent or <u>excessive talk</u>

vivacious [vɪˈveɪʃəs] *adj.* 活泼的，快活的：<u>lively</u> in temper, conduct, or spirit

specious [ˈspiːʃəs] *adj.* 似是而非的，欺骗性的：having a <u>false look of truth</u> or genuineness

judicious [dʒuˈdɪʃəs] *adj.* 明智的，慎重的：having or exhibiting sound <u>judgment</u>; <u>prudent</u>

officious [əˈfɪʃəs] *adj.* 多管闲事的：<u>thrusting oneself</u> where one is not welcome or invited

malicious [məˈlɪʃəs] *adj.* 恶意的：given to, marked by, or arising from malice; <u>deliberately harmful</u>

pernicious [pərˈnɪʃəs] *adj.* 有害的：highly <u>injurious</u> or destructive

auspicious [ɔːˈspɪʃəs] *adj.* 好兆头的：pointing <u>toward a happy outcome</u>

meretricious [ˌmerəˈtrɪʃəs] *adj.* 艳俗的，俗气的：attracting attention in a <u>vulgar manner</u>

vicious [ˈvɪʃəs] *adj.* 凶恶的，恶毒的：having or showing the <u>desire to inflict</u> severe pain and suffering on others

precocious [prɪˈkoʊʃəs] *adj.* 早熟的：occurring <u>before the usual</u> or expected time

ferocious [fəˈroʊʃəs] *adj.* 激烈的，爆发性的：marked by <u>bursts of destructive force</u> or intense activity
adj. 凶猛的，残暴的：violently <u>unfriendly or aggressive</u> in disposition

atrocious [əˈtroʊʃəs] *adj.* 极坏的，极其残忍的：<u>extremely wicked</u>, brutal, or cruel

174

tedious	[ˈtiːdiəs] *adj.* 冗长乏味的：tiresome because of length or dullness: boring
fastidious	[fæˈstɪdiəs] *adj.* 挑剔的，极仔细的，追求完美的：possessing or displaying careful, meticulous attention to detail
invidious	[ɪnˈvɪdiəs] *adj.* 惹人反感的：tending to cause discontent, animosity, or envy *adj.* 羡慕嫉妒恨的：having or showing mean resentment of another's possessions or advantages
commodious	[kəˈmoʊdiəs] *adj.* 宽敞舒适的：comfortably or conveniently spacious: roomy
contagious	[kənˈteɪdʒəs] *adj.* 传染的：communicable by contact; catching *adj.* (情绪等) 唤起共鸣的：exciting a similar feeling or reaction in others
prodigious	[prəˈdɪdʒəs] *adj.* 巨大的：impressively great in size, force, or extent; enormous *adj.* 惊人的，了不起的：causing wonder or astonishment
supercilious	[ˌsuːpərˈsɪliəs] *adj.* 高傲的，傲慢的：feeling or showing haughty disdain
punctilious	[pʌŋkˈtɪliəs] *adj.* 注意细节的，一丝不苟的：strictly attentive to minute details of form in action or conduct
abstemious	[əbˈstiːmiəs] *adj.* (吃喝等) 有节制的，节俭的：marked by restraint especially in the consumption of food or alcohol, sparing

音频

ingenious [ɪnˈdʒiːniəs] *adj.* 聪明的，有创造才能的：marked by originality, <u>resourcefulness</u>, and <u>cleverness</u> in conception or execution

euphonious [juːˈfoʊniəs] *adj.* 悦耳的：<u>pleasing</u> or agreeable to the ear

ceremonious [ˌserəˈmoʊniəs] *adj.* 讲究礼节的，庄重的：marked by or showing <u>careful attention to set forms</u> and details

acrimonious [ˌækrɪˈmoʊniəs] *adj.* 刻薄的，充满仇恨的：having or showing <u>deep-seated resentment</u>

parsimonious [ˌpɑːrsəˈmoʊniəs] *n.* 过度节俭的，吝啬的：frugal to the point of <u>stinginess</u>

sanctimonious [ˌsæŋktɪˈmoʊniəs] *adj.* 假装虔诚的：<u>hypocritically pious</u> or devout

harmonious [hɑːrˈmoʊniəs] *adj.* 和谐一致的：having the parts <u>agreeably related</u>

impecunious [ˌɪmpɪˈkjuːniəs] *adj.* 贫穷的：having very little or <u>no money</u>

pious [ˈpaɪəs] *adj.* （信仰上）虔诚的：marked by or showing reverence for deity and <u>devotion to divine worship</u>

impious [ˈɪmpiəs] *adj.* 不敬神的：<u>lacking reverence</u> for holy or sacred matters

copious [ˈkoʊpiəs] *adj.* 丰富的，大量的：large inquantity; <u>abundant</u>

precarious [prɪˈkeriəs] *adj.* 危险的，不稳定的：dangerously lacking in security or stability
adj. 可疑的，不明确的：dependent on uncertain premises

vicarious [vaɪˈkeriəs] *adj.* 代理的，取代的：performed or suffered by one person as a substitute for another or to the benefit or advantage of another

nefarious [nɪˈferiəs] *adj.* 极坏的，邪恶的：flagrantly wicked or impious

multifarious [ˌmʌltɪˈferiəs] *adj.* 多种多样的：being of many and various kinds

gregarious [grɪˈgeriəs] *adj.* 爱社交的：likely to seek or enjoy the company of others
adj. 群居的：tending to group with others of the same kind

hilarious [hɪˈleriəs] *adj.* 非常好笑的：marked by or causing hilarity: extremely funny

opprobrious [əˈproubriəs] *adj.* 辱骂的：expressing contemptuous reproach; scornful or abusive
adj. 臭名昭著的，令人鄙视的：bringing disgrace; shameful or infamous

lugubrious [ləˈguːbriəs] *adj.* (故作夸张的)悲哀的：mournful, dismal, or gloomy, especially to an exaggerated or ludicrous degree

salubrious [səˈluːbriəs] *adj.* 有益健康的：favorable to or promoting health or well-being

imperious [ɪmˈpɪriəs] *adj.* 傲慢的，专横的：arrogantly domineering or overbearing

deleterious [ˌdeləˈtɪriəs] *adj.* 有害的：harmful often in a subtle or unexpected way

laborious [ləˈbɔːriəs] *adj.* 勤奋的：hard-working; industrious *adj.* 费力的：marked by or requiring <u>long, hard work</u>

industrious [ɪnˈdʌstriəs] *adj.* 勤勉的：constantly, regularly, or habitually occupied, <u>diligent</u>

illustrious [ɪˈlʌstriəs] *adj.* 著名的，杰出的：well known and very <u>distinguished</u>

spurious [ˈspjʊriəs] *adj.* 假的，伪造的：<u>lacking authenticity</u> or validity in essence or origin; not genuine

luxurious [lʌgˈʒʊriəs] *adj.* 奢侈的：given to or marked by <u>excessive gratification</u> of one's desires

ostentatious [ˌɑːstenˈteɪʃəs] *adj.* 炫耀卖弄的：marked by or fond of <u>conspicuous</u> or vain glorious and sometimes <u>pretentious</u> display

fractious [ˈfrækʃəs] *adj.* 难以管束的：tending to be troublesome; <u>unruly</u>

rambunctious [ræmˈbʌŋkʃəs] *adj.* 喧闹的，骚乱的：being rough or <u>noisy</u> in a high-spirited way

facetious [fəˈsiːʃəs] *adj.* 喜欢开玩笑的，轻浮的：<u>joking</u> or jesting often inappropriately

seditious [sɪˈdɪʃəs] *adj.* 煽动性的，意在制造混乱的：tending to <u>excite political disorder</u> or insurrection

propitious [prəˈpɪʃəs] *adj.* 吉祥的：<u>favorably</u> disposed : pointing toward a <u>happy outcome</u>

fictitious [fɪkˈtɪʃəs] *adj.* 虚构的：<u>not real</u> and existing only in the imagination

repetitious [ˌrepəˈtɪʃəs] *adj.* 重复的，反复的：<u>repeated many times</u> and therefore boring

adventitious [ˌædvenˈtɪʃəs] *adj.* 外来的，后天的，非内在的：coming from another source and <u>not inherent or innate</u>

surreptitious [ˌsɜːrəpˈtɪʃəs] *adj.* 偷偷摸摸的，保密的：undertaken or done so as to <u>escape being observed</u> or known by others

178

licentious [laɪˈsenʃəs] *adj.* 放荡的，性欲强的：lacking legal or moral restraints; having a strong sexual, desire

tendentious [tenˈdenʃəs] *adj.* 有偏见的：marked by a tendency in favor of a particular point of view: biased

conscientious [ˌkɑːnʃiˈenʃəs] *adj.* 仔细的，一丝不苟的：taking, showing, or involving great care and effort
adj. 有良心的，正直的：governed by or conforming to the dictates of conscience

unpretentious [ˌʌnprɪˈtenʃəs] *adj.* 低调的，谦逊的：lacking pretension or affectation; modest
adj. 坦诚的，自然的：free from any intent to deceive or impress others

contentious [kənˈtenʃəs] *adj.* 引起争论的：likely to cause contention; argumentative
adj. 好争论的，好战的：exhibiting an perverse and wearisome tendency to quarrels and disputes

captious [ˈkæpʃəs] *adj.* 吹毛求疵的，爱挑毛病的：marked by an often ill-natured inclination to stress faults and raise objections

bumptious [ˈbʌmpʃəs] *adj.* 专横傲慢的，自以为是的：having a feeling of superiority that shows itself in an overbearing attitude

obsequious [əbˈsiːkwiəs] *adj.* 谄媚的，奴性的：marked by or exhibiting a fawning attentiveness

devious [ˈdiːviəs] *adj.* 狡猾的：willing to lie and trick people in order to get what is wanted

oblivious [əˈblɪviəs] *adj.* 不知道的，不知情的：lacking conscious awareness; not informed about or aware of something

impervious [ɪmˈpɜːrvɪəs] *adj.* 不可渗透的，不可穿透的：not allowing entrance or passage

adj. 不能被破坏的： not capable of being damaged or harmed

adj. 不为所动的：not capable of being affected or disturbed

noxious [ˈnɑːkʃəs] *adj.* 有害的，有毒的： harmful to living things; injurious to health

adj. 产生强烈厌恶的： causing intense displeasure, disgust, or resentment

scandalous [ˈskændələs] *adj.* 引起反感的，丢脸的：causing intense displeasure, disgust, or resentment

anomalous [əˈnɑːmələs] *adj.* 不普通的，不平常的： being out of the ordinary

libelous [ˈlaɪbələs] *adj.* 恶意中伤的，诽谤的：constituting or including a libel; defamatory

perilous [ˈperələs] *adj.* 危险的：involving potential loss or injury

scurrilous [ˈskɜːrələs] *adj.* 说粗话的：given to the use of vulgar, coarse, or abusive language

callous [ˈkæləs] *adj.* 无同情心的，冷漠的：emotionally hardened; unfeeling

frivolous [ˈfrɪvələs] *adj.* 轻浮的：marked by unbecoming levity

adj. 不重要的：of little weight or importance

fabulous [ˈfæbjələs] *adj.* 幻想中的，不真实的：not real and existing only in the imagination

adj. 极好的：extremely pleasing or successful

nebulous [ˈnebjələs] *adj.* 模糊的：indistinct, vague

meticulous [məˈtɪkjələs] *adj.* 极 为 谨 慎 的 ：marked by extreme or excessive care in the consideration or treatment of details

credulous	[ˈkredʒələs] *adj.* 轻信的，易受骗的：disposed to believe too readily; gullible
sedulous	[ˈsedʒələs] *adj.* 勤奋认真的：involving or accomplished with careful perseverance
scrupulous	[ˈskruːpjələs] *adj.* 正直的：guided by or in accordance with one's sense of right and wrong; principled *adj.* 一丝不苟的：taking, showing, or involving great care and effort
querulous	[ˈkwerələs] *adj.* 抱怨的，爱发牢骚的：habitually complaining
garrulous	[ˈɡærələs] *adj.* 啰嗦的，话多得令人厌烦的：given to excessive and often trivial or rambling talk; tiresomely talkative
infamous	[ˈɪnfəməs] *adj.* 臭名昭著的：having an extremely and deservedly bad reputation
pusillanimous	[ˌpjuːsɪˈlænɪməs] *adj.* 懦弱的，胆小得令人鄙视的：lacking courage and resolution, marked by contemptible timidity
unanimous	[juˈnænɪməs] *adj.* 一致同意的：having the agreement and consent of all
anonymous	[əˈnɑːnɪməs] *adj.* 匿名的：not named or identified
synonymous	[sɪˈnɑːnɪməs] *adj.* 同义的：having the same or a similar meaning
diaphanous	[daɪˈæfənəs] *adj.* 模糊的；非实在的：vague or insubstantial *adj.* （质地精致得）几乎透明的：of such fine texture as to be transparent or translucent
indigenous	[ɪnˈdɪdʒənəs] *adj.* 土产的，本地的：originating and living or occurring naturally in an area or environment *adj.* 与生俱来的，先天的：being a part of the innermost nature of a person or thing

ravenous ['rævənəs] *adj.* 食量大的，贪食的；贪婪的：having a huge appetite; greedy for gratification

heinous ['heɪnəs] *adj.* 可憎的，十恶不赦的：hatefully or shockingly evil, abominable

ominous ['ɑːmɪnəs] *adj.* 凶兆的：of or being an omen, especially an evil one

luminous ['luːmɪnəs] *adj.* 杰出的，重要的：standing above others in rank, importance, or achievement

voluminous [və'luːmɪnəs] *adj.* 卷数多的，大量的，庞大的：having great volume, fullness, size, or number

numinous ['nuːmɪnəs] *adj.* 神秘的，超自然的：having supernatural and mysterious qualities or powers

glutinous ['gluːtənəs] *adj.* 胶状的，粘的：of the nature of or resembling glue

synchronous ['sɪŋkrənəs] *adj.* 同时期的，同步的：having identical period and phase

monotonous [mə'nɑːtənəs] *adj.* 无聊的：tediously uniform or unvarying

pompous ['pɑːmpəs] *adj.* 浮夸的：excessively elevated or ornate
adj. 傲慢的：having or exhibiting self-importance

barbarous ['bɑːrbərəs] *adj.* 野蛮的，凶残的：mercilessly harsh or cruel

ludicrous ['luːdɪkrəs] *adj.* 荒唐的，可笑的：meriting derisive laughter or scorn as absurdly inept, false, or foolish

ponderous ['pɑːndərəs] *adj.* 沉重的：of very great weight

vociferous [vou'sɪfərəs] *adj.* 喧哗的，大叫大嚷的：making, given to, or marked by noisy and vehement outcry

treacherous ['tretʃərəs] *adj.* 背叛的：marked by betrayal of fidelity, confidence, or trust

cantankerous	[kæn'tæŋkərəs] *adj.* 脾气不好的：having or showing a habitually <u>bad temper</u>
onerous	['ɑːnərəs] *adj.* 费时间花心思的：<u>requiring much time, effort,</u> or careful attention
obstreperous	[əb'strepərəs] *adj.* 不听话的，任性的：stubbornly resistant to control; <u>unruly</u>; given to resisting authority or another's control
prosperous	['prɑːspərəs] *adj.* 成功的，繁盛的：marked by <u>vigorous growth</u> and <u>well-being</u> especially economically
boisterous	['bɔɪstərəs] *adj.* 喧嚷的，吵闹的：<u>noisily</u> turbulent
preposterous	[prɪ'pɑːstərəs] *adj.* 荒谬的，不符合常理的：<u>contrary</u> to nature, reason, or <u>common sense</u>
dexterous	['dekstrəs] *adj.* 动作灵活的：<u>ready</u> and <u>skilled</u> in physical movements *adj.* 头脑灵活的：<u>mentally adroit</u> and <u>skillful</u>: clever
chivalrous	['ʃɪvlrəs] *adj.* 有骑士风度的，(尤指对女性)彬彬有礼的：marked by <u>gracious courtesy and high-minded consideration</u>(especially to women)
decorous	['dekərəs] *adj.* 得体端正的：following the established traditions of <u>refined society and good tast</u>
indecorous	[ɪn'dekərəs] *adj.* 不合乎礼节的，不得体的：<u>conflicting with accepted standards</u> of good conduct or good taste
malodorous	[ˌmæl'oʊdərəs] *adj.* 恶臭的：having an <u>unpleasant smell</u>
vigorous	['vɪgərəs] *adj.* 精力旺盛的：having <u>active strength</u> of body or mind
dolorous	['doʊlərəs] *adj.* 忧伤的：causing, marked by, or expressing <u>misery</u> or <u>grief</u>
glamorous	['glæmərəs] *adj.* 迷人的：having an often mysterious or <u>magical power to attract</u>

183

音频

List 24

timorous	[ˈtɪmərəs] *adj.* 胆小的：of a timid disposition: fearful
sonorous	[ˈsɑːnərəs] *adj.* 声音洪亮的：marked by conspicuously full and rich sounds or tones
porous	[ˈpɔːrəs] *adj.* 多孔可渗透的：admitting the passage of gas or liquid through pores or interstices
lustrous	[ˈlʌstrəs] *adj.* 有光泽的：having a shiny surface or finish
covetous	[ˈkʌvətəs] *adj.* 贪婪的，渴求财富的：marked by inordinate desire for wealth or possessions or for another's possessions
infelicitous	[ɪnfɪˈlɪsɪtəs] *adj.* 不愉快的，不幸：not happy; unfortunate *adj.* 不适当的，不合时宜的：not appropriate or well-timed
solicitous	[səˈlɪsɪtəs] *adj.* 为他人操心，体谅他人的：given to or made with heedful anticipation of the needs and happiness of others
duplicitous	[djuːˈplɪsɪtəs] *adj.* 两面派的，奸诈的：given to or marked by cheating and deception
precipitous	[prɪˈsɪpɪtəs] *adj.* 非常陡峭的：very steep, perpendicular, or overhanging in rise or fall *adj.* 匆忙的：acting or done with excessive or careless speed
circuitous	[sərˈkjuːɪtəs] *adj.* 迂回的，不直接的：not being forthright or direct in language or action

ubiquitous [juː'bɪkwɪtəs] *adj.* 无所不在的，普通的：being everywhere at the same time; often observed or encountered

gratuitous [grə'tuːɪtəs] *adj.* 无根据的，无理由的：unnecessary or unwarranted
adj. 无报酬的，免费的：given or granted without return or recompense

momentous [moʊ'mentəs] *adj.* 极重要的：of utmost importance; of outstanding significance or consequence

portentous [pɔːr'tentəs] *adj.* 预兆性的，凶兆的：being or showing a sign of evil or calamity to come

vacuous ['vækjuəs] *adj.* 茫然的，愚蠢的：marked by lack of ideas or intelligence

conspicuous [kən'spɪkjuəs] *adj.* 显而易见的；吸引人的：obvious to the eye or mind; attracting attention

innocuous [ɪ'nɑːkjuəs] *adj.* 无害的：producing no injury
adj. 乏味的，不会引起敌意的：not likely to give offense or to arouse strong feelings or hostility

assiduous [ə'sɪdʒuəs] *adj.* 勤勉的，专心仔细的：marked by careful unremitting attention or persistent application; busy

arduous ['ɑːrdʒuəs] *adj.* 难以做到的，费劲的：hard to accomplish or achieve: difficult

ambiguous [æm'bɪɡjuəs] *adj.* 不确定的：open to more than one interpretation; doubtful or uncertain

contiguous [kən'tɪɡjuəs] *adj.* 接壤的，相邻的：sharing an edge or boundary; touching

mellifluous [me'lɪfluəs] *adj.* （曲调）优美的：smooth and sweet

superfluous [suː'pɜːrfluəs] *adj.* 多余的，过剩的：exceeding what is sufficient or necessary

ingenuous	[ɪnˈdʒenjuəs] *adj.* 天真淳朴的：lacking in cunning, guile, or worldliness
disingenuous	[ˌdɪsɪnˈdʒenjuəs] *adj.* 不真诚的，假惺惺的：not truly honest or sincere
strenuous	[ˈstrenjuəs] *adj.* 有活力的：vigorously active *adj.* 艰巨的，费力的：requiring considerable physical or mental effort
tenuous	[ˈtenjuəs] *adj.* 没有实际内容的，空洞的：having little substance; flimsy
sinuous	[ˈsɪnjuəs] *adj.* 蜿蜒的，迂回的：marked by a long series of irregular curves; not direct
fatuous	[ˈfætʃuəs] *adj.* 愚笨的，昏庸的：complacently or inanely foolish
unctuous	[ˈʌŋktʃuəs] *adj.* 油嘴滑舌的，谄媚的：overly or insincerely flattering
impetuous	[ɪmˈpetʃuəs] *adj.* 冲动的，性急的，轻率的：marked by impulsive vehemence or passion
sumptuous	[ˈsʌmptʃuəs] *adj.* 豪华的，奢侈的：extremely costly, rich, luxurious, or magnificent
presumptuous	[prɪˈzʌmptʃuəs] *adj.* 傲慢的：having a feeling of superiority that shows itself in an overbearing attitude
voluptuous	[vəˈlʌptʃuəs] *adj.* 奢侈逸乐的，沉溺酒色的：given to or spent in enjoyments of luxury, pleasure, or sensual gratifications
virtuous	[ˈvɜːrtʃuəs] *adj.* 品德高尚的，正直的：having or showing virtue, especially moral excellence
tortuous	[ˈtɔːrtʃuəs] *adj.* 转弯抹角的：marked by devious or indirect tactics: crooked, tricky
tempestuous	[temˈpestʃuəs] *adj.* 突然的，剧烈的：marked by sudden or violent disturbance

186

mischievous	[ˈmɪstʃɪvəs] *adj.* 调皮的，淘气的：playful in a naughty or teasing way
consensus	[kənˈsensəs] *n.* 一致同意：general agreement; unanimity
detritus	[dɪˈtraɪtəs] *n.* 废品，碎屑，遗骸：a product of disintegration, destruction, or wearing away: debris
nexus	[ˈneksəs] *n.* 连结：a means of connection *n.* 核心，最重要的地带：a thing or place that is of greatest importance to an activity or interest
offbeat	[ˌɔːfˈbiːt] *adj.* 不平常的：noticeably different from what is generally found or experienced
upbeat	[ˈʌpbiːt] *adj.* 心情好的：having or showing a good mood or disposition *adj.* 给人希望的，象征好运的：having qualities which inspire hope
browbeat	[ˈbraʊbiːt] *vt.* 恐吓：to intimidate by a stern manner or arrogant speech: bully
entreat	[ɪnˈtriːt] *vt.* 恳求：to plead with especially in order to persuade, ask urgently
caveat	[ˈkæviæt] *n.* 警告，告诫：a warning of a specific limitation of something such as information or an agreement
éclat	[eɪˈklæ] *n.* 辉煌成就：brilliant or conspicuous success
turncoat	[ˈtɜːrnkoʊt] *n.* 叛徒：one who switches to an opposing side or party; specifically: traitor
gloat	[gloʊt] *vi.* 幸灾乐祸，自鸣得意：a feeling of great, often malicious, pleasure or self-satisfaction
spat	[spæt] *n.* (小的)争吵：a brief petty quarrel or angry outburst

squat	[skwɑːt] *adj.* 又矮又胖的：being compact and <u>broad in build</u> and often <u>short in stature</u>
enact	[ɪˈnækt] *vt.* 制定或颁布（法律）：to <u>establish</u> by legal and authoritative act
detract	[dɪˈtrækt] *vt.* 贬低，降低价值：to <u>diminish</u> the importance，value，or effectiveness of something *vt.* 使分心：to <u>draw</u> the <u>attention</u> or mind to something else
retract	[rɪˈtrækt] *vt.* 收回，否认：to <u>take back</u>
contract	[ˈkɑːntrækt] *n.* 契约，合同：a <u>binding agreement</u> between two or more persons or parties, especially one that is written and enforceable by law [kənˈtrækt] *v.* 收缩：to <u>reduce</u> in <u>size</u> by drawing together; shrink *v.* 感染疾病：to <u>become affected</u> by a disease or disorder
protract	[prəˈtrækt] *vt.* 延长，拖长：to draw out or <u>lengthen</u> in time; <u>prolong</u>
abstract	[æbˈstrækt] *vt.* 做总结，概括：to make an <u>abstract</u> of, <u>summarize</u> *vt.* 使分心：to draw <u>away</u> the <u>attention</u> of
distract	[dɪˈstrækt] *vt.* 转移（注意力），使分心：to <u>draw</u> or <u>direct</u>（as one's attention）to a <u>different</u> object
extract	[ɪkˈstrækt] *vt.* 用力拔出：to pull or <u>take out</u> forcibly
tact	[tækt] *n.* 机敏，精明，不冒犯：a <u>keen sense</u> of what to do or say in order to <u>maintain good relations</u> with others or avoid offense
disinfect	[ˌdɪsɪnˈfekt] *vt.* 消毒，使无菌：to <u>free from infection</u> especially by destroying harmful microorganisms

abject	[ˈæbdʒekt] *adj.* （地位、身份）悲惨、凄凉的：sunk to or exist-ing in a <u>low state</u> or condition *adj.* 卑微的，讨好的：expressing or offered in a <u>humble</u> and often ingratiating spirit
subject	[ˈsʌbdʒekt] *adj.* 取决于(其他因素)的，受制于：contingent on or <u>under the influence</u> of some later action
deject	[dɪˈdʒekt] *vt.* 使沮丧：to <u>lower the spirits</u> of；<u>dishearten</u>
project	*vt.* 预测，预计：to calculate, estimate, or predict (something in the future), <u>based on present data or trends</u>
deflect	[dɪˈflekt] *vt.* 使偏斜，使转向：to <u>turn aside</u> especially <u>from a straight course</u> or fixed direction
reflect	[rɪˈflekt] *vt.* 反映，显露：to <u>make manifest</u> or apparent: show *vi.* 思考：to <u>think seriously</u>
aspect	[ˈæspekt] *n.* 外表，容貌：<u>appearance</u> to the eye or mind
circumspect	[ˈsɜːrkəmspekt] *adj.* 谨慎的，小心的：<u>careful</u> to consider all circumstances and possible consequences: prudent
prospect	[ˈprɑːspekt] *v.* 探查，勘探：to <u>go into</u> or range over for purposes of <u>discovery</u>
resurrect	[ˌrezəˈrekt] *vt.* 使重生，使复苏：to <u>bring back to life</u>, practice, or activity
dissect	[dɪˈsekt] *vt.* 仔细分析：to <u>examine</u>, <u>analyze</u>, or criticize in <u>minute</u> detail
contradict	[ˌkɑːntrəˈdɪkt] *vt.* 否认，反驳；与…相矛盾：to assert the <u>contrary</u> of; to imply the opposite or a denial of

addict [ə'dɪkt] *v.* 沉溺，上瘾：to devote or surrender (oneself) to something habitually or obsessively
['ædɪkt] *n.* 对某事上瘾的人：a person with a strong and habitual liking for something

indict [ɪn'daɪt] *vt.* 起诉，控告：to accuse of wrong-doing; charge

interdict ['ɪntərdɪkt] *vt.* 禁止：to forbid in a usually formal or authoritative manner

derelict ['derəlɪkt] *adj.* 玩忽职守的，不认真的：lacking a sense of duty; marked by a carelessly easy manner

evict [ɪ'vɪkt] *vt.* 赶出，逐出：to put out (a tenant, for example) by legal process; expel

sacrosanct ['sækrousæŋkt] *adj.* 极为神圣的，不可侵犯的：most sacred or holy

succinct [sək'sɪŋkt] *adj.* 简明的，简洁的：characterized by clear, precise expression in few words

extinct [ɪk'stɪŋkt] *adj.* 灭绝的：no longer existing or living

adjunct ['ædʒʌŋkt] *n.* 附属物，非必须部分：something joined or added to another thing but not essentially a part of it

concoct [kən'kɑːkt] *v.* 捏造，编造：to invent or develop especially in order to deceive someone

obstruct [əb'strʌkt] *vt.* 妨碍，给…制造困难：to impede, retard, or interfere with; hinder; to create difficulty for the work or activity of

construct [kən'strʌkt] *vt.* 建造，建立：to form by assembling or combining parts
vt. 创造，想出：to create or think of by clever use of the imagination

abet [ə'bet] *v.* 鼓励：to actively encourage (as an activity or plan)

190

dulcet	['dʌlsɪt] *adj.* 悦耳的，令人愉悦的：pleasing to the ear; <u>melodious</u>; generally pleasing or agreeable
fleet	[fliːt] *adj.* 迅速的：moving, proceeding, or acting <u>with great speed</u>
meet	[miːt] *adj.* 合适的：precisely adapted to a particular situation, need, or circumstance: <u>very proper</u>
discreet	[dɪ'skriːt] *adj.* （言行）谨慎的：having or showing <u>good judgment and restraint</u> especially in conduct or speech
cachet	[kæ'ʃeɪ] *n.* 同意：an indication of <u>approval</u> carrying great prestige *n.* 威望，声望：<u>prestige</u>; a <u>mark or quality</u>, as of distinction, individuality, or authenticity
epithet	['epɪθet] *n.* 外号，绰号：a <u>descriptive</u> or familiar <u>name</u> given instead of or in addition to the one belonging to an individual; a disparaging or abusive word or phrase
whet	[wet] *vt.* 磨快：to <u>sharpen</u> by rubbing on or with something (as a stone)
plummet	['plʌmɪt] *vi.* 突然下降：to <u>decline suddenly</u> and steeply
gourmet	['gʊrmeɪ] *n.* 美食家：a <u>connoisseur</u> of <u>food</u> and drink
martinet	[ˌmɑːrtn'et] *n.* 纪律严明之人：a <u>strict</u> disciplinarian
trumpet	['trʌmpɪt] *v.* 大声说出或宣告：to <u>make known</u> openly or publicly
beset	[bɪ'set] *vt.* 使苦恼，骚扰：to <u>cause persistent suffering</u> to *vt.* 攻击，袭击：to <u>set upon</u>
onset	['ɑːnset] *n.* 起始，开始：the point at which something <u>begins</u>
cosset	['kɑːsɪt] *vt.* 宠爱：to treat as a pet; <u>pamper</u>

outset	[ˈaʊtset] *n.* 开端，开始：<u>beginning</u>，start
daft	[dæft] *adj.* 不明智的：showing or marked by a <u>lack of good sense</u> or judgment
graft	[grɑːft] *vt.* 移植，移接：to <u>implant</u> (living tissue) <u>surgically</u> or as if surgically
waft	[wɑːft] *v.* 飘荡，漂浮：to <u>float</u> easily and gently, as on the air
deft	[deft] *adj.* 灵巧的，熟练的：characterized by facility and <u>skill</u>
rift	[rɪft] *n.* 分裂，不和：a <u>break</u> in <u>friendly</u> relations *vt.* 使开裂：to cause to split open or <u>break</u>
spendthrift	[ˈspendθrɪft] *n.* 挥霍者，败家子：a person who <u>spends improvidently</u> or wastefully *adj.* 挥霍的，不节俭的：given to <u>spending money freely</u> or foolishly
sift	[ˈsɪft] *v.* 审查：to <u>examine</u> and sort carefully
aloft	[əˈlɔːft] *adv.* 在空中：in the air especially：<u>inflight</u> (as in an airplane)
blight	[blaɪt] *v.* (使)枯萎：to <u>affect</u> (as a plant) with blight *v.* 损害：to <u>impair</u> the quality or effect of
plight	[plaɪt] *n.* 困境：a situation, especially a bad or <u>unfortunate</u> one
slight	[slaɪt] *adj.* 不重要的：<u>deficient in weight</u>, importance

vt. 轻蔑，看不起：to treat with disdain or indifference

vt. 忽略，疏忽：to fail to give proper attention to

forthright [ˈfɔːrθraɪt] *adj.* 直率的，说话率真的：free in expressing one's true feelings and opinions

adj. 直接的，不绕弯子的：free from ambiguity or evasiveness: going straight to the point

airtight [ˈertaɪt] *adj.* 无瑕疵的：having no noticeable weakness, flaw, or loophole

fraught [frɔːt] *adj.* 充满的：full of or accompanied by something

distraught [dɪˈstrɔːt] *adj.* 精神狂乱的，极疯狂的：deeply agitated, as from emotional conflict; insane

overwrought [ˌoʊvərˈrɔːt] *adj.* 十分激动的，非常不安的：being in a state of increased activity or agitation

adj. (装饰、文风等)过分华丽的：elaborately and often excessively decorated

bait [beɪt] *vt.* 引诱：to lead away from a usual or proper course by offering some pleasure or advantage

n. 诱饵：something (as food) used in luring especially to a hook or trap

tacit [ˈtæsɪt] *adj.* 暗示的：implied or indicated (as by an act or by silence) but not actually expressed

elicit [iˈlɪsɪt] *vt.* 激起，唤起：to draw forth or bring out

implicit [ɪmˈplɪsɪt] *adj.* 不言而喻的，心照不宣的：capable of being understood from something else though unexpressed

explicit [ɪkˈsplɪsɪt] *adj.* 表达清晰的：fully revealed or expressed without vagueness, implication, or ambiguity

adj. 成熟的，完全形成的：<u>fully developed</u> or formulated

credit [ˈkredɪt] *n.* 信任，信赖：<u>mental conviction of the truth</u> of some statement or the reality of some being or phenomenon

n. 表扬，赞扬：public <u>acknowledgment or admiration</u> for an achievement

discredit [dɪsˈkredɪt] *vt.* 羞辱，使丧失名誉：to <u>damage in reputation; disgrace</u>

vt. 怀疑，不相信：to think <u>not</u> to be <u>true</u> or <u>real</u>

pundit [ˈpʌndɪt] *n.* 权威人士，专家：a person who gives <u>opinions</u> in an <u>authoritative</u> manner usually through the mass media

counterfeit [ˈkaʊntərfɪt] *adj.* 仿制的，假冒的：made in <u>imitation</u> of something else with intent to deceive

vt. 仿制：to make a <u>fraudulent replica</u> of

forfeit [ˈfɔːrfət] *n.* 罚金：a sum of money to be paid as a <u>punishment</u>

surfeit [ˈsɜːrfɪt] *v./n.* (使)过量，(使)饮食过度：to feed or <u>supply</u> to <u>excess</u>

discomfit [dɪsˈkʌmfɪt] *vt.* 使尴尬：to put into a state of perplexity and <u>embarrassment</u>

vt. 阻碍：to <u>prevent</u> from achieving a goal

flit [flɪt] *vi.* 快速或突然地经过：to <u>pass quickly</u> or abruptly from one place or condition to another

summit [ˈsʌmɪt] *n.* 顶点：the <u>highest point</u>

manumit [ˌmænjuˈmɪt] *vt.* 解放（奴隶）：to <u>release from slavery</u> or bondage

knit [nɪt] *vt.* 连接，联系：to <u>join closely</u>; unite securely

exploit [ˈeksplɔɪt] *n.* 英雄行为：a <u>notable</u> or heroic <u>act</u>

[ɪkˈsplɔɪt] *vt.* 最大程度地利用：to <u>employ</u> to the greatest possible advantage

maladroit [ˌmælə'drɔɪt] *adj.* 笨拙的：lacking or showing a lack of nimbleness in using one's hands

decrepit [dɪ'krepɪt] *adj.* 虚弱的，衰老的，破旧的：weakened, worn out, impaired, or broken down by old age, illness

grit [grɪt] *n.* （面对困难时所表现出来的）毅力：the strength of mind that enables a person to endure pain or hardship

posit ['pɑːzɪt] *vt.* 假定，断定：to assume or affirm the existence of

deposit [dɪ'pɑːzɪt] *n.* 自然积累，沉积，矿藏：a natural accumulation (as of iron ore, coal, or gas)
vt. 存钱：to put in an account

bruit ['bruːt] *vt.* （未经证实地）散播（消息）：to make (as a piece of information) the subject of common talk without any authority or confirmation of accuracy

wit [wɪt] *n.* 机智，智慧：the natural ability to perceive and understand
n. 智者，有智慧的人：a person of exceptional intelligence

outwit [ˌaʊt'wɪt] *vt.* 瞒骗，以智取胜：to surpass in cleverness or cunning; outsmart

exalt [ɪg'zɔːlt] *vt.* 赞扬：to glorify, praise, or honor

heartfelt ['hɑːrtfelt] *adj.* 真心实意的：genuine in feeling

tilt [tɪlt] *v.* 倾斜：to set or cause to be at an angle
n. 倾斜：the act of positioning or an instance of being positioned at an angle

wilt [wɪlt] *vi.* 精神萎靡，憔悴：to feel or exhibit the effects of fatigue or exhaustion

dolt [doʊlt] *n.* 笨蛋：a stupid person

jolt	[dʒoʊlt] *vt.* 惊吓：to cause an unpleasant surprise for
molt	[moʊlt] *vi.* 脱（羽、皮等）：to shed hair, feathers, shell, horns, or an outer layer periodically
revolt	[rɪˈvoʊt] *vt.* 使厌恶，使反感：to fill with disgust or abhorrence
default	[dɪˈfɔːlt] *n.* 不履行义务，玩忽职守：the nonperformance of an assigned or expected action
occult	[əˈkʌlt] *adj.* 难以理解的：not easily apprehended or understood: abstruse, mysterious
tumult	[ˈtuːmʌlt] *n.* 骚动，暴动：a disorderly commotion or disturbance, a riot
exult	[ɪgˈzʌlt] *vi.* 感到欢喜：to rejoice especially with feelings or display of triumph or self-satisfaction
recant	[rɪˈkænt] *vt.* 撤回，放弃，改变：to withdraw or repudiate（a statement or belief）formally and publicly
intoxicant	[ɪnˈtɑːksɪkənt] *n.* 使人陶醉的东西（尤指酒精饮料）：an agent that intoxicates, especially an alcoholic beverage
scant	[skænt] *adj.* 不足的，缺乏的：barely or scarcely sufficient
pedant	[ˈpednt] *n.* 书呆子，墨守成规之人：one who pays undue attention to book learning and formal rules
ascendant	[əˈsendənt] *adj.* 有影响力的，主宰的：dominant in position or influence; superior
abundant	[əˈbʌndənt] *adj.* 大量的：marked by great plenty（as of resources）
redundant	[rɪˈdʌndənt] *adj.* 多余的，冗余的：exceeding what is necessary or normal

verdant	[ˈvɜːrdnt] *adj.* (因长满植物而)翠绿的，郁郁葱葱的：<u>green with vegetation</u>; covered with green growth
mordant	[ˈmɔːrdnt] *adj.* 尖酸刻薄的：<u>biting</u> and <u>caustic</u> in thought, manner, or style
miscreant	[ˈmɪskriənt] *n.* 恶棍，罪犯：one who <u>behaves criminally</u> or viciously
extravagant	[ɪkˈstrævəgənt] *adj.* 挥霍的：given to <u>spending money freely</u> or foolishly *adj.* 过度的，不必要的：going <u>beyond</u> a <u>normal</u> or <u>acceptable limit</u> in degree or amount
penchant	[ˈpentʃənt] *n.* 嗜好，迷恋：a <u>strong</u> and continued <u>inclination</u>
trenchant	[ˈtrentʃənt] *adj.* (言辞)一针见血的：vigorously effective and <u>articulate</u>
disenchant	[ˌdɪsɪnˈtʃænt] *vt.* 使清醒：to <u>free from illusion</u>
sycophant	[ˈsɪkəfænt] *n.* 马屁精：a servile self-seeking <u>flatterer</u>
insouciant	[ɪnˈsuːsiənt] *adj.* 无忧虑的，不在乎的：<u>free from concern</u>, worry, or anxiety
valiant	[ˈvæliənt] *adj.* 勇敢的，英勇的：possessing or acting with <u>bravery</u> or boldness
pliant	[ˈplaɪənt] *adj.* 易弯曲的：<u>easily bent</u> or flexed *adj.* 顺从的：<u>yielding</u> readily to influence or domination
compliant	[kəmˈplaɪənt] *adj.* 顺从的：ready or disposed to comply: <u>submissive</u>
nonchalant	[ˌnɑːnʃəˈlɑːnt] *adj.* 冷漠的：having an air of easy unconcern or <u>indifference</u>
jubilant	[ˈdʒuːbɪlənt] *adj.* 喜悦的：exultingly <u>joyful</u>
vigilant	[ˈvɪdʒɪlənt] *adj.* 警醒的，警惕的：<u>alertly watchful</u> especially to avoid danger

gallant	[ˈɡælənt] *adj.* 英勇的：<u>brave</u>, spirited；nobly <u>chivalrous</u> and often self-sacrificing
supplant	[səˈplænt] *vt.* 排挤，篡夺⋯的位置：to <u>usurp the place of</u>, especially through intrigue or underhanded tactics
slant	[slænt] *n.* （看待问题、思考的）角度，看法：<u>a way of looking</u> at or thinking about something *adj.* 倾斜的：running in a <u>slanting</u> direction
petulant	[ˈpetʃələnt] *adj.* 易怒的，爱发脾气的：<u>easily irritated</u> or annoyed
adamant	[ˈædəmənt] *adj.* 固执的，不可动摇的：<u>unshakable</u> or insistent especially in maintaining a position or opinion, <u>unyielding</u>；<u>inflexible</u>
dormant	[ˈdɔːrmənt] *adj.* 静止的，不活跃的：in a state of rest or <u>inactivity</u>；<u>inoperative</u>；<u>inabeyance</u>
stagnant	[ˈstæɡnənt] *adj.* 停滞不前的：<u>not advancing</u> or developing
pregnant	[ˈpreɡnənt] *adj.* 重要的，意味深长的：weighty or significant；<u>full of meaning</u>
malignant	[məˈlɪɡnənt] *adj.* 恶毒的，邪恶的：having or showing a <u>desire to cause someone pain</u> or suffering for the sheer enjoyment of it; disposed to do evil
poignant	[ˈpɔɪnjənt] *adj.* 令人感伤的：<u>causing</u> a strong feeling of <u>sadness</u>
repugnant	[rɪˈpʌɡnənt] *adj.* 令人厌恶的：<u>arousing</u> disgust or <u>aversion</u>
dominant	[ˈdɑːmɪnənt] *adj.* 处于支配地位的：commanding, <u>controlling</u>, or prevailing over all <u>others</u> *adj.* （基因）显性的：of, relating to, or exerting ecological or <u>genetic dominance</u>
remnant	[ˈremnənt] *n.* 残余，剩余物：something <u>left over</u>

198

resonant	[ˈrezənənt] *adj.* (声音)洪亮的，共鸣的：strong and deep in tone
consonant	[ˈkɑːnsənənt] *adj.* 和谐一致的：being in agreement or harmony; free from elements making for discord
rampant	[ˈræmpənt] *adj.* （植物）生长茂盛的：growing thickly and vigorously
rant	[rænt] *n.* （尤指长时间的）训斥，责骂：a long angry speech or scolding
protuberant	[proʊˈtuːbərənt] *adj.* 隆起的，凸出的：thrusting out from a surrounding or adjacent surface often as a rounded mass
exuberant	[ɪɡˈzuːbərənt] *adj.* 非常高兴的，热情洋溢的：joyously unrestrained and enthusiastic
preponderant	[prɪˈpɑːndərənt] *adj.* 占优势的，更重要的：having superior weight, force, importance, or influence
itinerant	[aɪˈtɪnərənt] *adj.* 巡游的，巡回的：traveling from place to place
aspirant	[əˈspaɪərənt] *n.* 有抱负者，有野心者：one who aspires, as to advancement, honors, or a high position
warrant	[ˈwɔːrənt] *vt.* 批准，认可：to give official acceptance of as satisfactory
errant	[ˈerənt] *adj.* 误入歧途的，犯错误的：straying from the proper course or standards

音频

List 26

aberrant	[æˈberənt] *adj.* 异常的，非常规的：deviating from the usual or natural type
recalcitrant	[rɪˈkælsɪtrənt] *adj.* 顽抗的，不顺从的：marked by stubborn resistance to and defiance of authority or guidance
tyrant	[ˈtaɪrənt] *n.* 暴君：a ruler who exercises absolute power oppressively or brutally
conversant	[kənˈvɜːrsnt] *adj.* 熟悉的：having frequent or familiar association
incessant	[ɪnˈsesnt] *adj.* 无间断的：continuing or following without interruption
blatant	[ˈbleɪtnt] *adj.* (让人生厌地)惹人注目的：very noticeable especially for being incorrect or bad
reluctant	[rɪˈlʌktənt] *adj.* 不情愿的，反感的：feeling or showing aversion, hesitation, or unwillingness
exorbitant	[ɪgˈzɔːrbɪtənt] *adj.* 过度的：exceeding the customary or appropriate limits in intensity, quality, amount, or size
incogitant	[ɪnˈkɑːdʒɪtənt] *adj.* 考虑不周的，不体谅的：thoughtless; inconsiderate
concomitant	[kənˈkɑːmɪtənt] *adj.* 伴随的,同时发生的：present at the same time and place
repentant	[rɪˈpentənt] *adj.* 悔过的：feeling sorrow for a wrong that one has done
extant	[ekˈstænt] *adj.* 现存的：still in existence；not destroyed, lost, or extinct

200

piquant [ˈpiːkənt] *adj.* 令人振奋的：appealingly provocative

truant [ˈtruːənt] *adj./ n./ vi.* 逃避责任（的）；逃避责任者：shirking responsibility; one who shirks duty

savant [sæˈvɑːnt] *n.* 博学之士，学者：a person of learning

relevant [ˈreləvənt] *adj.* 有关系的，重要的：having a bearing on or connection with the matter at hand

observant [əbˈzɜːrvənt] *adj.* 警惕的，警觉的：paying close attention usually for the purpose of anticipating approaching danger or opportunity

flamboyant [flæmˈbɔɪənt] *adj.* 艳丽夺目的，炫耀的，充满装饰的：marked by or given to strikingly elaborate or colorful display or behavior; ornate

buoyant [ˈbuːjənt] *adj.* 心情好的：having or showing a good mood or disposition

cognizant [ˈkɑːgnɪzənt] *adj.* 知道的，意识到的：fully informed; conscious; aware

recumbent [rɪˈkʌmbənt] *adj.* 躺着的：lying down, especially in a position of comfort or rest

incumbent [ɪnˈkʌmbənt] *adj.* 义不容辞的，必须的：imposed as an obligation or duty

complacent [kəmˈpleɪsnt] *adj.* 自满的，自鸣得意的：feeling or showing an often excessive or unjustified satisfaction and pleasure in one's status, possessions, or attainments

beneficent [bɪˈnefɪsnt] *adj.* 仁慈的，好慈善的：characterized by or performing acts of kindness or charity
adj. (对个人或社会)有益的：promoting or contributing to personal or social well-being

magnificent	[mæg'nɪfɪsnt] *adj.* 壮丽的：strikingly beautiful or impressive	
munificent	[mjuː'nɪfɪsnt] *adj.* 慷慨的：very liberal in giving	
reticent	['retɪsnt] *adj.* 沉默不语的：inclined to be silent or uncommunicative in speech	
nascent	['næsnt] *adj.* 新生的：coming or having recently come into existence	
iridescent	[ˌɪrɪ'desnt] *adj.* 五颜六色的：displaying a play of lustrous colors like those of the rainbow	
incandescent	[ˌɪnkæn'desnt] *adj.* 明亮灿烂的：strikingly bright, radiant, or clear *adj.* 热情饱满的，感情强烈的：characterized by glowing zeal	
quiescent	[kwi'esnt] *adj.* 平静的，静止的：being quiet, still, or at rest; inactive	
evanescent	[ˌevə'nesnt] *adj.* 逐渐消失的，短暂的：tending to vanish like vapor	
reminiscent	[ˌremɪ'nɪsnt] *adj.* 怀旧的，引发回忆的：provoking a memory or mental association	
translucent	[træns'luːsnt] *adj.* 透明的：permitting the passage of light; clear, transparent	
dent	[dent] *vt.* (数量、程度上)削弱：to make smaller in amount, volume, or extent	
decadent	['dekədənt] *adj.* 堕落的，腐败的：having or showing lowered moral character or standards *n.* 道德上堕落的人：a person in a condition or process of mental or moral decay	
precedent	['presɪdənt] *n.* 先例，前例：an earlier occurrence of something similar *adj.* 先前的：prior in time, order, arrangement, or significance	
strident	['straɪdnt] *adj.* 刺耳的：characterized by harsh, insistent, and discordant sound	

provident	[ˈprɑːvɪdənt] *adj.* 节俭的：frugal; economical *adj.* 有远见的：having or showing awareness of and preparation for the future
resplendent	[rɪˈsplendənt] *adj.* 华丽辉煌的：shining brilliantly
impudent	[ˈɪmpjədənt] *adj.* 放肆大胆的，无礼的：marked by contemptuous or cocky boldness or disregard of others
prudent	[ˈpruːdnt] *adj.* 明智的：marked by wisdom or judiciousness; wise *adj.* 小心谨慎的，审慎的：marked by circumspection
imprudent	[ɪmˈpruːdnt] *adj.* 不明智的：lacking discretion, wisdom, or good judgment
indigent	[ˈɪndɪdʒənt] *adj.* 贫穷的：lacking money or material possessions
negligent	[ˈneglɪdʒənt] *adj.* 疏忽大意的：failing to give proper attention or care
diligent	[ˈdɪlɪdʒənt] *adj.* 勤勉的，辛勤的：characterized by steady, earnest, and energetic effort: painstaking
intransigent	[ɪnˈtrænzɪdʒənt] *adj.* 不妥协的，固执的：characterized by refusal to compromise or to abandon an extreme position
exigent	[ˈeksɪdʒənt] *adj.* 紧急的：requiring immediate aid or action
indulgent	[ɪnˈdʌldʒənt] *adj.* (对己)放纵的，(对他人)纵容的：showing, characterized by, or given to indulgence
refulgent	[rɪˈfʌldʒənt] *adj.* 辉煌的，灿烂的：shining radiantly; resplendent
effulgent	[ɪˈfʌldʒənt] *adj.* 光辉灿烂的：shining brilliantly; resplendent

plangent ['plændʒənt] *adj.* 凄凉的，哀伤的：having an expressive and especially plaintive quality

tangent ['tændʒənt] *n./adj.* 离题（的），不相关（的）：diverging from an original purpose of course: irrelevant

stringent ['strɪndʒənt] *adj.* 严格的：marked by rigor, strictness, or severity especially with regard to rule or standard

pungent ['pʌndʒənt] *adj.* 辛辣的，讽刺的：marked by the use of wit that is intended to cause hurt feelings

cogent ['koʊdʒənt] *adj.* 令人信服的：appealing forcibly to the mind or reason: convincing
adj. 相关的：pertinent, relevant

insurgent [ɪn'sɜːrdʒənt] *n.* 叛乱分子：one who breaks with or opposes constituted authority or the established order

proficient [prə'fɪʃnt] *adj.* 熟练的，精通的：having or marked by an advanced degree of competence, as in an art, vocation, profession, or branch of learning

omniscient [ɑːm'nɪsiənt] *adj.* 无所不知的：possessed of universal or complete knowledge

obedient [ə'biːdiənt] *adj.* 服从的，顺从的：submissive to the restraint or command of authority

salient ['seɪliənt] *adj.* 显著的，最突出的：standing out conspicuously

emollient [i'mɑːliənt] *adj.* 起缓和作用的：making less intense or harsh

ebullient [ɪ'bʌliənt] *adj.* 热情奔放的：zestfully enthusiastic

lenient ['liːniənt] *adj.* 宽大仁慈的：inclined not to be harsh or strict; merciful, generous, or indulgent

sapient [ˈseɪpiənt] *adj.* 聪明的，有洞察力的：having or showing deep understanding and intelligent application of knowledge

incipient [ɪnˈsɪpiənt] *adj.* 起初的，初现的：beginning to come into being or to become apparent

orient [ˈɔːriənt] *vt.* 使确定方向，使熟悉或适应：to set or arrange in any determinate position especially in relation to the points of the compass; to make familiar with or adjusted to facts, principles, or a situation

transient [ˈtrænʃnt] *adj.* 短暂的，瞬时的：passing with time; transitory

insentient [ɪnˈsentiənt] *adj.* 无感觉的，无知觉的：lacking perception, consciousness, or animation
adj. 一知半解的，略懂的：not having or showing a deep understanding of something

subservient [səbˈsɜːrviənt] *adj.* 奉承的，屈从的：obsequiously submissive

prevalent [ˈprevələnt] *adj.* 流行的，普遍的：widely or commonly occurring, existing, accepted, or practiced

ambivalent [æmˈbɪvələnt] *adj.* （尤指感情、态度）矛盾的：having a mixture of opposing feelings

equivalent [ɪˈkwɪvələnt] *adj./n.* 等价的，相等的：equal in force, amount, or value

redolent [ˈredələnt] *adj.* 芳香的：having or emitting fragrance

indolent [ˈɪndələnt] *adj.* 懒惰的：averse to activity, effort, or movement

insolent [ˈɪnsələnt] *adj.* 粗野的，无礼的：audaciously rude or disrespectful

malevolent [məˈlevələnt] *adj.* 恶意的，恶毒的：having, showing, or arising from intense often vicious ill will, spite, or hatred

turbulent	['tɜːrbjələnt] *adj.* 动荡的：marked by sudden or violent disturbance
truculent	['trʌkjələnt] *adj.* 好战的，好斗的：feeling or displaying eagerness to fight
fraudulent	['frɔːdʒələnt] *adj.* 欺诈的：characterized by, based on, or done by fraud
virulent	['vɪrələnt] *adj.* 有毒的：extremely poisonous or venomous
lament	[lə'ment] *v.* 为…哀悼，表达痛苦或遗憾：to express sorrow or regret; mourn
cement	[sɪ'ment] *n./v.* 粘合，粘合剂：a uniting or binding force or influence
commencement	[kə'mensmənt] *n.* 开始：a beginning; a start *n.* 毕业典礼：the ceremonies or the day for conferring degrees or diplomas
rapprochement	[ˌræprouʃ'mɑːn] *n.* 和睦，友好：establishment of or state of having cordial relations
vehement	['viːəmənt] *adj.* (情感)强烈的，热情的：having or expressing great depth of feeling
clement	['klemənt] *adj.* 宽容的，善良的：tolerant and kind in the judgment of and expectations for others *adj.* 气候温和的：marked by temperatures that are neither too high nor too low
inclement	[ɪn'klemənt] *adj.* (天气等)恶劣的：lacking mildness *adj.* 无情的，严酷的：showing no clemency; unmerciful
implement	['ɪmplɪment] *vt.* 执行，实施：to put into practical effect; carry out
supplement	['sʌplɪmənt] *n./v.* 增补，补充：something that serves to complete or make up for a deficiency in something else

self-abasement	[ˌselfə'beɪsmənt] *n.* 自卑，自谦：degradation or humiliation of oneself
segment	['segmənt] *vt./n.* 分割；部分：to separate into segments
figment	['fɪgmənt] *n.* 虚构的事物，幻觉：something made up or contrived
pigment	['pɪgmənt] *n.* 颜料：a substance that imparts black or white or a color to other materials *vt.* 给…上颜色：to color with or as if with pigment
blandishment	['blændɪʃmənt] *n.* 甜言蜜语，讨好某人的话：something that tends to coax or cajole
compliment	*n.* ['kɑːmplɪmənt] *v.* ['kɑːmplɪment] *n./vt.* 称赞，恭维：an expression of praise, admiration, or congratulation *n.* 敬意，免费赠送的礼物：formal and respectful recognition: honor
foment	[foʊ'ment] *vt.* 助长，煽动：to promote the growth or development of
commitment	[kə'mɪtmənt] *n.* 致力，投入：the state or an instance of being obligated or emotionally impelled *n.* 承诺，表态：the act of revealing one's view of
document	['dɑːkjument] *v.* 证实：to show the existence or truth of by evidence
argument	['ɑːrgjumənt] *n.* 争吵，争论：an often noisy or angry expression of differing opinions *n.* (逻辑上的)论证：a coherent series of statements leading from a premise to a conclusion

音频

List 27

immanent	[ˈɪmənənt] *adj.* 内在的：being a part of the innermost nature of a person or thing
permanent	[ˈpɜːrmənənt] *adj.* 永恒的：<u>continuing or enduring</u> without fundamental or marked change; lasting <u>forever</u>
eminent	[ˈemɪnənt] *adj.* 杰出的：exhibiting eminence especially in standing <u>above others</u> in some quality or position
preeminent	[priˈemɪnənt] *adj.* 优秀的，重要的：having <u>paramount</u> rank, dignity, or importance
pertinent	[ˈpɜːrtnənt] *adj.* 相关的，恰当的：having a clear decisive <u>relevance</u> to the matter in hand
impertinent	[ɪmˈpɜːrtnənt] *adj.* 无关紧要的：<u>not having</u> a clear decisive <u>relevance</u> to the matter in hand *adj.* 粗鲁无礼的，大胆的：given to or characterized by <u>insolent rudeness</u>
proponent	[prəˈpoʊnənt] *n.* 建议者，支持者：one who argues in <u>support</u> of something; an advocate
exponent	[ɪkˈspoʊnənt] *n.* 倡导者，支持者：one that speaks for, represents, or <u>advocates</u>
spent	[spent] *adj.* 精疲力竭的：<u>drained of energy</u> or effectiveness
transparent	[trænsˈpærənt] *adj.* 没有歧义的，清晰易懂的：<u>not subject to misinterpretation</u> or more than one interpretation
indifferent	[ɪnˈdɪfrənt] *adj.* 不感兴趣的，冷漠的：marked

by a <u>lack of interest</u>, enthusiasm, or concern for something

belligerent [bə'lɪdʒərənt] *adj.* 好斗的，好战的：inclined to or exhibiting <u>assertiveness</u>, <u>hostility</u>, or <u>combativeness</u>

inherent [ɪn'hɪrənt] *adj.* 内在的，本质的：involved in the constitution or <u>essential</u> character of something

resent [rɪ'zent] *v.* 怨恨，憎恨：to be <u>angry or upset</u> about (someone or something that you think is unfair)

misrepresent [ˌmɪsˌreprɪ'zent] *vt.* 误传，篡改：to <u>give</u> an incorrect or <u>misleading representation</u> of

consent [kən'sent] *n.* 同意，赞同：the <u>approval</u> by someone in authority for the doing of something

assent [ə'sent] *vi.* 同意：to <u>agree</u> to something especially after thoughtful consideration

dissent [dɪ'sent] *vi.* 持异议，不同意：to <u>differ</u> in opinion
n. 反对正统：<u>departure</u> from a generally <u>accepted</u> theory, opinion, or practice

latent ['leɪtnt] *adj.* 潜在的，不活跃的：present or <u>potential</u> but <u>not evident</u> or active

patent ['peɪtnt] *adj.* 显而易见的，明显的：<u>readily visible</u> or intelligible: obvious

penitent ['penɪtənt] *adj.* 悔过的：feeling or expressing humble or <u>regretful</u> pain or sorrow for sins or offenses

impenitent [ɪm'penɪtənt] *adj.* 不悔悟的：<u>not</u> feeling or expressing humble or <u>regretful</u> pain or sorrow for sins or offenses

content [kən'tent] *vt.* 使满足：to <u>appease</u> the desires of
['kɑːntent] *n.* 主题：a <u>major object of interest</u> or concern (as in a discussion or artistic composition)

malcontent [ˌmælkən'tent] *n.* 不满分子：one who is in active opposition to an established order or government
adj. 不满的：dissatisfied with the existing state of affairs

impotent ['ɪmpətənt] *adj.* 无力的，无能的：lacking in power, strength, or vigor

inadvertent [ˌɪnəd'vɜːrtənt] *adj.* 偶然发生的：happening by chance
adj. 疏忽的，不留意的：marked by unintentional lack of care

inconsistent [ˌɪnkən'sɪstənt] *adj.* 不一致的，矛盾的：not being in agreement or harmony

intermittent [ˌɪntər'mɪtənt] *adj.* 断断续续的：coming and going at intervals, not continuous

fluent ['fluːənt] *adj.* 表达流利的：able to express oneself clearly and well

affluent ['æfluənt] *adj.* 富裕的：having a generously sufficient and typically increasing supply of material possessions

grandiloquent [græn'dɪləkwənt] *adj.* (语言等)浮夸的：a lofty, extravagantly colorful, pompous, or bombastic style, manner, or quality especially in language

congruent ['kɑːŋgruənt] *adj.* 和谐一致的：being in agreement, harmony, or correspondence; congruous
adj. 全等的：coinciding exactly when superimposed

incongruent [ɪn'kɑːŋgruənt] *adj.* 不全等的；不一致的：not coinciding exactly when superimposed; not conforming to the circumstances or requirements of a situation

solvent ['sɑːlvənt] *adj.* 有偿付能力的：able to pay all legal debts *n.* 溶剂：a substance in which <u>another sub-stance is dissolved</u>, forming a solution

circumvent [ˌsɜːrkəmˈvent] *vt.* 躲避，不遵从：to <u>avoid</u> having to <u>comply</u> with（something）especially through cleverness

fervent [ˈfɜːrvənt] *adj.* 充满感情的，热情洋溢的：exhibiting or marked by <u>great intensity of feeling</u>

taint [teɪnt] *vt.* 使（品质）污损：to affect slightly with something <u>morally bad</u> or undesirable

mint [mɪnt] *adj.* 无损坏的：<u>unmarred</u> as if fresh from a mint

pinpoint [ˈpɪnpɔɪnt] *adj.* 非常精确的：located, fixed, or directed with <u>extreme precision</u>
vt. 精确定位或确认：to locate, fix, determine, or <u>identify with precision</u>

blueprint [ˈbluːprɪnt] *vt.* 事先计划：to <u>work out</u> the details of（something）<u>in advance</u>

stint [stɪnt] *vi.* 吝惜，节省：to <u>be</u> sparing or <u>frugal</u>

confront [kənˈfrʌnt] *vt.* 直接对抗，直面：to come <u>face to face</u> with, especially with defiance or hostility

daunt [dɔːnt] *vt.* 使胆怯，吓倒：<u>to lessen the courage</u> or confidence of

haunt [hɔːnt] *vt.* 常去拜访：to visit often; <u>frequent</u>
vt. 不断地想起，萦绕心头：to come to mind continually; <u>obsess</u>

taunt [tɔːnt] *vt.* 嘲弄性质疑，挑衅：to reproach or <u>challenge</u> in a mocking or insulting manner: <u>jeer at</u>

vaunt [vɔːnt] *vi.* 吹嘘：to speak <u>boastfully</u>

blunt [blʌnt] *vt.* 使变钝：to make <u>less sharp</u> or definite
adj. 直率的：being or characterized by <u>direct</u>, <u>brief</u>, and potentially rude speech or manner

| paramount | [ˈpærəmaʊnt] *adj.* 最重要的：of chief concern or importance |

| tantamount | [ˈtæntəmaʊnt] *adj.* 等价的，与…相等的：equivalent in value, significance, or effect |

| surmount | [sərˈmaʊnt] *vt.* 战胜，获得胜利：to achieve a victory over |

| stunt | [stʌnt] *vt.* 阻碍（成长）：to hinder the normal growth, development, or progress of |

| bigot | [ˈbɪgət] *n.* 固执己见者，有偏见的人：a person obstinately devoted to his own opinions and prejudices |

| riot | [ˈraɪət] *n.* 喧闹，暴乱：public violence, tumult, or disorder |

| patriot | [ˈpeɪtriət] *n.* 爱国者：one who loves his or her country and supports its authority and interests |

| jot | [dʒɑːt] *vt.* 简要记录：to write briefly or hurriedly |

| zealot | [ˈzelət] *n.* 狂热者：a zealous person; especially a fanatical partisan |

| clot | [klɑːt] *n.* 密集的一群：a number of things considered as a unit
v. 凝结：to turn from a liquid into a substance resembling jelly |

| pilot | [ˈpaɪlət] *adj.* 初步的，试验性的：serving as a tentative model for future experiment or development
vt. 带领通过：lead or conduct over a usually difficult course |

| parrot | [ˈpærət] *vt.* （机械地）模仿，复制：to repeat or imitate, especially without understanding |

| apt | [æpt] *adj.* 恰当的，合适的：exactly suitable; appropriate
adj. 聪明的：keenly intelligent and responsive |

| adapt | [əˈdæpt] *v.* 修改，使（适应）：to modify according with the changing circumstances |

212

| rapt | [ræpt] *adj.* 狂喜的，狂热的：experiencing or marked by overwhelming usually <u>pleasurable</u> <u>emotion</u> |

| inept | [ɪˈnept] *adj.* 愚笨的，荒谬的：displaying a <u>lack</u> <u>of judgment</u>, sense, or reason
adj. 不称职的，无能力的：generally <u>incompetent</u> |

| nondescript | [ˈnɑːndɪskrɪpt] *adj.* 平凡的，不吸引人的：<u>lacking distinctive</u> or <u>interesting</u> qualities |

| manuscript | [ˈmænjuskrɪpt] *n.* 手稿：a book, document, or other composition <u>written by hand</u> |

| preempt | [priˈempt] *vt.* 预先占有：to appropriate, <u>seize</u>, or take for oneself <u>before others</u> |

| unkempt | [ˌʌnˈkempt] *adj.* 凌乱的，无序的：<u>lacking in order</u>, neatness, and often cleanliness |

| contempt | [kənˈtempt] *n.* 蔑视，鄙视：open dislike for someone or something considered <u>unworthy of</u> <u>one's concern or respect</u> |

| exempt | [ɪgˈzempt] *vt.* 使免除：to <u>release</u> or deliver from some <u>liability</u> or requirement to which others are subject |

| dart | [dɑːrt] *vi.* 突然移动，猛冲，狂奔：to move <u>suddenly</u> and rapidly
n. 公开侮辱：an act or expression showing scorn and usually <u>intended to hurt another's feelings</u> |

| counterpart | [ˈkaʊntərpɑːrt] *n.* (地位、功能)对等的人或物：one having the <u>same function or characteristics</u> as another |

| thwart | [θwɔːrt] *vt.* 阻挠：to <u>oppose</u> successfully |

| stalwart | [ˈstɔːlwərt] *adj.* 坚定的：<u>firm</u> and <u>resolute</u> |

| disconcert | [ˌdɪskənˈsɜːrt] *vt.* 使不安：to <u>disturb</u> the composure of |

inert [ɪˈnɜːrt] *adj.* (人)懒惰缺乏活力的；(物品)惰性的：sluggish in action or motion; deficient in active properties

assert [əˈsɜːrt] *vt.* 断言，肯定地说出：to state or declare positively and often forcefully or aggressively

subvert [səbˈvɜːrt] *vt.* 颠覆：to overturn or overthrow from the foundation

advert [ədˈvɜːrt] *vi.* 引起注意；提到：to call attention; refer

divert [daɪˈvɜːrt] *vt.* 使转向：to turn from one course or use to another: deflect

vt. 使消遣：to cause (someone) to pass the time agreeably occupied

convert [kənˈvɜːrt] *vt.* 改变，转化：to alter the physical or chemical nature or properties of especially in manufacturing

overt [oʊˈvɜːrt] *adj.* 明显的，公开的：open and observable; not hidden, concealed, or secret

covert [ˈkoʊvɜːrt] *adj.* 隐蔽的，秘密的：not openly shown, engaged in, or avowed

skirt [skɜːrt] *vt.* 绕行，避开：to go around or keep away from in order to avoid danger or discovery

flirt [flɜːrt] *vi.* 调情：to behave amorously without serious intent

escort [ɪˈskɔːrt] *vt.* 同行，护送：to go along with in order to provide assistance, protection, or companionship

exhort [ɪgˈzɔːrt] *vt.* 敦促，力劝：to urge by strong, often stirring argument, admonition, advice, or appeal

rapport [ræˈpɔːr] *n.* 和睦，友好：a friendly relationship marked by ready communication and mutual understanding

purport [ˈpɜːrpɔːrt] *v.* 声称，打算：to state as a fact usually forcefully

consort [kənˈsɔːrt] *v.* 结交：to come or be together as friends

retort [rɪˈtɔːrt] *n.* （尤指机智的）回应，回答：something spoken or written in reaction especially to a question, especially a quick, witty, or cutting reply

contort [kənˈtɔːrt] *vt.* 扭曲：to twist, wrench, or bend severely out of shape

distort [dɪˈstɔːrt] *vt.* 扭曲，歪曲：to twist out of the true meaning or proportion

extort [ɪkˈstɔːrt] *vt.* 勒索：to obtain from a person by force, intimidation, or undue or illegal power

curt [kɜːrt] *adj.* 言词简略的，直接（以至显得粗鲁）的：being or characterized by direct, brief, and potentially rude speech or manner
adj. 言简意赅的：marked by the use of few words to convey much information or meaning

blurt [blɜːt] *vt.* 突然说出，冲动地说：to utter abruptly and impulsively

court [kɔːrt] *vt./n.* 追求，献殷勤：to seek the affections of

bombast [ˈbɑːmbæst] *n.* 夸大的言辞：grandiloquent, pompous speech or writing

cast [kæst] *vt.* 提出：to put forth, give off, to place as if by throwing
v. 抛弃：to get rid of as useless or unwanted

abreast [ə'brest] *adj.* 熟知的：up to a particular standard or level especially of knowledge of recent developments

fast [fæst] *n.* 绝食；斋戒：an act of abstaining from food

adj. 忠诚的：firm in one's allegiance to someone or something

音 频

steadfast	[ˈstedfæst] *adj.* 坚定的，忠诚的：firm in belief, determination, or adherence
blast	[blæst] *n.* 爆炸：an explosion or violent detonation *vt.* 炸裂，爆破：to cause to break open or into pieces by or as if by an explosive *vt.* 斥责，抨击：to criticize harshly and usually publicly
iconoclast	[aɪˈkɑːnəklæst] *n.* 特立独行的人：a person who does not conform to generally accepted standards or customs
manifest	[ˈmænɪfest] *adj.* 显然的，明显易懂的：clearly apparent to the sight or understanding; obvious *v.* 显现，显露：to make evident or certain by showing or displaying
ingest	[ɪnˈdʒest] *vt.* 摄入，咽下：to take into the body by the mouth for digestion or absorption
jest	[dʒest] *n.* 轻浮的态度，戏谑：a frivolous mood or manner
earnest	[ˈɜːrnɪst] *adj.* 严肃认真的：characterized by or proceeding from an intense and serious state of mind, grave
crest	[krest] *n.* 顶部，浪尖，山顶：the top, as of a hill or wave
arrest	[əˈrest] *n./v.* 停止：the stopping of a process or activity; to bring to a standstill

217

v. 逮捕：to take or keep under one's control by authority of law

v. 吸引（某人）注意力：to hold the attention of as if by a spell

wrest [rest] *vt.* 辛苦地获得：to gain with difficulty by or as if by force, violence, or determined labor

detest [dɪ'test] *v.* 厌恶：to dislike (someone or something) very strongly

attest [ə'test] *vt.* 证实，为…作证：to give evidence or testimony to the truth or factualness of

gist [dʒɪst] *n.* 要点：the main point or part

anarchist ['ænərkɪst] *n.* 反抗权威的人：a person who rebels against any authority, established order, or ruling power

list [lɪst] *v.* （使）倾斜：to set or cause to be at an angle

jingoist ['dʒɪŋɡoʊɪst] *n.* 极端爱国激进分子（通常表现为好战的对外政策）：extreme chauvinism or nationalism marked especially by a belligerent foreign policy

exhaust [ɪɡ'zɔːst] *vt.* 耗尽：to consume entirely: to make complete use of

robust [roʊ'bʌst] *adj.* 精力充沛的；强壮的，健康的：full of health and strength

gust [ɡʌst] *n.* 情感爆发：a sudden intense expression of strong feeling

august [ɔː'ɡʌst] *adj.* 威严的，庄重的：having or showing a formal and serious or reserved manner

oust [aʊst] *vt.* 驱逐：to drive or force out

boycott ['bɔɪkɑːt] *vt.* 联合抵制，拒绝参与：to engage in a concerted refusal to have dealings with (as a person, store, or organization) usually to express disapproval or to force acceptance of certain conditions

juggernaut	[ˈdʒʌgərnɔːt] *n.* 无法阻挡的力量，摧毁一切的强大力量：an <u>overwhelming</u>, advancing <u>force</u> that crushes everything in its path
taut	[tɔːt] *adj.* 紧绷的：<u>not loose</u> or flabby
debut	[deɪˈbjuː] *n.* 初次登台，出道：a <u>first</u> public <u>appearance</u>
glut	[glʌt] *vt.* 使过量，使充满：to fill <u>beyond capacity</u>, especially with food
clout	[klaʊt] *n.* 权力，影响力：<u>influence</u>; pull
flout	[flaʊt] *n./v.* 嘲弄性不理会，蔑视：to <u>treat with</u> contemptuous <u>disregard</u>
pout	[paʊt] *vi.* （尤指撅嘴或板着脸）表示不悦：to <u>show displeasure</u>, especially by thrusting out the lips or wearing a sullen expression
tout	[taʊt] *vt.* 极力赞扬：to promote or <u>praise</u> energetically; publicize
devout	[dɪˈvaʊt] *adj.* 忠诚的：firm in one's <u>allegiance</u> to someone or something
strut	[strʌt] *vi.* 趾高气扬地走：to <u>walk</u> with a <u>pompous</u> and affected air
plateau	[plæˈtoʊ] *n.* 高原：a usually extensive level land area <u>raised</u> sharply <u>above</u> adjacent land on at least one side *n.* 稳定时期，平台期：a relatively <u>stable level</u>, period, or state
milieu	[miːˈljɜː] *n.* 环境，氛围：the <u>physical or social setting</u> in which something occurs or develops
purlieu	[ˈpɜːrluː] *n.* 常去的地方：a place for spending time or for <u>socializing</u> *n.* 临近的地区：an <u>adjoining region</u> or space
impromptu	[ɪmˈprɑːmptuː] *n.* 即席的表演：something, such as a speech, that is made or <u>done extemporaneously</u>

adj. 即席的，即兴的：composed <u>without previ-</u>
<u>ous preparation</u>

flaw [flɔː] *n.* 瑕疵，缺点：an <u>imperfection</u>, often
concealed, that impairs soundness
v. 降低，破坏，使不完美：to <u>reduce</u> the soundness, effectiveness, or <u>perfection</u> of

withdraw [wɪðˈdrɔː] *v.* 撤退：to <u>take back</u> or away

hew [hjuː] *vi.* 遵守：<u>confirm</u>, adhere, to <u>hold to</u>
<u>something firmly</u> as if by adhesion

eschew [ɪsˈtʃuː] *vt.* 刻意避开；戒绝：to <u>avoid</u> habitually
especially on moral or practical grounds

askew [əˈskjuː] *adj./adv.* 不成直线的（地），歪的（地）：
out of line, <u>awry</u>

slew [sluː] *n.* 大量，许多：a <u>large amount</u> or number

sinew [ˈsɪnjuː] *n.* 活力，力量：<u>vigorous strength</u>；mu-
scular power

cow [kaʊ] *vt.* 恐吓，威胁：to <u>frighten</u> with threats or
a show of force

shadow [ˈʃædoʊ] *vt.* 偷偷尾随：to <u>follow</u> especially
<u>secretly</u>: <u>trail</u>
v. 遮蔽，（使）变暗：to （cause to） become
<u>gloomy</u> or dark

foreshadow [fɔːrˈʃædoʊ] *vt.* 预示：to represent, indicate, or
typify beforehand; <u>prefigure</u>

overshadow [ˌoʊvərˈʃædoʊ] *vt.* （在重要性上）超越，超过：to
<u>exceed in importance</u>

callow [ˈkæloʊ] *adj.* 不老练的，不成熟的：<u>lacking</u> in
adult <u>experience</u> or maturity

fallow [ˈfæloʊ] *adj.* 休耕的：left <u>untilled</u> or unsown
after plowing

hallow [ˈhæloʊ] *vt.* 尊敬，把…视为神圣：to <u>respect</u> or
honor greatly; revere

winnow [ˈwɪnoʊ] *v.* 筛选：to <u>examine closely</u> in order to
separate the good from the bad

220

row [rou] *n.* 争吵，争执：an often noisy or angry expression of differing opinions

crow [krou] *vi.* 感到高兴：to feel or express joy or triumph

harrow ['hærou] *vt.* 折磨，使苦恼：to inflict great distress or torment on

disavow [ˌdɪsə'vau] *vt.* 拒绝承认，否认：to disclaim knowledge of, responsibility for, or association with; to declare not to be true

lax [læks] *adj.* 松弛的，不紧的，不严格的：not tense, firm, or rigid
adj. 懈怠的，漫不经心的：failing to give proper care and attention

coax [kouks] *v.* 哄骗：to persuade or try to persuade by pleading or flattery; cajole

hoax [houks] *n./vt.* 欺骗：to cause to believe what is untrue

wax [wæks] *vi.* 增大，增强：to increase in size, numbers, strength, prosperity, or intensity

annex [ə'neks] *vt.* 添加，合并：to join (something) to a mass, quantity, or number so as to bring about an overall increase

vex [veks] *vt.* 使烦恼，使恼怒：to bring trouble, distress, or agitation to

affix [ə'fɪks] *vt.* 粘合：to attach physically

prolix ['proulɪks] *adj.* 啰嗦的，冗长的：tending to speak or write at excessive length

paradox ['pærədɑːks] *n.* 矛盾，悖论：a statement that is seemingly contradictory or opposed to common sense and yet is perhaps true

orthodox ['ɔːrθədɑːks] *adj.* 传统的：following or agreeing with established form, custom, or rules

heterodox [ˈhetərədɑːks] *adj.* 非正统的，异端的：holding unorthodox opinions or doctrines, not rigidly following established form, custom, or rules

influx [ˈɪnflʌks] *n.* 涌入：a coming in

crux [krʌks] *n.* 中心，关键点：the basic, central, or critical point or feature

allay [əˈleɪ] *vt.* 减轻：to subdue or reduce in intensity or severity, alleviate

downplay [ˌdaʊnˈpleɪ] *vt.* 轻描淡写，不予重视：to minimize the significance of, play down

waylay [weɪˈleɪ] *vt.* 埋伏，伏击：to lie in wait for or attack from ambush

dismay [dɪsˈmeɪ] *vt.* 使失去勇气：to cause to lose courage or resolution

vt. 使不安，使焦虑：to trouble the mind of; to make uneasy

defray [dɪˈfreɪ] *vt.* 支付：to undertake the payment of

array [əˈreɪ] *n.* 排列，阵列：a regular and imposing grouping or arrangement

vt. 排列，摆放：to arrange or display in or as if in an array

disarray [ˌdɪsəˈreɪ] *n.* 混乱，无秩序：a lack of order or sequence

vt. 使混乱：to undo the proper order or arrangement of

stray [streɪ] *adj.* 漫无目的的：lacking a definite plan, purpose, or pattern

gainsay [ˌɡeɪnˈseɪ] *vt.* 否认：to declare false

naysay [ˈneɪseɪ] *vt.* 拒绝，否认：to oppose, deny, or take a pessimistic or negative view of

lullaby [ˈlʌləbaɪ] *vt.* 使镇静，使安心：to free from distress or disturbance

flabby [ˈflæbi] *adj.* 疲软的，无力的：lacking strength or determination; weak and ineffective; feeble

222

delicacy [ˈdelɪkəsi] *n.* (外貌、结构等)精致；极度兴奋，发狂：<u>fineness</u> of appearance, construction, or execution; elegance

legacy [ˈlegəsi] *n.* 遗产：something <u>handed down</u> from an <u>ancestor</u> or a predecessor or from the past

racy [ˈreɪsi] *adj.* 活泼生动的：<u>vigorous</u>; lively

autocracy [ɔːˈtɑːkrəsi] *n.* 独裁政府：<u>government</u> in which a person possesses <u>unlimited power</u>

illiteracy [ɪˈlɪtərəsi] *n.* 文盲：the condition of being <u>unable to read and write</u>

discrepancy [dɪsˈkrepənsi] *n.* (在事实和宣称之间的)差异或矛盾：<u>divergence</u> or <u>disagreement</u>, as between facts or claims

flippancy [ˈflɪpənsi] *n.* 轻率，无礼：<u>unbecoming levity</u> or pertness especially in respect to grave or sacred matters

complacency [kəmˈpleɪsnsi] *n.* 自满，无忧患意识：a feeling of <u>self-satisfaction</u>, coupled with an <u>unawareness of trouble</u>

contingency [kənˈtɪndʒənsi] *n.* 可能发生的事：something (such as an emergency) that <u>might happen</u>

deficiency [dɪˈfɪʃnsi] *n.* 缺乏，不足：the quality or state of being deficient: <u>inadequate</u>

expediency [ɪkˈspiːdiənsi] *n.* 应急手段，权宜之计：doing what is <u>convenient</u> rather than what is morally right

toady [ˈtoʊdi] *n./v.* 马屁精；拍马屁：one who <u>flatters</u> in the hope of <u>gaining favors</u>

giddy [ˈgɪdi] *adj.* 轻率不严肃的：<u>lacking in seriousness</u> or maturity

muddy [ˈmʌdi] *adj.* 浑浊的，不清晰的：<u>lacking</u> in <u>clarity</u> or brightness

223

vt. 使难以理解：to make (something) unclear to the understanding

needy ['niːdi] *adj.* 贫困的：being in need; impoverished, poor

perfidy ['pɜːrfədi] *n.* 不忠，背信弃义：an act or an instance of disloyalty

subsidy ['sʌbsədi] *n.* 补助金，津贴：monetary assistance granted by a government to a person or group in support of an enterprise regarded as being in the public interest

dandy ['dændi] *n.* 纨绔子弟，爱打扮的人：a man who gives exaggerated attention to personal appearance

windy ['wɪndi] *adj.* 冗长的：characterized by wearisome verbosity

parody ['pærədi] *n.* （以嘲笑原作作者的）模仿作品：a literary or musical work in which the style of an author or work is closely imitated for comic effect or in ridicule

v. 模仿（以嘲弄）：to copy or exaggerate (someone or something) in order to make fun of

音频

hardy	[ˈhɑːrdi] *adj.* 顽强的：able to withstand hardship, strain, or exposure
jeopardy	[ˈdʒepərdi] *n.* 危险：risk of loss or injury; peril or danger
tardy	[ˈtɑːrdi] *adj.* 缓慢的，迟缓的：moving slowly: sluggish
sturdy	[ˈstɜːrdi] *adj.* 强健的，结实的：marked by or reflecting physical strength or vigor; substantially made or built
gaudy	[ˈgɔːdi] *adj.* 俗丽的：ostentatiously or tastelessly ornamented, excessively showy
cagey	[ˈkeɪdʒi] *adj.* 不乐意说话的：not willing to say everything that you know about something
off-key	[ˌɔːf ˈkiː] *adj.* 不寻常的，不合适的：being out of accord with what is considered normal or appropriate
medley	[ˈmedli] *adj.* 大杂烩，混合物：an unorganized collection or mixture of various things
motley	[ˈmɑːtli] *adj.* 混杂的，富于变化的：(especially of colors) having elements of great variety or incongruity
purvey	[pərˈveɪ] *v.* (大量)供给，供应：to supply (food, for example); furnish
defy	[dɪˈfaɪ] *vt.* 蔑视：to go against the commands, prohibitions, or rules of
rarefy	[ˈrerfaɪ] *vt.* 使稀薄：to make rare, thin, porous, or less dense: to expand without the addition of matter

225

pacify	[ˈpæsɪfaɪ] vt. 使平静，安慰：to ease the anger or agitation of
calcify	[ˈkælsɪfaɪ] vt. 使僵化：to make inflexible or unchangeable
deify	[ˈdeɪɪfaɪ] vt. 尊敬，尊崇：to assign a high status or value to
qualify	[ˈkwɑːlɪfaɪ] vt. 限定：to reduce from a general to a particular or restricted form vt. 使有资格，使有能力：to make competent (as by training, skill, or ability) for a particular office or function
vilify	[ˈvɪlɪfaɪ] vt. 诽谤，辱骂：to utter slanderous and abusive statements against
mollify	[mɑːlɪfaɪ] vt. 平息，抚慰，缓和：to calm in temper or feeling
verify	[ˈverɪfaɪ] vt. 校验，证实：to determine or test the truth or accuracy of, as by comparison, investigation, or ref-erence
petrify	[ˈpetrɪfaɪ] vt. 使僵化，使失去活力：to cause to become stiff or stone-like; deaden
intensify	[ɪnˈtensɪfaɪ] vt. 加强，激化：to make intense or more intensive
ossify	[ˈɑːsɪfaɪ] v. (使)硬化，(使)僵化：to (cause to) become hardened or conventional and opposed to change
ratify	[ˈrætɪfaɪ] vt. (官方地)认可，批准：to give official acceptance of as satisfactory
gratify	[ˈɡrætɪfaɪ] vt. 使满足：to give what is desired to, to please or satisfy
stratify	[ˈstrætɪfaɪ] vt. 将…分成各种等级：to divide into classes, castes, or social strata
sanctify	[ˈsæŋktɪfaɪ] vt. 使神圣，将…敬为神：to make holy

226

stultify	['stʌltɪfaɪ] *vt.* 使无效，抑制：to deprive of vitality and <u>render futile</u> especially by enfeebling or repressive influences
fortify	['fɔːrtɪfaɪ] *vt.* 加固，鼓励：to <u>give physical strength</u>, courage, or endurance to
justify	['dʒʌstɪfaɪ] *vt.* 证明…的合理性，为…辩解：to <u>prove</u> or show <u>to be just</u>, <u>right</u>, or reasonable
stodgy	['stɑːdʒi] *adj.* 平庸的，乏味的：<u>dull</u>, unimaginative, and commonplace
elegy	['elədʒi] *n.* 哀歌（诗），挽歌（诗）：a song or poem <u>expressing sorrow</u> or lamentation
groggy	['grɑːgi] *adj.* 虚弱的，(走路)不稳的：<u>weak and unsteady</u> on the feet or in action
mangy	['meɪndʒi] *adj.* 卑劣的：mean; <u>contemptible</u>
tangy	['tæŋi] *adj.* 刺激的：having a <u>powerfully stimulating</u> odor or flavor
dingy	['dɪndʒi] *adj.* 昏暗的；肮脏的：<u>darkened</u> with smoke and grime; <u>dirty</u> or discolored
stingy	['stɪndʒi] *adj.* 小气的，吝啬的：being <u>unwilling</u> or showing unwillingness <u>to share</u> with others
terminology	[ˌtɜːrmə'nɑːlədʒi] *n.* 专业术语：the <u>special terms or expressions</u> of a particular group or field
calligraphy	[kə'lɪgrəfi] *n.* （优美的）书法：artistic, stylized, or <u>elegant handwriting</u> or lettering
demography	[dɪ'mɑːgrəfi] *n.* 人口统计学：the study of <u>changes</u> (such as the number of births, deaths, marriages, and illnesses) that occur over a period of time <u>in human populations</u>
atrophy	['ætrəfi] *vi.* 萎缩，衰退：to <u>waste away</u>; wither or deteriorate
apathy	['æpəθi] *n.* 缺乏兴趣，不关心：<u>lack</u> of <u>interest</u> or <u>concern</u>

antipathy	[æn'tɪpəθi] *n.* 厌恶，反感：settled <u>aversion</u> or <u>dislike</u>
pithy	['pɪθi] *adj.* 精练的，简洁的：precisely meaningful; forceful and <u>brief</u>
frothy	['frɔːθi] *adj.* （内容等）欢乐轻佻、不严肃的：<u>gaily frivolous</u> or light in content or treatment
finicky	['fɪnɪki] *adj.* 过分讲究的，挑剔的：<u>extremely</u> or excessively particular, exacting, or <u>meticulous</u> in taste or standards
balky	['bɔːlki] *adj.* 不服管束的，倔强的：<u>refusing</u> or likely to refuse to proceed, act, or function as directed or expected
quirky	['kwɜːrki] *adj.* 古怪，奇葩的：<u>different from the ordinary</u> in a way that causes curiosity or suspicion
murky	['mɜːrki] *adj.* 模糊的，晦涩的：<u>lacking clarity</u> or distinct-ness
husky	['hʌski] *adj.* （尤指声音）沙哑的，粗糙的：hoarse or <u>rough</u> in quality
fluky	['fluːki] *adj.* 侥幸的：coming or <u>happening by good luck</u> especially unexpectedly
gawky	['gɔːki] *adj.* （举止）笨拙的：having or showing an <u>inability to move in a graceful manner</u>
worldly	['wɜːrldli] *adj.* 世间的，世俗的：of this world <u>rather than spiritual</u> or religion affairs *adj.* 老练的：<u>experienced</u> in human affairs
timely	['taɪmli] *adj.* 恰到好处的，合乎适宜的：<u>appropriate</u> or adapted to the times or the occasion
homely	['hoʊmli] *adj.* 其貌不扬的，朴素简单的：<u>not attractive</u> or good-looking
gadfly	['gædflaɪ] *n.* 刺激物：one that acts as a <u>provocative stimulus</u>

228

homily	['hɑːməli] *n.* 冗长乏味的道德讲演或训诫：a tedious moralizing lecture or admonition
wily	['waɪli] *adj.* 狡诈的，狡猾的：clever at attaining one's ends by indirect and often deceptive means
ally	['ælaɪ] *n.* 盟友，支持者：one in helpful association with another [ə'laɪ] *v.* 加入联盟：to enter into an alliance
dally	['dæli] *vi.* 虚度时光：to spend time doing nothing
willy-nilly	[ˌwɪli 'nɪli] *adj.* 无秩序的，随意的：without order or plan
bully	['bʊli] *n.* 欺凌弱小者，恶霸：a person who habitually treats others in an overbearing or intimidating manner
seemly	['siːmli] *adv.* 得体的，遵守礼节的：following the established traditions of refined society and good taste
slovenly	['slʌvnli] *adj.* 邋遢的，不整洁的：lacking neatness in dress or person
ungainly	[ʌn'ɡeɪnli] *adj.* 笨拙的，不雅的：having or showing an inability to move in a graceful manner
miserly	['maɪzərli] *adj.* 吝啬的：marked by grasping meanness and penuriousness
surly	['sɜːrli] *adj.* 脾气不好的：irritably sullen and churlish in mood or manner
sly	[slaɪ] *adj.* 狡猾的：clever or cunning, especially in the practice of deceit
measly	['miːzli] *adj.* 少得可怜的，微不足道的：so small or unimportant as to warrant little or no attention
grisly	['ɡrɪzli] *adj.* 令人反感的，令人恐惧的：inspiring repugnance; gruesome

sprightly	['spraɪtli] *adj.* 活泼的，充满活力的：full of spirit and vitality
unruly	[ʌn'ruːli] *adj.* 难驾驭的，不守规矩的：difficult or impossible to discipline, control, or rule
seamy	['siːmi] *adj.* 肮脏的，堕落的：sordid; base *adj.* 僻静的，隐蔽的：screened or hidden from view
grimy	['graɪmi] *adj.* 肮脏的：not clean
palmy	['pɑːmi] *adj.* 繁荣的：marked by prosperity
autonomy	[ɔː'tɑːnəmi] *n.* 政治上的独立：the quality or state of being self-governing *n.* 自我主导的自由，（尤其是）精神独立：self-directing freedom and especially moral independence
gloomy	['gluːmi] *adj.* 忧郁的：low in spirits
dichotomy	[daɪ'kɑːtəmi] *n.* 对立：a division into two especially mutually exclusive or contradictory groups or entities
smarmy	['smɑːrmi] *adj.* 虚情假意的，过分恭维的：hypocritically, complacently, or effusively earnest
ignominy	['ɪgnəmɪni] *n.* 耻辱：the state of having lost the esteem of others
spiny	['spaɪni] *adj.* 棘手的，麻烦的：requiring exceptional skill or caution in performance or handling
canny	['kæni] *adj.* 精明的，聪明的：careful and shrewd, especially where one's own interests are concerned
uncanny	[ʌn'kæni] *adj.* 离奇的，奇异的：being so extraordinary or abnormal as to suggest powers which violate the laws of nature
cacophony	[kə'kɑːfəni] *n.* 刺耳的声音：loud, confused, and usually inharmonious sound

felony ['feləni] *n.* 重罪：one of several <u>grave crimes</u>, such as murder, rape, or burglary, punishable by a more stringent sentence than that given for a misdemeanor

hegemony [hɪ'dʒemoʊni] *n.* 霸权，统治权：<u>preponderant</u> influence or <u>authority</u> over others

testimony ['testɪmoʊni] *n.* 证词，声明：firsthand <u>authentication</u> of a fact

thorny ['θɔːrni] *adj.* 棘手的：full of <u>difficulties</u> or controversial points: ticklish

puny ['pjuːni] *adj.* 微小的，弱小的：of <u>inferior size</u>, strength, or significance; <u>weak</u>

coy [kɔɪ] *adj.* 不愿与人交往的，内向的：<u>tending to avoid people</u> and social situations

alloy ['ælɔɪ] *n.* 合金；混合物：a distinct entity formed by the <u>combining of two or more different things</u>
[ə'lɔɪ] *vt.* 掺杂，降低…的纯度：to <u>debase by the addition</u> of an inferior element

ploy [plɔɪ] *n.* 计策，手段：<u>a clever often underhanded means</u> to achieve an end

deploy [dɪ'plɔɪ] *v.* （有目的地）展开；调度，部署：to <u>spread out</u>, utilize, or arrange for a deliberate purpose

annoy [ə'nɔɪ] *vt.* 不断烦扰：to <u>disturb</u> or irritate especially by <u>repeated</u> acts

toy [tɔɪ] *vi.* 草率或不认真地对待：to <u>handle thoughtlessly</u>, ignorantly, or mischievously

buoy [bɔɪ] *vt.* 使充满勇气和力量，使振作：to fill with <u>courage or strength</u> of purpose

scrappy ['skræpi] *adj.* 好斗的，好吵架的：having an <u>aggressive</u> and determined spirit, quarrelsome

sloppy	[ˈslɑːpi] *adj.* 邋遢的，不整洁的：lacking neatness in dress or person *adj.* 混乱的：lacking in order, neatness, and often cleanliness
raspy	[ˈræspi] *adj.* 声音刺耳的：harsh and dry in sound
quandary	[ˈkwɑːndəri] *n.* 困惑，窘境：a state of perplexity or doubt
dreary	[ˈdrɪri] *adj.* 单调乏味的：having nothing likely to provide cheer, comfort, or interest

音 频

| vagary | [ˈveɪɡəri] *n.* 不可预测的思想或行为：an <u>erratic</u>, <u>unpredictable</u>, or extravagant manifestation, action, or notion |

| chary | [ˈtʃeri] *adj.* 非常谨慎的：very <u>cautious</u> |

| intermediary | [ˌɪntərˈmiːdieri] *n.* 中间人：one who works with opposing sides in order to <u>bring about an a-greement</u> |

| subsidiary | [səbˈsɪdieri] *adj.* 次要的：of <u>secondary importance</u> |

| incendiary | [ɪnˈsendieri] *n.* 煽动者：a <u>person who stirs up</u> public feelings especially of discontent
adj. 煽动性的：<u>tending to inflame</u> |

| pecuniary | [pɪˈkjuːnieri] *adj.* 金钱上的：of or relating to <u>money</u>, banking, or investments |

| ancillary | [ˈænsəleri] *adj.* 次要的：of <u>secondary importance</u>
adj. 辅助的，补充的：<u>auxiliary, supplementary</u> |

| exemplary | [ɪɡˈzempləri] *adj.* 榜样的，值得效仿的：constituting, serving as, or worthy of <u>being a pattern</u> to be <u>imitated</u> |

| mercenary | [ˈmɜːrsəneri] *adj.* 唯利是图的，贪婪的：motivated solely by a desire for <u>monetary or material gain</u> |

| luminary | [ˈluːmɪneri] *n.* 杰出人物：a person who has achieved <u>eminence</u> in a specific field |

| visionary | [ˈvɪʒəneri] *adj.* 空想的，不切实际的：having or marked by a tendency to be <u>guided</u> more <u>by ideals</u> than by reality |

233

adj. 有远见的：having or marked by <u>foresight</u> and imagination

reactionary [riˈækʃəneri] *adj.* 反对变革的，极保守的：characterized by reaction, especially <u>opposition to progress</u> or liberalism; extremely conservative

discretionary [dɪˈskreʃəneri] *adj.* 自主决定的：left to discretion: exercised at <u>one's own discretion</u>

eleemosynary [ˌelɪɪˈmɑːsiːnəri] *adj.* 慈善的：of, relating to, or supported by <u>charity</u>

hoary [ˈhɔːri] *adj.* 极老的：<u>extremely old</u>

arbitrary [ˈɑːrbətreri] *adj.* 专横的，独断专行的：having or showing a tendency to <u>force one's will on others</u> without any regard to fairness or necessity

adj. 缺乏计划的，随意的：<u>lacking a definite plan</u>, purpose, or pattern

adversary [ˈædvərseri] *n.* 敌手，对手：one that contends with, opposes, or <u>resists</u>: <u>enemy</u>

proprietary [prəˈpraɪəteri] *adj.* 私营的：<u>privately owned</u> and managed and run as a profit-making organization

sanitary [ˈsænəteri] *adj.* 健康的，清洁的：of or relating to <u>health</u>

sedentary [ˈsednteri] *adj.* 固定不动的：<u>not migratory</u>: settled

complementary [ˌkɑːmplɪˈmentri] *adj.* 互补的：mutually <u>supplying each other's</u> lack

rudimentary [ˌruːdɪˈmentri] *adj.* 初始的，未发展的：being in the <u>earliest</u> stages of <u>development</u>

adj. 最根本的，基础的：consisting in <u>first principles</u>: fundamental

votary ［'voʊtəri］*n.* 崇拜者，信徒：a person who is <u>fervently devoted</u>, as to a leader or ideal; a faithful follower

salutary ［'sæljəteri］*adj.* 有益健康的：beneficial, <u>promoting health</u>
adj. 有利的，利好的：<u>promoting</u> or contributing to personal or social <u>well-being</u>

sanctuary ［'sæŋktʃueri］*n.* 避难所：a place of refuge and <u>protection</u>

wary ［'weri］*adj.* 小心的，机警的，谨慎的：marked by keen <u>caution</u>, cunning, and watchfulness

decry ［dɪ'kraɪ］*vt.* 强烈反对，否定：to express <u>strong disapproval</u> of

tawdry ［'tɔːdri］*adj.* 俗丽的，花哨而庸俗的：cheap and <u>gaudy</u> in appearance or quality; ignoble

leery ［'lɪri］*adj.* 怀疑的，不信任的：<u>suspicious</u> or distrustful; wary

drudgery ［'drʌdʒəri］*n.* 苦工；单调、卑贱或无趣的工作：<u>tedious</u>, menial, or unpleasant <u>work</u>

skullduggery ［skʌl'dʌgəri］*n.* 欺诈，诡计：the <u>use of clever</u> <u>underhanded actions</u> to achieve an end

mockery ［'mɑːkəri］*n.* 鄙视，嘲弄：scornfully contemptuous <u>ridicule</u>
n. 以嘲笑为目的的模仿：a false, <u>derisive</u>, or impudent <u>imitation</u>

chicanery ［ʃɪ'keɪnəri］*n.* 诡计多端，欺骗：<u>deception</u> by artful subterfuge or sophistry

slippery ［'slɪpəri］*adj.* 光滑的：causing or tending to cause something to <u>slide</u> or fall
adj. 意义不明确的：<u>not precise</u> or fixed <u>in meaning</u>, elusive or tricky

235

effrontery	[ɪˈfrʌntəri] *n.* 厚颜无耻，放肆大胆：flagrant <u>disregard</u> of <u>courtesy</u> or propriety and an arrogant assumption of privilege
mastery	[ˈmæstəri] *n.* 技艺超群，精通：possession or display of <u>great skill</u> or technique
pillory	[ˈpɪləri] *vt.* 当众嘲弄：to expose to <u>public contempt</u>, ridicule, or scorn
provisory	[prəˈvaɪzəri] *adj.* 有附带条件的；临时的：depending on a proviso; <u>conditional</u>; serving in a position for the time being
cursory	[ˈkɜːrsəri] *adj.* 匆忙的，不注意细节的：acting or done with <u>excessive or careless speed</u>
accessory	[əkˈsesəri] *adj.* 辅助的，附属的：having a <u>secondary</u>, <u>supplementary</u>, or <u>subordinate</u> function
illusory	[ɪˈluːsəri] *adj.* 幻觉的，虚幻的：produced by, based on, or having the nature of an <u>illusion</u>
mandatory	[ˈmændətɔːri] *adj.* 强制的：<u>forcing</u> one's <u>compliance</u> or participation
laudatory	[ˈlɔːdətɔːri] *adj.* 表示赞扬的：of, relating to, or expressing <u>praise</u>
obligatory	[əˈblɪɡətɔːri] *adj.* 强制性的：of the nature of an obligation; <u>compulsory</u>
nugatory	[ˈnuːɡətɔːri] *adj.* 无关紧要的：of little or no <u>consequence; inconsequential</u>
dilatory	[ˈdɪlətɔːri] *adj.* 拖延的，磨蹭的：tending or intended to <u>cause delay</u>, characterized by <u>procrastination</u>
minatory	[ˈmɪnətɔːri] *adj.* 带来威胁的，有凶兆的：being or showing <u>a sign of evil</u> or calamity to come
migratory	[ˈmaɪɡrətɔːri] *adj.* 迁移的：having a way of life that involves <u>moving from one region to another</u> typically on a seasonal basis

236

conservatory [kən'sɜːrvətɔːri] *n.* 温室：a greenhouse for growing or displaying plants

n. 艺术学院：a school specializing in one of the fine arts

refractory [rɪ'fræktəri] *adj.* 倔强的，不顺从的：resisting control or authority

perfunctory [pər'fʌŋktəri] *adj.* 敷衍的，呵呵的：characterized by routine or superficiality and often done merely as a duty

transitory ['trænsətɔːri] *adj.* 短暂的：existing or lasting only a short time; short-lived or temporary

desultory ['desəltɔːri] *adj.* 无计划的，无目的的：lacking a definite plan, purpose, or pattern

inventory ['ɪnvəntɔːri] *n.* （包含要点的）简介：a short statement of the main points

peremptory [pə'remptəri] *adj.* 不容反抗的：not allowing contradiction or refusal; imperative

adj. 傲慢的：having a feeling of superiority that shows itself in an overbearing attitude

savory ['seɪvəri] *adj.* 令人愉悦的：giving pleasure or content-ment to the mind or senses

pry [praɪ] *vi.* 刺探，打听：to look or inquire closely, curiously, or impertinently

harry ['hæri] *vt.* 不断烦扰，骚扰：to disturb or distress by or as if by repeated attacks; harass

parry ['pæri] *vi.* 躲避（问题）：to evade especially by an adroit answer

symmetry ['sɪmətri] *n.* 对称：balanced proportions

paltry ['pɔːltri] *adj.* 无价值的；微不足道的：lacking in importance or worth

fury ['fjʊri] *n.* 暴怒：intense, disordered, and often destructive rage

penury	[ˈpenjəri] *n.* 贫穷：extreme <u>dearth</u>; barrenness or insufficiency *n.* 吝啬，节俭：extreme and often niggardly <u>frugality</u>
wry	[raɪ] *adj.* 坚持错误的：<u>stubborn</u> in adherence <u>to wrong</u> opinion or principles
awry	[əˈraɪ] *adj./adv.* 出差错的（地）：<u>off</u> the correct or expected <u>course</u>
idiosyncrasy	[ˌɪdiəˈsɪŋkrəsi] *n.* 独特而奇怪的习惯：an <u>odd or peculiar habit</u>
fantasy	[ˈfæntəsi] *n.* 幻想：<u>imaginative fiction</u> featuring especially strange settings and grotesque characters *vt.* 产生幻想：to <u>form a mental picture</u> of
ecstasy	[ˈekstəsi] *n.* 狂喜：<u>intense joy</u> or delight
apostasy	[əˈpɑːstəsi] *n.* 背叛：<u>abandonment</u> of a <u>previous loyalty</u>: defection
heresy	[ˈherəsi] *n.* 异教，和普遍观点相悖的说法：a <u>controversial or unorthodox opinion</u> or doctrine, departure from a generally accepted theory, opinion, or practice
clumsy	[ˈklʌmzi] *adj.* 笨拙的：<u>lacking</u> or showing a lack of <u>nimbleness</u> in using one's hands; a lack of <u>skill</u> and tact
rosy	[ˈroʊzi] *adj.* 乐观的：having qualities which in-<u>spire hope</u>
brassy	[ˈbræsi] *adj.* 厚脸皮的，不知羞耻的：displaying or marked by <u>rude boldness</u>
glossy	[ˈɡlɑːsi] *adj.* 平滑的，有光泽的：<u>smooth</u>, shiny, lustrous <u>surface</u>
fussy	[ˈfʌsi] *adj.* 谨慎的：taking, showing, or <u>involv-ing great care</u> and effort *adj.* 挑剔的：<u>hard to please</u>

238

frowsy ['frauzi] *adj.* 邋遢的：having a <u>slovenly</u> or uncared-for appearance

nicety ['naisəti] *n.* 准确，精确：<u>careful</u> attention to <u>details</u>; delicate exactness

notoriety [ˌnoutə'raiəti] *n.* 坏名声：the quality or condition of being notorious; <u>ill fame</u>

propriety [prə'praiəti] *n.* 适当，得体：the quality or state of being especially <u>suitable or fitting</u>

rickety ['rikəti] *adj.* 不稳的：<u>lacking stability</u> or firmness

shifty ['ʃifti] *adj.* (显得)狡诈的，(显得)欺诈的：having, displaying, or suggestive of <u>deceitful character</u>

lofty ['lɔːfti] *adj.* 崇高的：<u>elevated</u> in character and spirit, noble
adj. 自大的：having a feeling of <u>superiority</u> that shows itself in an overbearing attitude

probity ['proubəti] *n.* 正直：faithfulness to high <u>moral standards</u>

paucity ['pɔːsəti] *n.* 少量，缺乏：smallness of number; <u>dearth</u>

vitality [vai'tæləti] *n.* 活力，生命力：physical or mental <u>vigor</u> especially when highly developed

sensuality [ˌsenʃu'æləti] *n.* 感官享乐：excessive <u>pursuit of fleshly pleasures</u>

fidelity [fi'deləti] *n.* 忠诚：the quality or state of <u>being faithful</u>

liability [ˌlaiə'biləti] *n.* 责任：the quality or state of being <u>liable</u>

agility [ə'dʒiləti] *n.* (身手)敏捷：<u>quickness, ease and grace</u> in physical activity

tranquility [træŋ'kwiləti] *n.* 宁静，淡定：a state of <u>freedom from storm</u> or disturbance

civility [səˈvɪləti] *n.* 彬彬有礼：<u>courteous</u> behavior；<u>politeness</u>

amity [ˈæməti] *n.* 友好关系，亲善和睦：<u>friendship</u>; especially: <u>friendly</u> relations between nations

calamity [kəˈlæməti] *n.* 大灾难：a <u>disastrous event</u> marked by great loss and lasting distress and suffering

enmity [ˈenməti] *n.* 敌意：positive, active, and typically <u>mutual hatred</u> or ill will

comity [ˈkɑːməti] *n.* 友好，社会和谐：<u>friendly</u> social atmosphere: social <u>harmony</u>

sanity [ˈsænəti] *n.* 心智健全，神志正常：the normal or <u>healthy condition</u> of the mental abilities

amenity [əˈmenəti] *n.* (环境、设备等的)舒适，人性化：something that conduces to <u>comfort</u>, convenience, or enjoyment
n. 融洽，和谐：the quality of being <u>pleasant</u> or <u>agreeable</u>

affinity [əˈfɪnəti] *n.* 喜欢，倾向：a habitual <u>attraction</u> to some activity or thing
n. 相似：the fact or state of having something <u>in common</u>

indemnity [ɪnˈdemnəti] *n.* (损害、伤害等的)保险补偿：<u>compensation</u> for damage, loss, or injury suffered

solemnity [səˈlemnəti] *n.* 庄严，严肃：the quality or condition of being <u>solemn</u>

音 频

impunity [ɪmˈpjuːnəti] *n.* 免责，免受处罚：exemption or freedom from punishment, harm, or loss

serendipity [ˌserənˈdɪpəti] *n.* 意外发现珍奇(或称心)事物的本领：the faculty of making fortunate discoveries by accident

peculiarity [pɪˌkjuːliˈærəti] *n.* 特征，特点：a distinguishing characteristic

clarity [ˈklærəti] *n.* 清晰，清楚：the quality or state of being clear: lucidity

parity [ˈpærəti] *n.* 相称，同等，平等：the quality or state of being equal or equivalent

alacrity [əˈlækrəti] *n.* 反应迅速，乐意，欣然：promptness in response: cheerful readiness

temerity [təˈmerəti] *n.* 鲁莽，冒失：foolhardy disregard of danger; recklessness

asperity [æˈsperəti] *n.* (举止、性情)粗暴：roughness of manner or of temper
n. (环境)艰苦：rigor, severity

integrity [ɪnˈtegrəti] *n.* 正直：steadfast adherence to a strict moral or ethical code, devotion to telling the truth
n. 完整性：the quality or condition of being whole or undivided

authority [əˈθɔːrəti] *n.* (某领域的)权威人士：a person with a high level of knowledge or skill in a field
n. 管辖权，控制：lawful control over the affairs of a political unit (as a nation)

propensity [prə'pensəti] *n.* 倾向，癖好：an often intense natural inclination or preference

adversity [əd'vɜːrsəti] *n.* 厄运，逆境：a state, condition, or instance of serious or continued difficulty or adverse fortune

diversity [daɪ'vɜːrsəti] *n.* 多样性：variety or multiformity

nonentity [nɑː'nentəti] *n.* 不重要的人：a person or thing of little consequence or significance

perspicuity [ˌpɜːrspɪ'kjuːəti] *n.* 清晰明了：the quality of being perspicuous; clearness and lucidity

equity ['ekwəti] *n.* 不偏不倚，公平：lack of favoritism toward one side or another

iniquity [ɪ'nɪkwəti] *n.* 邪恶，不公正：gross immorality or injustice

depravity [dɪ'prævəti] *n.* 道德败坏：immoral conduct or practices harmful or offensive to society

levity ['levəti] *n.* 轻浮：excessive or unseemly frivolity

brevity ['brevəti] *n.* 简短，简洁：shortness of duration

proclivity [prə'klɪvəti] *n.* 癖性，偏好：a natural propensity or inclination; predisposition

royalty ['rɔɪəlti] *n.* 皇家身份：regal character or bearing
n. 版税；专利权税：a payment to an author or composer for each copy of a work sold or to an inventor for each item sold under a patent

jaunty ['dʒɔːnti] *adj.* 轻快的，活泼的：sprightly in manner or appearance: lively

hasty ['heɪsti] *adj.* 轻率的：fast and typically superficial; acting or done with excessive or careless speed

tasty ['teɪsti] *adj.* 美味的；令人愉悦的：giving pleasure or contentment to the mind or senses

242

testy	['testi] *adj.* 易怒的，暴躁的：easily annoyed; irritable
travesty	['trævəsti] *n./v.* 拙劣的、嘲弄性模仿：an exaggerated or grotesque imitation, such as a parody of a literary work
zesty	[zesti] *adj.* 刺激的，开胃的：appealingly piquant or lively
feisty	['faɪsti] *adj.* 好斗的，好争论的：having or showing a lively aggressiveness
frosty	['frɔːsti] *adj.* 寒冷的：having a low or subnormal temperature
	adj. 无强烈感情的，冷淡的：lacking in friendliness or warmth of feeling
fusty	['fʌsti] *adj.* 过时的：rigidly old-fashioned or reactionary
	adj. 腐臭的：saturated with dust and stale odors
natty	['næti] *adj.* 整洁的，时髦的：trimly neat and tidy
tatty	['tæti] *adj.* 破旧的，褴褛的：somewhat worn, shabby, or dilapidated
petty	['peti] *adj.* 细微的，不重要的：of small importance; trivial
knotty	['nɑːti] *adj.* 复杂的，困难的：marked by or full of knots especially: so full of difficulties and complications as to be likely to defy solution
obloquy	['ɑːbləkwi] *n.* 谩骂，诽谤：abusively detractive language or utterance; calumny
	n. 恶名，耻辱：the state of having lost the esteem of others
soliloquy	[sə'lɪləkwi] *n.* （尤指自言自语的）独白：a dramatic or literary form of discourse in which a character talks to himself or herself or reveals his or her thoughts without addressing a listener

243

scurvy	['skɜːrvi] *adj.* 下流的，让人鄙视的：mean; contemptible
topsy-turvy	[ˌtɑːpsi'tɜːrvi] *adj.* 混乱的：lacking in order, neatness, and often cleanliness
savvy	['sævi] *n.* 老练，机智：knowledge gained by actually doing or living through something *adj.* 有见识的，精明能干的：having or showing a practical cleverness or judgment
frenzy	['frenzi] *n.* 疯狂，狂怒：a violent mental or emotional agitation

索 引

245

264

Note

Note

Note

Note